STUDENT TEACHING CASEBOOK

for Supervising Teachers and Teaching Interns

Patricia J. Wentz
James R. Yarling

University of West Florida

Merrill, an imprint of
Macmillan Publishing Company
New York

Maxwell Macmillan Canada
Toronto

Maxwell Macmillan International
New York   Oxford   Singapore   Sydney

Cover art: Suzanne Whitaker
Editor: Linda James Scharp
Production Editor: Laura Messerly
Art Coordinator: Ruth A. Kimpel
Text Designer: Susan E. Frankenberry
Cover Designer: Cathleen Norz
Production Buyer: Pamela D. Bennett
Illustrations: Suzanne Whitaker

This book was set in Baskerville by American–Stratford Graphic Services, Inc., and was printed and bound by Semline, Inc., a Quebecor America Book Group Company. The cover was printed by Phoenix Color Corp.

Macmillan Publishing Company
866 Third Avenue
New York, NY 10022

Macmillan Publishing Company is part of the
Maxwell Communication Group of Companies.

Maxwell Macmillan Canada, Inc.
1200 Eglinton Avenue East, Suite 200
Don Mills, Ontario M3C 3N1

Library of Congress Cataloging-in-Publication Data
Wentz, Patricia J.
    Student teaching casebook for supervising teachers and teaching
interns / Patricia J. Wentz and James R. Yarling.
        p.   cm.
    Includes bibliographical references and index.
    ISBN 0-02-425491-6
    1. Student teachers—Supervision of—United States—Case studies.
    I. Yarling, James R.   II. Title.
    LB2157.U5W46   1994
    370'.7'33—dc20   92-44326
                                                                          CIP

Printing: 1 2 3 4 5 6 7 8 9   Year: 4 5 6 7 8

Credits: "A Teacher's Influence," p. 7, by Myrtle B. Beavers, and "A Letter from a Supervising Teacher," p. 11, by Kathy Brake, both reprinted by permission.

PREFACE

This book addresses the practical, day-to-day induction into the classroom of the student teacher/intern. It guides the beginning teacher from the first visit in the classroom through the certification and job application processes.

The special recommendations given as Guidelines are meant as suggestions that may stimulate the process and give more confidence to both the student teaching intern and the supervising teacher. In this book, the term *supervising teacher* refers to the classroom teacher with whom the student teaching intern is placed for the assignment. The term *coordinator* is used in reference to the individual assigned from the college or university. Both individuals work in strong support of the student teaching intern.

The case studies presented in each chapter introduce real life school experiences for the student teacher/intern. These cases should stimulate discussion and afford opportunities for small and large group discussions and role playing. Most of the cases that are included, even though some appear to be extreme, have actually occurred.

The short chapters presented are compact and to the point. The limited time of both supervisors and interns makes this an important consideration. The suggestions that are presented to both the supervising teachers and the intern have been proven practical. It is recognized that they cannot possibly accomplish all of the suggestions that are given; these suggestions can be used as springboards for discussion, however. The brevity of this book also makes it more affordable for potential buyers.

The current, annotated bibliography found at the end of each chapter offers references for interns and supervisors seeking additional ideas. In the Recommended Readings, those readings especially pertinent to interns are noted by an I in parentheses, those for supervising teachers by an S, and those for both by I&S. It is hoped that experiences reflected in the real-life case studies and our fifty-six years of combined experience in working with student teachers and their supervisors will give assistance to both. This book attempts to bring together the necessary ingredients for a meaningful student teaching experience.

We recommend this book for undergraduate and graduate classes dealing with general methods and the preparation for student teaching. This material has been used successfully as a text for the training of supervising teachers and it would benefit inservice and staff development programs in public and private schoool districts.

We give special thanks to Myrtle Beavers and Kathy Brake, who have allowed us to use their materials, and to the many students who have given us feedback concerning these cases. The information in this book has been field tested and numerous students (both undergraduate and graduate), supervising teachers, and coordinators have given us feedback.

We are grateful to our spouses, Marty Yarling and Charlie Wentz, who have encouraged and assisted us throughout the preparation of this material.

Working with supervising teachers and student teaching interns has been a continuing source of joy, amazement, and satisfaction to the authors. It is our desire that our work may be of some assistance as our profession moves toward improved schooling for all children and youth.

CONTENTS

APPENDIXES   171

INDEX   193

1 GETTING OFF TO A GOOD START

Many people—representing colleges, communities, and schools—are involved in the cooperative venture of training teachers. They spend much time and effort on teacher training programs and take their responsibilities very seriously.

The basic purpose of any student teaching program is to provide a situation in which interns learn and practice varied techniques of teaching while working with "real students" under the direction of a regular teacher in a public or private school. The length of student teaching has normally been one quarter or semester; however, many programs are now year-long internships.

The general atmosphere in every school differs. In most schools, interns receive a warm welcome from the staff, but if a supervising teacher is assigned an intern without having the opportunity to volunteer, problems can result that affect the intern. Normally, a supervising teacher is quite eager to have the opportunity to work with an intern who, it is hoped, will bring fresh ideas into the classroom.

Interns usually begin student teaching wondering whether they will be able to complete the assignment satisfactorily. The possibility of failure does exist. Some of the questions in the mind of the beginning intern are: Will I perform satisfactorily for my supervising teacher? Will we have a personality conflict? Will I be able to be myself, or must I become a clone of my supervisor? Will I be able to control a classroom full of students? Will my supervisor assist me in filling in the gaps? Will the pupils accept me as another teacher or see me as a student?

The supervising teacher, especially if this is the first intern, also has questions in mind: Will the intern be critical of my teaching? Will I perform as a satisfactory supervisor? Will I be able to turn my teaching over to an intern? How will my pupils feel about having another adult in the classroom? How will I get along with my new intern? Will the intern be competent enough to work with my class? How will I get along with the university coordinator?

The decision to become a professional educator carries with it the responsibility to appear professional both in appearance and habits. Dress and physical appearance are important when working in a teaching role. Most school districts have written dress codes, and the intern should comply with these cooperatively and completely.

Subject matter and classroom equipment often dictate types of clothing interns should wear. Vocational education teachers frequently find a necktie to be a safety hazard and science teachers and art teachers sometimes find in laboratory situations that loose-fitting clothes with floppy sleeves or long scarves can be dangerous. Female kindergarten teachers often discover that wearing a dress is impractical.

Interns begin their student teaching with an orientation period during which they become acquainted with the community, school, staff, and students.

These first few weeks of student teaching are crucial for the interns. First impressions are often unchanged.

It is important that interns and supervising teachers believe that student teaching is going to be worthwhile and even enjoyable. This is absolutely true in most student teaching assignments. Supervising teachers are usually pleased with the addition of two adult hands, and interns find that student teaching is the most beneficial experience they have had in college.

▼ GUIDELINES FOR THE SUPERVISING TEACHER

1. Consider it an honor to be assigned an intern. Not only your pupils but also your intern will adopt some of your ideas and concerns in life. In this way you will become immortalized.
2. Approach this opportunity with confidence and trust. If you consider your intern as a worthy, unique individual, you should do well as a supervising teacher. Interns produce better results if you express confidence in them.
3. Enter the student teaching experience with the frame of mind that you are going to have another teacher in the classroom. Let your intern know that you hope to pursue the ''we'' process. Effective team teaching can use the strengths of both individuals and, therefore, benefit your pupils.
4. Consider your intern a beginner. There are many tasks an intern has not experienced in the process of teaching; only experience can fill these gaps.
5. Prepare your pupils for the intern. Explain to them that they are going to have the benefit of another teacher. Some supervisors refer to their ''intern'' rather than ''student teacher.'' (In the early weeks, interns usually think of themselves as students rather than teachers.)
6. Show warmth and openness when you first meet your intern. Your attitude toward the intern will be detected easily at this meeting.
7. Specify to your intern what you expect. A good early project is to decide jointly on a lesson plan and journal format (see sample formats in the Appendix) and to stress to the intern the need to keep a journal. Planning should be done carefully and creatively.
8. Involve your intern early and gradually. Assign routine tasks and encourage work with individual pupils or small groups. Allow routines to vary to provide for the special needs and abilities of your intern.
9. If possible, provide your intern with a table or desk.
10. Encourage creative thinking by your intern and pupils. Interns should be expected to show initiative and to try out their ideas.
11. Provide for planned and unplanned conferences. Suggest that your intern keep notes during observations, and give your intern guidelines for taking notes that will be discussed at the next conference.
12. Strive for open communication with your intern to assure professional growth. This can happen only in an environment of mutual trust and helpfulness.

▼ GUIDELINES FOR THE INTERN

1. Go into student teaching with a positive attitude and a determination to do your very best. Although you still consider yourself a student, you are well on your way to becoming a professional. An average performance will not be good enough.

2. Be determined to show enthusiasm and to prove you have definite contributions to make to the teaching profession. If you do not feel good about yourself, chances are your impression on others will be negative.

3. Consider student teaching a full-time task. Part-time jobs, heavy social engagements, and college courses should be avoided if at all possible. You owe it to your pupils to be available to concentrate on student teaching.

4. Make specific preparations prior to student teaching. This could involve reading through pertinent curriculum guides or preparing teaching units that your supervisor has suggested. Such preparations would impress your supervisor and make you feel more confident.

5. Try to be congenial at all times. Pleasant interns make the best impressions. Make the most of each day's opportunities.

6. Keep in mind that you are about to enter a very noble profession, one that involves the responsibility of guiding young lives to their optimum.

7. Look the part of a professional. Determine what is considered appropriate dress in your particular school. By all means, be neat and clean. As a teacher-to-be, you must be an example to your pupils.

8. Learn the names of your pupils. They will be impressed if you call them by name the first few days. It will also work to your advantage if you learn the names of the school staff.

9. Follow the rules of the school. Be punctual and call if you will be tardy or absent. Be at school when you are supposed to be there if not before. Under normal conditions, it would be good to remain at school until your supervisor is ready to leave.

10. Attend all required meetings: faculty, grade level, PTA, and others involving your supervising teacher. These meetings can be informative and help give you the total picture of the teaching profession.

11. Become familiar with instructional materials. This is time-consuming but a necessary task.

12. While observing your supervising teacher, take notes for use at later conferences. Supervising teachers become upset if you spend time observing but fail to see what is taking place. Be an alert observer.

13. As you start student teaching, look interested and be curious. Look for ways to be helpful in the classroom. Volunteer special assistance for individual students or small groups. Your involvement should be active rather than passive.

CASE 1–1
▼

Mrs. Van Dyke's intern, Camille, has been approximately a half hour late each of the first 3 days of her second grade teaching assignment. Camille appears to be quite upset over the matter but feels she has a legitimate excuse. Her 2-year-old has the flu, and she considers home responsibilities her first obligation.

Mrs. Van Dyke has strong feelings that an intern's first responsibility is the student teaching assignment. She is a conscientious supervising teacher and expects her intern to arrive at school on time. She and Camille discuss the matter, and emotions run high. Each party holds her ground, and the problem is not resolved.

Camille calls the college coordinator.

1. What reaction do you feel the coordinator will have?
2. What steps could the coordinator take?
3. Do you feel that Mrs. Van Dyke has been fair with her intern? Explain.
4. How could Camille have planned for unforeseen emergencies such as this before beginning her internship?
5. Should Camille have called the coordinator in the first place?
6. Under what conditions should the principal be consulted? ▼

CASE 1–2
▼

Tom is in his second week as an intern in a fifth grade classroom. His supervising teacher encourages him to look for ways to get more involved in classroom activities and suggests he work with individual students having difficulty with mathematics.

One week goes by and Tom shows little or no involvement. He appears listless and constantly complains about his lack of knowledge in certain subjects, especially mathematics.

The supervising teacher contacts Tom's coordinator to discuss the problem.

1. What do you consider to be Tom's problem?
2. If you were Tom's coordinator, what would you do?
3. If Tom does not show more interest, in what ways would his student teaching program be affected?
4. What options are available to the supervising teacher?
5. How could this problem be avoided for student teachers in the future? ▼

CASE 1–3
▼

Mrs. Chang's intern, Anna, is very sure of herself during the first week of student teaching. She has been one big smile from the very start, giving the impression that she is living in another world. The fact is that three of Mrs. Chang's seventh grade social studies classes are most difficult to handle even for an experienced teacher.

Mrs. Chang wonders how Anna will ever win the respect of her classes. Anna seems to have decided that teaching is all roses and sugar and that negative factors should be overlooked.

Of course, the giggly seventh-graders think the intern is very amusing. Some are quite eager to assist her in losing her smile. Mrs. Chang knows from experience that the seventh-graders will make life unbearable for Anna when she begins teaching unless some changes are made. However, Mrs. Chang does not want to discourage her intern's positive attitude.

1. A positive attitude is an asset in an intern. What do you see to be the problem with Anna?
2. How should Mrs. Chang address Anna's problem?
3. What changes could Anna make in order to be more successful?
4. How could the coordinator define the problem for Anna?
5. How would teachers you have known have dealt with such a problem? ▼

CASE 1–4
▼

Paul began his student teaching as a loner. He avoided talking to teachers and, in fact, had difficulty communicating with his supervising teacher, Mr. Evans. Although Mr. Evans suggested Paul work with individual students and assume minor classroom chores, he has avoided all types of responsibility.

Most of Paul's comments are negative. He hints periodically that he really does not know if teaching is what he wants to do. Mr. Evans is quite alarmed when he mentions that he has not gotten anything out of his methods classes.

1. What could cause Paul to be so negative?
2. What steps can Mr. Evans take to change Paul's pattern?
3. How can a teacher have a negative disposition and still be effective?
4. What effect would more involvement with other interns have on Paul's attitude?
5. Why should a supervising teacher spend time trying to train someone to be a teacher when the person is not sure that he wants to be one? ▼

CASE 1-5 ▼

Betty has entered student teaching with a great deal of enthusiasm. She projects much more self-confidence than the typical intern.

During her introduction to the class, she states that she has a few rules she expects to enforce. One of the rules is in definite conflict with the supervising teacher's procedures.

1. How could Betty be approached tactfully?
2. Should an intern ever be permitted to be in conflict with the supervising teacher's procedures? Why or why not?
3. Most student teaching interns are quite cautious at the beginning. Why do you think Betty started with such confidence?
4. What could the supervising teacher have done to have avoided this situation?
5. How could this problem indicate possible related difficulties in the future? ▼

CASE 1-6 ▼

Marilyn is student teaching in a suburban high school, and her academic preparation seems to be satisfactory. The major problem with Marilyn is the way she dresses; she always looks like a Fifth Avenue model, and this disturbs both the students and the faculty. The students think some of her clothes are funny, and members of the faculty consider some of her outfits to be too revealing.

Although Marilyn always wears the latest fashion, she is dressing inappropriately for the classroom and for teaching.

1. How could Marilyn's apparel affect the students?
2. What should the supervising teacher do?
3. How can she avoid hurting Marilyn's feelings?
4. Would she seem envious herself if she suggests that Marilyn tone down her wardrobe?
5. To what extent should the coordinator be involved? ▼

RECOMMENDED READING

Readings especially pertinent for interns are followed by the notation ''I'' and for supervising teachers by the notation ''S.''

Boyer, Ernest. (1990). Teaching in America. In Marcella L. Kysilka (Ed.), *Honor in Teaching: Reflections* (pp. 3–6). West Lafayette, IN: Kappa Delta Pi. (I&S)

Boyer implores us to accord teaching the dignity it deserves. Reading this essay will give student teaching interns a zest for entering the profession and encouragement to assist with its renewal.

Deal, Terrence E., & Chatman, Reva. (1989, Spring). Learning the ropes alone: Socializing new teachers. *Action in Teacher Education, 11*(1), 21–30. (I&S)
Deal and Chatman give specific examples of how to assist in the orientation of new teachers. These techniques can be used in acclimating the student teaching intern.

Morris, John E., Pannell, Sue K., & Houston, W. Robert. (1988). Standards for professional laboratory and field experiences: Review and recommendations. In John Sikula (Ed.), *Action in teacher education* (pp. 147–152). Reston, VA: Association of Teacher Educators. (I&S)
The authors provide an analysis of the current standards for laboratory and field experiences; these standards have originated primarily from historically successful practices. The discussion and set of recommendations speak to the improvement of teacher education through a revision of these standards.

Odel, Sandra J. (1990). Support for new teachers. In Teresa M. Bey & C. Thomas Holmes (Eds.), *Mentoring: Developing successful new teachers* (pp. 3–23). Reston, VA: Association of Teacher Educators. (I&S)
An explanation of the mentoring concept, a table that gives mentoring roles from literature, and methods of applying the mentoring concept to the beginning teacher-experienced teacher situation are given. The importance of the careful choice of a mentor and the maintenance of such a relationship are stressed.

Sorenson, Virgina M., & Veele, Mary L. (1978). The student teaching team. In *Student teacher's handbook* (pp. 3–14). Holmes Beach, FL: Learning Publications, Inc. (I)
This overview gives the student teaching intern a good idea of the responsibilities of the student teaching team and where the intern fits into the team. The school administrator is included as a member of the team, in addition to the university coordinator, the supervising teacher, and the student teaching intern.

Tyler, Ralph. (1990). Placing teaching in the proper perspective. In Marcella L. Kysilka (Ed.), *Honor in teaching: Reflections* (pp. 15–18). West Lafayette, IN: Kappa Delta Pi. (I&S)
This brief essay by Ralph Tyler, the father of curriculum development in modern education, speaks to the honor of the profession of teaching. He refers to the value of teaching to our civilization and indicates that the public should understand and respect more of what teachers currently do.

2 ROLE OF THE SUPERVISING TEACHER

A Teacher's Influence

So you want a student teacher—
To offer your wisdom and such,
To train the novice in the role
That you enjoy so much!

The task before you can be fun,
If you follow some simple rules:
Set good examples for your charge,
Both in and out of school.

Give good advice—encouragement, too,
During these trying days—
Let your novice know you're there
To help in many ways.

Perhaps a few short years from now
You'll be so glad to hear
The novice guided and inspired by you
Is "Teacher of the Year!"

Myrtle Beavers
High School Teacher

The supervising teacher is the key facilitator in the professional development of any future teacher. Everything that the intern learns in college courses fuses during the term of student teaching, and it is the supervising teacher who assists more than anyone else in fitting all the pieces together to form a complete picture in the novice teacher's professional development.

The supervising teacher is a mentor, an example, a guide, a critical adviser, and a good friend to the intern during the student teaching experience. It is only with a great deal of faith and trust that a supervising teacher is able to turn a class over to an intern. Teachers become emotionally involved with their own classes and usually become rather possessive about them. It serves the intern well to realize this while working with the students in the supervising teacher's classroom. The development of a team-teaching partnership at the beginning is one method of dealing with this possessiveness.

Initially, the supervising teacher prepares the students for the arrival of the student teaching intern. Often such activities as preparing name tags for the elementary students to wear on the first few days the intern is there helps the students anticipate the arrival of the intern. In secondary schools, seating charts are helpful. When the intern arrives at school for the first observation, the supervising teacher should give a welcome to the classroom and an introduction to the classes, to the principal, and to the office staff. A brief tour of the school plant, including such important sites as the cafeteria, the teachers' lounge, and the location of rest rooms is beneficial.

To alleviate some initial concerns, the supervising teacher should give the intern copies of all materials the students will be using, including teacher tests and resource lists. Having the materials in hand makes it easier for the intern.

Being able to observe the supervising teacher in actual teaching situations is the second greatest aid to quiet the anxieties of the intern. Offering the interns the opportunity to observe the other classrooms in the school tends to make them feel more at home in the school and see themselves as an integral part of the total school picture.

Planning is critical. The intern may not yet be aware that the secret to being a successful teacher is effective planning. The supervising teacher should explain this point, demonstrating just how important planning really is to the success of the teaching act. Sharing current lesson plans also helps. It is reassuring to the intern if the supervising teacher can, on the very first visit, confer and make tentative written plans for the entire term. Such plans do not have to be detailed, but they can give some closure that would make the intern feel more comfortable. Occasionally, supervising teachers carry their plans around in their heads, but this is not a good example to set. Planning is extremely important, and the supervising teacher and intern should spend time on the subject during the term. It is better to overplan than for the students to have spare time on their hands and become behavior problems.

The supervising teacher should have the intern work into the teaching situation gradually by assigning work with individuals who need help, with small groups, with portions of the day's lesson with the entire class, and then with the entire class for the entire period or lesson.

The supervising teacher should plan specific times for uninterrupted conferences with the intern. Frequency is more desirable than length. From the very beginning, there should be an air of friendly criticism, with the supervising teacher using positive reinforcement whenever possible. If a specific point that may seem rather harsh needs to be shared with the intern, the supervising teacher should use the "sandwich" technique: sandwiching the criticism between two compliments. Tactfully done, this can be professionally developmental for the intern.

During conferences, the supervising teacher should help the intern look back as well as forward. In discussing those classes already taught, share feelings and ideas so that in planning for the future the intern can capitalize on successful techniques. Maintaining a journal (see Appendix A for sample journal format) assists both the intern and the supervising teacher.

It is the responsibility of the supervising teacher to keep a watchful eye on all that is happening in the classroom. Being accessible at all times is also important. After the intern takes over the teaching responsibility, it may be appropriate for supervising teachers to stay out of the classroom as much as they remain in it, gauging their decision on the capability of the intern. Some interns follow supervising teachers when they leave the room but others will blossom when supervising teachers are out of the room. Some classes of students cannot divide the supervising teacher's authority to include the intern; in such cases, the students will not see the intern as their teacher until such leadership in the classroom is established. Deciding when to intervene in a situation is one of the most difficult decisions for the supervising teacher to make.

The supervising teacher should evaluate continuously and maintain a folder of notes relative to the intern. Some supervising teachers keep a steno pad record, using one page per day with one side of the page for the intern and the other side for the supervising teacher. Both can jot down ideas and questions that come to them during the day so that when conference time comes, there is much to be discussed. This serves well as a reminder when the time arrives for the supervising teacher to evaluate the intern. The intern is more able to self-evaluate by having sufficient notes throughout the term (see Appendix B for format).

Most colleges ask the supervising teacher to formally evaluate the intern during the middle of the term and again at the end of the term. Although some colleges use only grades of "pass" or "fail," other colleges request that the supervising teacher assign a letter grade. Usually all grades are derived in conjunction with the college coordinator to maintain continuity between the intern's college work and the work in the supervising teacher's classroom.

▼ GUIDELINES FOR THE SUPERVISING TEACHER

1. You have accepted a tremendous responsibility in agreeing to work with an intern.
2. Some interns arrive at the supervising teacher's door well prepared and ready to teach and conduct themselves in a professional manner. Some are not as well prepared as others although they may have had the same college courses and teachers.
3. As a supervising teacher you have the right at any time to request that the intern be withdrawn from your classroom.
4. Most interns have areas of weaknesses and areas that need much development. If you can picture the intern as a diamond in the rough that needs some polishing, and that you, as the supervising teacher, are the jeweler, then the task may be less difficult.
5. The supervising teacher should never complain to peers about an intern; however, it would certainly be appropriate to boast if the occasion arose. Problems can be discussed with the college coordinator.
6. Most interns do not know exactly where to start; usually they are somewhat overwhelmed by the reality of the profession they have chosen for themselves. The supervising teacher should guide explicitly and carefully until it is obvious that the intern can maneuver alone.
7. Avoid the loss of precious time at the beginning of the term as you wait for the intern to act; not knowing what to do, the intern may be waiting for directions from you. Too often the supervising teacher feels the intern is lazy when it really is a case of the intern's not knowing what to do.
8. Be patient with your intern, but be firm in demanding professional standards in performance. Understand the stress under which the intern works.
9. Be helpful when help is requested; remember that the objective of student teaching is to help the intern learn to stand alone. Encourage the development of those qualities that will make the intern independent, not more dependent.

▼ GUIDELINES FOR THE INTERN

1. Your supervising teacher is devoted to the profession and would like to help another see the rewards of teaching. Do not add to your supervising teacher's burden; lighten it.
2. Do not wait to be told what to do. If you see something that needs to be

done, do it. However, do nothing without clearing it with your supervising teacher first.

3. Think ahead. Anticipate your responsibilities. Plan for ways in which you can best fit into the classroom.

4. Naturally, you will be anxious about your own performance in the classroom. When you begin to work with the students who need you, you will gradually begin to lose yourself. By your helping them, you will become more confident in yourself and more skilled in teaching and dealing with students.

5. Try to make life as easy for the supervising teacher as possible. Be professional; avoid having to be reminded of deadlines.

6. Learn as much as you can from your supervising teacher, both in classroom management techniques and in content delivery; you will find that your internship will be a profitable experience.

A LETTER FROM A SUPERVISING TEACHER

Dear Intern:

I am so excited and pleased that you will be joining me in my classroom. The children are so lucky to be getting another teacher to help them learn. I'm also a little worried. I'm not worried about your abilities or preparation, but about myself. Will I be able to make you feel welcomed and comfortable? Will I be able to communicate with you in a way that will make you grow confidently into the kind of teacher you want to be? Will I be able to answer all of your questions fully?

Trust and honesty are important qualities in a teacher. I promise to trust you and be honest with you. Will you be honest with me? If you need special help in an area, will you trust me enough to ask? If you are scared, unsure, and worried, will you be honest with yourself and tell me?

I promise to introduce you to the other members of our school team and to make you feel welcomed. I won't leave you out of conversations and make you feel like a third wheel. There are times when I might want to be alone with other teachers. I'm not going to talk about you. Remember, you can trust me.

I don't expect you to become me. You will teach differently. I hope you will want to do some things that I do, but then again, you have just completed your college education and should have some new and exciting ideas to share with me. Teach me. Share with me. I will share all my ideas with you. Remember, there is so much that I can share with you.

There is one area that you will have to show me that I can trust you. That's with my children. They are my world to me. Every one of them has become a part of me—an extension of my soul. Through your planning and preparation, your promptness, your interest, your concern for their welfare, your giving that little bit of extra effort, you can show me that they have also become a part of you. I love them and you will grow to love them, too.

Yes, I am called your supervisor, but I hope that I can also be called your friend.

Kathy Brake
Elementary Teacher

CASE 2–1
▼

Bert, the new intern in Mrs. Lambert's journalism class, arrived at the school on time and hurried past the office to the classroom. When he arrived, Mrs. Lambert was in conversation with some neighbor teachers. Bert approached the group and with a large smile and a loud "Hello, folks," he proceeded to slap one of the male teachers on the shoulder and peer directly into the eyes of the pretty young female teacher talking to Mrs. Lambert. Both teachers, never having met Bert, were somewhat appalled and backed away.

1. What do you think causes Bert to be overly friendly?
2. How should Mrs. Lambert react?
3. What impressions has Bert made on the neighbor teachers?
4. How can Bert make up for such a beginning?
5. What responsibility does Mrs. Lambert have concerning Bert's actions? ▼

CASE 2–2
▼

Since the initial visit, the supervising teacher, Mrs. Strong, had suggested to her intern that she preferred that he develop his plans in detail at least a week before he planned to implement them. As the time approached for the intern to take over his first class, Mrs. Strong repeatedly asked the intern if she could see his plans and if they could discuss them. The intern always put her off with remarks to the effect that he was not happy with the plans yet; he had not finished working with them.

The day before he was to begin teaching, he still refused to allow her to see the plans or to discuss them with her. Mrs. Strong told him that she would be at school 45 minutes early the next day for the specific purpose of reviewing his plans with him before he taught or she would not allow him to take over her classroom. The next morning, she arrived at school early but the intern came at his usual time. When she asked him about his plans for teaching the class that day, he shrugged his shoulders and said, "Oh, I know what I'm going to do; I've got it all in my mind."

1. How do you think Mrs. Strong reacted?
2. What would have been the best action to have taken in this situation? Why?
3. How should the supervising teacher report the intern's actions to the university coordinator?
4. What kind of attitude changes should the intern have in order for this to be a successful experience?
5. How could the supervising teacher build on the planning strategies the intern had developed in methodology courses? ▼

CASE 2–3
▼

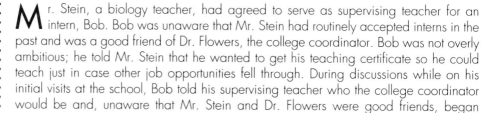

Mr. Stein, a biology teacher, had agreed to serve as supervising teacher for an intern, Bob. Bob was unaware that Mr. Stein had routinely accepted interns in the past and was a good friend of Dr. Flowers, the college coordinator. Bob was not overly ambitious; he told Mr. Stein that he wanted to get his teaching certificate so he could teach just in case other job opportunities fell through. During discussions while on his initial visits at the school, Bob told his supervising teacher who the college coordinator would be and, unaware that Mr. Stein and Dr. Flowers were good friends, began discussing Dr. Flowers in an unfavorable light.

Back on the college campus, as Bob was preparing to intern, he asked Dr. Flowers if he could discuss with him some possible problems. He then related some inappropriate details about Mr. Stein to Dr. Flowers, who realized that the intern was deceiving only himself in establishing the triangle.

1. Whose responsibility is it to discuss the truth with the intern?
2. Why should the intern not be allowed to play his game further?
3. As supervising teacher, what approach would you have taken?
4. Why is it wise for interns to avoid criticizing their coordinator or their supervisor?
5. How would a change of coordinator affect the situation? ▼

CASE 2–4
▼

Mr. Lyons, a fifth grade teacher, had made arrangements for Nyasha, his new intern, to observe in several teachers' classes during her first 2 weeks in the new assignment. The observations went well until one of the observed teachers reported to Mr. Lyons that Nyasha had wanted to discuss with her what she referred to as different attitudes and methods of approach of the teacher previously observed.

1. How should Mr. Lyons approach the intern without indicating where he obtained his information?
2. What should he say to her?
3. How could he verify with other teachers if this pattern of behavior existed elsewhere?
4. How could he keep this type of behavior from occurring in the future?
5. Why would it be important for evaluation sessions to be restricted to the coordinator and/or supervising teacher? ▼

CASE 2–5
▼

Maria, the new intern in Ms. Elbert's fourth grade classroom, really wanted to be a good teacher. She was enthusiastic about her future as a teacher; she was also enthusiastic about her wedding that was scheduled for the week following the end of the term. At the beginning of the term, Maria explained that she was spending much time in the evenings getting things organized for the wedding but that she would soon be finished with that and be able to spend plenty of time on lesson preparation.

As the weeks wore on, Maria seemed less and less prepared with materials.

Ms. Elbert habitually arrived at school early and organized materials for the day. Maria had become lax and frequently came in at the last minute with her arms full of papers. Often she would ask Ms. Elbert to watch the class while she went to the teachers' work room and prepared materials; then while the students were working on those, Maria would prepare the next materials. This hurt Ms. Elbert and she feared for her students' achievement. Until this point, Ms. Elbert had not shared her concern with the college coordinator because she had hoped Maria would improve.

As things got worse instead of better, Ms. Elbert confronted Maria with the problem. Maria explained that she just did not know any way to improve, that she could not get everything done that she was responsible for, and she felt that she should withdraw from student teaching.

1. What alternatives should Ms. Elbert offer Maria?
2. Should Ms. Elbert take over any of Maria's responsibility in the classroom?
3. What assistance could the college coordinator offer?
4. What should be the limit of the principal's involvement in this case?
5. In what ways would an intern's attention to personal affairs affect professionalism? ▼

CASE 2–6
▼

Eric was assigned to student teach with a young female coach. Although his major was physical education, he resented being placed to student teach with a female. During his initial observations and early visits with his supervising teacher, he expressed to her the possibility that he might be placed with another teacher, since it just did not seem appropriate to him to be placed with a female.

As the term wore on, week after week, his remarks and hints became less subtle. The supervising teacher, exasperated, decided she had all she could take of the student teacher's attitude.

1. What procedure should the supervising teacher follow?
2. What alternatives are available to the supervising teacher? To the student teaching intern?
3. Under what conditions should the supervising teacher be expected to allow the student teacher to complete the term?
4. In what ways would Eric's attitude affect his professional relationships with females?
5. How could the attitude have been identified earlier? ▼

RECOMMENDED READING

Balch, Pamela M., & Balch, Patrick E. (1987). The responsibilities of a cooperating teacher. In *The cooperating teacher: A practical approach for the supervision of student teachers* (pp. 29–47). New York: University Press of America. (S)
The variety of roles and responsibilities of the cooperating (supervising) teacher are explained. Helpful, practical suggestions are given for supervisory style and time management.

Good, Thomas L., & Brophy, Jere E. (1991). Instruction. In *Looking in classrooms (5th ed.)* (pp. 439–520). New York: Harper Collins Publishers. (I&S)
This chapter on instruction is excellent reading and reference for both the supervising teacher and the student teaching intern. Research on instructional methods, on teacher behavior related to learning, and on higher order thinking and problem solving strategies is a valu-

able resource for establishing competence in teaching.

Posner, George J. (1989). What is the situation with the cooperating teacher and the classroom? In *Field experiences: Methods of reflective teaching* (2nd ed.) (pp. 47–59). New York: Longman. (I&S)
Posner shows the student teaching intern how to see the cooperating (supervising) teacher and the classroom from the perspective of a teacher instead of from a student. Taking a fresh look at the teacher, the room itself, the students, and the activities enhances the readiness of the student teaching intern.

Rohrkemper, Mary M. (1982). Teacher self-assessment. In Daniel L. Duke (Ed.), *Helping teachers manage classrooms* (pp. 77–96). Alexandria, VA: Association for Supervision and Curriculum Development. (S)
As supervising teachers begin to assess the classroom activities of the student teaching intern, they begin to review their own assessment more critically. This chapter assists supervising teachers to be more aware of the relationships between their intentions and the student behaviors.

Ryan, Kevin (1982). The cooperating teacher: Who? what? why? when? how? and whither? In Gary A. Griffin & Sara Edwards (Eds.), *Student teaching: problems and promising practices* (pp. 57–68). Austin, TX: Research and Development Center for Teacher Education, the University of Texas at Austin. (S)
The author discusses the role of the cooperating teacher (referred to in this book as the supervising teacher) and two possible scenarios related to involvement in student teaching assignments. A number of questions are considered, and he concludes by recommending that the current orthodoxies of student teaching be questioned.

3 ROLE OF THE COLLEGE COORDINATOR

The college coordinator serves as the liaison between the schools where student teaching is taking place and the college or university that is sponsoring the experience. Furthermore, the college coordinator is ultimately responsible for recommending the intern for certification to the college or university. Coordinators serve as public relations agents and may be the only people from the college to work directly with the schools. Often they are asked to explain specific services of their institution.

An additional responsibility of the coordinator is to provide interpretation of the university program to assigned interns. This involves visiting the interns in the school, conducting seminars, and conferring with principals, supervisors, and supervising teachers.

Coordinators guide interns through the realization of teaching skills. The one-to-one relationship between coordinator and intern should present an ideal teaching atmosphere; the unique problems faced by each intern can be considered and suitable courses of action prescribed. Education majors seldom experience this one-to-one assistance until student teaching. Working closely with both a supervising teacher and a coordinator during the last term can enhance this type of individualization. The coordinator should be considered a friend and helper who is always accessible.

It should be clarified that a coordinator is not primarily an "evaluator" during the supervisory visits. It is unrealistic to think that a coordinator can size

up the total teaching-learning situation during the typical four or five visits. The supervising teacher must be the major evaluator. The coordinator, relying heavily on the supervising teacher, is usually responsible for the final evaluation of the intern, however.

The trouble-shooting role of the coordinators is quite evident. They serve as intermediaries in situations that may arise between interns and supervisors. Because many interns face difficulties, they should feel free to confide in the coordinators, who, by virtue of their positions, must keep confidences.

Interns and/or supervising teachers possibly have not had previous contacts with their assigned coordinator. Each coordinator should represent expertise in certain academic areas and should be recognized and used as a professional resource during student teaching, both in and outside class. One of the most important tasks of a coordinator is to ensure close communication, getting all involved persons to give their best efforts in providing a successful learning experience for the student teaching intern.

▼ GUIDELINES FOR THE SUPERVISING TEACHER

1. Do everything you can to facilitate open communication with your intern and college coordinator. Do not protect your intern from the life experiences of teaching.
2. Interns should have the opportunity to try out their ideas during student teaching and experience failures as well as successes. Discuss openly the strengths and weaknesses of your intern with the college coordinator.
3. Use the strengths of the coordinator who could possibly provide some alternative plans of action to enrich your classroom. However, the coordinator will not present suggestions for change unless specifically asked and is not there to evaluate a supervisor's teaching methods.
4. Make arrangements for a three-way conference (supervising teacher, intern, coordinator) after the initial observation by the college coordinator. Coordinators usually prefer three-way conferences, particularly at the beginning of student teaching, because this will enhance communication. If such a conference cannot be arranged, provide time and a place for suitable two-way conferences between you and the coordinator and between the intern and the coordinator. (See Appendixes C and D.)
5. Be helpful by convincing the intern that the college coordinator is there to assist. It enriches the student teaching program to involve as many professionals as practical.
6. Call your coordinator if major concerns develop. Coordinators expect supervising teachers to communicate with them and seek help when necessary. Although coordinators normally visit each intern four or five times, they could be available more frequently if necessary.

▼ GUIDELINES FOR THE INTERN

1. Communicate openly with your coordinator. One purpose of student teaching is to meet and resolve problems. A successful student teaching experience cannot be void of conflicts; it is a strength to be able to recognize

problems and to discuss them with your coordinator. You should also have many joys and successes to share.

2. Meet with your coordinator very early in the student teaching experience. Coordinators usually visit schools during the first or second week. There is a good possibility that a group meeting with your coordinator and other student teaching interns will be scheduled on campus prior to the time you report to the school.

3. Consider your coordinator as a friend and helper. An effective coordinator is well aware of the emotional aspects of teaching with its highs and lows and is always ready to listen.

4. Make your coordinator feel welcomed when first visiting your classroom. Introduce your coordinator to your supervising teacher and to your students, if feasible. An acceptable time to present your coordinator to the students is immediately before the first observation. If you prefer not to make a formal introduction, be sure to explain to your students the purpose of the coordinator.

5. Keep your lesson plans and other information in a folder or notebook for inspection by your coordinator, allowing for a discussion of your teaching tasks. An effective coordinator helps you learn to evaluate your performance and can be invaluable in the development of instructional techniques.

6. Be yourself when your coordinator visits. Coordinators can easily recognize a dramatic presentation; they want to see a normal classroom situation. Be at your best for your students and yourself.

7. Appreciate and encourage the two- and three-way conferences with your coordinator and supervising teacher. Tremendous professional growth can take place during these conferences. Although you may experience in years to come teaching that will lack supervisory assistance, during student teaching you will know that you have at least two people who are deeply interested in your teaching skills.

8. Your coordinator will probably hold seminars during student teaching. This would be a good opportunity to compare notes with other interns. Morale is improved when you discover that others like you are struggling and working hard to accomplish the same goals.

CASE 3–1
▼

Juan was assigned as one of Dr. Jones's interns. At their meeting on the first day of the semester, Dr. Jones explained that he would drop in unannounced during student teaching. He felt that he would see a more normal situation if interns and supervisors did not know when he would visit. Juan expressed his displeasure over this arrangement and stated it would be more fair if the interns were informed, at least for the first two or three visits.

1. Why should the intern be informed of the time of the coordinator's first observation?
2. Why is the coordinator's first observation a big deal in the mind of an intern?
3. What is the primary role of a college coordinator?
4. What are the advantages/disadvantages of the intern knowing when the visits will take place?
5. How important are the evaluations of a coordinator? ▼

CASE 3-2
▼

During his first observation of Sally, her coordinator, Dr. Brown, made some comments on his observation report that stirred up the supervising teacher. Dr. Brown wondered why the third grades were not grouped for reading instruction to provide for the wide range of reading levels.

Sally is quite concerned because she was only following her supervising teacher's guidelines. She feels that she is caught between two differing philosophies and cannot possibly come out a winner.

The supervising teacher is fighting mad and threatens to discontinue working with her intern.

1. Why was Dr. Brown wrong about raising the question about the teaching of reading?
2. How should the supervising teacher confront Dr. Brown concerning her displeasure?
3. How could Dr. Brown raise the question without upsetting the supervisor?
4. What could be done to prevent Sally's situation from becoming unbearable?
5. What measures should Dr. Brown take to reduce the tension? ▼

CASE 3-3
▼

Phong, a technology education intern, was in his second week of student teaching. His coordinator, Dr. Randolph, arrived on the scene to discover that the supervising teacher was spending very little time in the classroom because he had explained to Phong that he wanted him to get the feel of complete control of the situation.

Dr. Randolph was quite concerned. He felt that this intern was not ready to take over the class. In fact, he was hardly familiar with the safety precautions in the shop. Dr. Randolph also wondered how effective supervision is with the supervising teacher gone most of the day.

1. Is there ever a valid reason for the supervising teacher to stay out of the classroom for long periods of time during the beginning of student teaching?
2. How could Phong accomplish his goals during student teaching with his supervising teacher out of the room most of the time?
3. Why is it important for a supervising teacher to leave the intern periodically?
4. How should Phong's problem be resolved?
5. What role should the principal and or/the coordinator take in this situation? ▼

CASE 3-4
▼

Beatrice was not pleased when Dr. Jacobson was assigned as her coordinator. Beatrice had received poor grades in two of his classes; she felt that he was most unfair in his evaluations.

After Dr. Jacobson's first observation of Beatrice, he wrote up a very negative observation report. Beatrice was quite upset because she thought she had taught an excellent science lesson with her third-graders that day. It was Beatrice's opinion that Dr. Jacobson gave her a negative report because of preconceived notions of her abilities. She discussed the matter with her supervising teacher after Dr. Jacobson left the school.

1. How should the supervising teacher handle this matter?
2. Why do you think Beatrice did not discuss this matter with Dr. Jacobson during their conference?
3. Is there any way that Beatrice could win the approval of Dr. Jacobson? How?
4. Because Dr. Jacobson will be responsible for Beatrice's final grade, should she drop out of student teaching and hope for a different coordinator next time? Why?
5. What situations require that the coordinator be changed during a student teaching assignment? ▼

CASE 3–5
▼

Helen was assigned as an intern in a second grade classroom. On arriving at school the first day, she was informed by her supervising teacher that she felt Helen was too immature to work with her low math group. She did not want her to experience failure so she planned to send her to another classroom to work with an above-average math group during the first part of the morning.

Helen, a top-notch teacher candidate, was distraught. She felt that her supervisor had little faith in her abilities and had already labeled her a failure. She wanted the experience of working with the low math group and wondered how she could be fairly evaluated while working in another classroom.

Feeling that she had no chance to succeed, she called her coordinator to explain the situation. She requested a change of assignment. The coordinator made plans to visit Helen the next day.

1. Were Helen's objections justified?
2. Was the supervising teacher unfair in assigning Helen to another classroom for math?
3. How could communication have been improved in this situation?
4. Why would it be advantageous to work out the problem rather than change Helen's assignment?
5. What could the coordinator do to resolve this conflict? ▼

CASE 3–6
▼

Bradford had not passed his first student teaching assignment but was given another chance in an eighth grade English class. It was the opinion of Bradford's first supervising teacher that he had potential as a teacher but had not been able to get his act together.

Bradford's newly assigned coordinator observed one of his classes during the third week of this second assignment. The coordinator felt that his teaching was satisfactory but noticed some definite idiosyncracies of behavior that bothered her considerably. She felt too embarrassed to discuss the matter with Bradford and decided to videotape his next lesson. Bradford was quite distraught at the idea of being videotaped and wondered why he had been singled out.

1. Is it unrealistic that Bradford's coordinator would not discuss the matter with him?
2. What kind of idiosyncracies could cause this much confusion?
3. Why did the coordinator feel that a videotape would be helpful?
4. Should interns be given a second chance to student teach? If so, under what conditions?
5. What would be the advantages and disadvantages of giving Bradford the same supervising teacher and coordinator he had during the first assignment? ▼

RECOMMENDED READING

Balch, Pamela M., & Balch, Patrick E. (1987). Establishing professional relationships. In *The cooperating teacher: A practical approach for the supervision of student teachers* (pp. 143–157). New York: University Press of America. (S) *This chapter includes a discussion on the relationship between the college coordinator and the supervising teacher. Of special note is the discussion of collaboration necessary for this team.*

Colton, Amy Bernstein, & Lander, Georgia Sparks. (1992). Restructuring student teaching experiences. In Carl D. Glickman (Ed.), *Supervision in transition: 1992 yearbook of the Association for Supervision and Curriculum Development* (pp. 155–168). Alexandria, VA: Association for Supervision and Curriculum Development. (I&S)

This article proposes to help to develop thoughtful and self-directed educational professionals, including student teaching interns, by initially structuring the basis of the perception of the student teaching intern experience. The second step is to train supervisors and coordinators who can use these restructured experiences. This model was developed through work with the Ann Arbor (Michigan) Public School teachers and faculty of Eastern Michigan University.

Hevener, Fillmer, Jr. (1981). Relating to the college student teaching counselor. In *Successful student teaching: A handbook for elementary and secondary student teachers* (pp. 54–61). Palo Alto, CA: R. & E. Research Associates, Inc. (I&S)
Hevener refers to the university student teaching coordinator as the college student teaching counselor. The roles of the coordinator are explored. Student teaching interns are encouraged to expect three-way conferences, conferences between the coordinator and the supervising teacher, and post-lesson conferences to evaluate the teaching skill of the intern.

Machado, Jeanne M., & Meyer, Helen C. (1984). Common problems of student teachers. In *Early childhood practicum guide: A sourcebook for beginning teachers of young children* (pp. 98–106). Albany, NY: Delmar Publishers, Inc. (I&S)
Areas of conflict that may occur involving the college coordinator, the supervising teacher, and the student teaching intern are considered in this chapter. Suggested activities are listed and reassurances are provided for the intern.

Sorenson, Virginia, & Veele, Mary. (1978). The student teaching team. In *The student teacher's handbook* (pp. 7–14). Holmes Beach, FL: Learning Publications, Inc. (I&S)
This brief chapter contains suggestions for the student teaching team: the university coordinator, the supervising teacher, the school administrator, and the student teacher. These responsibilities are listed in an effort to improve the communications among the entire team.

4 ROLE OF THE INTERN

Student teaching is designed to be a very rewarding experience for well-prepared interns. Each intern is placed in a public or private school under the direct and continuous supervision of a teacher who has expressed willingness to participate in the student teaching program. The supervising teacher, because of experience and background, can assist the intern in becoming a competent and caring teacher.

Opportunities are provided in the student teaching program that ensure interns an acquaintance with the responsibilities of teaching. These experiences in student teaching provide realistic evaluations of interns' strengths and weaknesses as prospective teachers and help develop competencies in classroom management skills. Successful interns should progress to the level of expertise needed for independent performance in the classroom as they are in the process of becoming rather than moving toward a finished product.

The student teaching experience consists of three phases: (1) orientation and observation, (2) assisting, and (3) assuming responsibility in the total school program. Interns need to observe in their own classroom as well as in other grades and areas such as Learning Disabilities (LD), Educable Mentally Handicapped (EMH), Physical Education, Art, and Music. These observations give interns a chance to observe a variety of teaching techniques and learning styles as well as allow them to get acquainted with the school's policies and procedures.

After observing for at least a week, interns should begin assisting students on an individual or small group basis. Some level of assistance should begin the first day in order for the intern to feel at ease in the classroom. This period of assisting gives the intern the feel of teaching in that particular environment.

After interns have progressed through the first two phases, the supervising teachers should gradually provide opportunities for them to assume greater responsibilities. Interns begin teaching a particular subject, depending on their experience. If they have had several years' experience in a classroom as aides and/or feel comfortable in the classroom, they may be capable of assuming greater responsibilities faster. This schedule should be worked out among the intern, supervising teacher, and coordinator.

If interns show initiative, enthusiasm, and adequate preparation, they may stay ahead of the schedule suggested by the college. As long as they are showing quality teaching, the supervising teachers may relinquish more and more responsibilities. During the latter part of student teaching, interns should be in full charge of the classroom.

The prime consideration of the interns should be the welfare of the students in the classroom. The supervising teacher has a master plan to meet the students' needs; the interns must learn to operate within the framework of this plan.

One of the first tasks of interns is to determine the goals and objectives of their assigned class. Supervising teachers should explain the goals and objectives that have been completed prior to the arrival of the interns, those planned for use during the internship, and those that will be realized after the interns leave.

Adequate planning is essential for a successful student teaching experience. Interns soon learn that there is a high positive correlation between effective planning and successful teaching.

Interns need to know how to identify best long-range goals for given subject areas as well as how to develop and place in proper sequence the related short-range objectives. The specific format of lesson plans should be agreed on by the supervising teacher and intern, and lesson plans should be presented to the supervising teacher well in advance so that necessary revision can be made. This meeting of minds concerning the lesson plans can be a major part of the evaluation process. (See Appendixes E through H.)

After instructional objectives have been developed, interns need to select, adapt, and/or develop the necessary materials. Not only will the interns use materials available in the school and district, but they should also bring in supplemental materials from the college, community, and other sources.

The personal qualities of the intern are extremely important; promptness and dependability are qualities that will be observed closely. Maintaining a punctual and regular attendance record is a must. A very important quality is enthusiasm toward teaching because responses and contributions of students depend a great deal on this enthusiasm.

Interns should formulate a standard for student classroom behavior that maintains the classroom atmosphere already developed by the supervising teacher. Drastic changes in classroom management tends to add to the students' insecurity. Interns should demonstrate skills that help students develop positive self-concepts and respect for the dignity and worth of other ethnic, linguistic, cultural, and economic groups.

Interns are responsible for certain forms and reports, which should be completed and returned promptly. It has been stated that most teachers dislike keeping records. Even though they consider it a necessary task, they feel that it is an unproductive aspect of accountability (Charles, 1983). Many interns report that the whole area of record keeping was not discussed during their university work, and they are quite shocked at the variety and amount of paperwork required of a classroom teacher.

Good records are valuable to teachers in many ways. They provide information about academic instructional levels, specific strengths and weaknesses, progress that has occurred in the various subject areas, social behavior, and future plans for individual students. Formats for keeping good records easily include objectives, progress forms, graphs to show progress, work samples, and individual student folders in which to keep the forms and samples (Charles, 1983).

Competency in subject matter should be expected of all interns. Knowledge of subject matter is reflected in areas such as effective lesson plans, success of students, and recognition of various levels of abilities among the students. Most problems encountered during student teaching, however, have been found to be in the area of interpersonal relations rather than subject matter adequacy.

Interns are expected to exhibit skill in using various instructional techniques. Procedures used by the supervising teacher should be continued, but they should be supplemented by the special skill of the intern. The interns should use methods and materials that are consistent with the philosophy of the school in which they are teaching.

▼ GUIDELINES FOR THE SUPERVISING TEACHER

1. You should be well aware of the purposes of a student teaching program when you agree to participate in it. Although you feel the responsibility of helping to train future teachers, recognize that your first responsibility will be to your students.

2. Taking time to prepare for the intern can produce positive results. The initial orientation of the intern sets the tone of the whole experience. Creating an atmosphere of acceptance of the intern in the classroom is most important. The words you use in preparing your students for the intern are also critical.

3. Guide your intern into teaching gradually but steadily. It is sometimes difficult to give up your classroom to another teacher, but it is necessary for your intern to assume a leadership role. On occasions when you may be tempted to interrupt the teaching of the intern, try to resist doing so unless absolutely necessary.

4. Involve your intern as soon as possible. This not only benefits your program but also helps to get the intern's mind off feelings of anxiety. Arrange observation in a few other classrooms during the early part of student teaching. Guiding the intern in determining what to observe and holding post-observation conferences is also helpful.

5. Be certain to review your total program goals and objectives. Provide your intern with the necessary curriculum guides and teachers' manuals.

6. Introduce the intern to classroom routines and instructional procedures. Acquaint the intern with available instructional materials, supplies, and equipment.

7. Make your intern aware of your record-keeping responsibilities and acquaint them with pupil personnel records and the manner in which they are kept and used. Let your intern assist you in simplifying your records management.

8. Require that your intern provide lesson plans prior to teaching. Assist your intern with initial lesson planning. There is no excuse for inadequate planning on the part of the intern.

9. Involve your intern in the total school program. Provide opportunities for professional growth through attendance at professional meetings, including staff meetings. Give interns as many opportunities as possible to transfer theory into practice in a variety of classroom and extra-class activities.

10. After your objectives have been attained cooperatively, continuously evaluate the intern. Hold frequent conferences, both planned and unplanned. Interns are disappointed if they do not receive feedback concerning their successes and failures. Open communication is a most important factor.

▼ GUIDELINES FOR THE INTERN

1. Take your student teaching assignment very seriously. You must do your very best; average work is not acceptable.

2. Look for ways to become involved from the very first day. Expect to give more assistance than you receive. Expect and even ask to be allowed to participate in all normal teaching duties: playground, lunchroom, field trips, and clubs.

3. Be a good listener. You will be learning a great deal about your class during

a short period of time. The more you learn about the goals and objectives and your students, the better you will do when you begin your teaching. Getting to know the students helps you to identify the causes of classroom misbehavior and to employ corrective techniques.

4. Carefully observe the organizational patterns and teaching techniques of your supervising teacher. It is possible for one to spend time observing but see very little. Get together with your supervising teacher and determine objectives for your observation; afterward, discuss your concerns and learnings from the observations. Keeping a proper journal is a big help in preparing for these conferences.

5. When you teach your first lesson, provide your supervising teacher with a thorough lesson plan. This plan not only shows your supervising teacher that you are aware of the importance of planning but also provides information for constructive feedback. Discussing these plans provides an excellent opportunity for evaluation and professional growth. After you begin teaching a full schedule, your plans will be shortened, but still they should be clear-cut and concise.

6. Discipline in the classroom will be a big concern for you. It is most important that you operate within the framework that has been developed by your supervising teacher.

7. Develop a receptive attitude toward suggestions and criticisms. If errors are to be avoided and/or corrected, you must be receptive; however, it is not your task to become a duplicate of your supervising teacher. It is a unique opportunity to get feedback concerning your teaching style from a professional teacher.

8. Keep in mind that you are another professional person in the classroom. Try to keep your enthusiasm at a high level as you go about your teaching duties. You are fortunate in being given the opportunity to work with these young minds.

CASE 4–1
▼

Susan was a successful intern in a high school English class. She had developed an excellent rapport with her students and had been very happy with her own progress. Everything went well until one of her students yelled out while leaving her class: "Good-bye, Susan!" She was shocked but let the matter drop. Word of this spread around the school rapidly. On her way to her car at the close of the school day, Susan was called by her first name at least three times by students.

When Susan arrived home, she was distraught. Things had gone so well until then.

1. What would be the advantages/disadvantages of Susan's ignoring such comments?
2. What could Susan do to solve this problem?
3. How could Susan involve her supervising teacher, principal, or college coordinator in this matter?
4. As Susan's supervising teacher, what would you do even if Susan did not seek your involvement?
5. How should this be handled with the students? ▼

CASE 4–2
▼

Bill had been dependable about turning his lesson plans in early and had undoubtedly spent a great deal of time on them. Today he presented a good introduction to his lesson, gave some valuable information, and assigned his students a work sheet. The problem was that the class was composed of students with varying abilities who finished the worksheet at different times. Students finishing first were not provided anything to do; therefore, discipline problems resulted. This had happened before, but Bill had not developed any solution.

1. Why is this likely to be a common problem of student teaching interns?
2. What could Bill have done when this happened?
3. When planning for a similar lesson, what additional plans should be included?
4. What should the supervising teacher do to help Bill?
5. Why should the college coordinator be informed about the problem? ▼

CASE 4–3
▼

Bob is successfully completing an internship in high school history. Everything was going fine until he began dating one of his students in his fifth period class. She was a senior who undoubtedly was infatuated with the new intern. Several of the students in the fifth period class began to tease Bob about his extracurricular affairs.

1. Do you feel that it is proper for interns to date their students? Why or why not?
2. What attitude should the supervising teacher have concerning this situation?
3. How could this situation have been avoided in the first place?
4. How do you feel the university coordinator will react to this?
5. What is the role of the principal in a situation such as this? ▼

CASE 4–4
▼

Mr. Muller's intern had designed a dynamic lesson and had motivated the students. While using the blackboard, he misspelled a word. None of the students said anything to the intern. However, one of the students privately mentioned it to Mr. Muller.

1. Why should an intern be a model for students?
2. What action, if any, should be taken by Mr. Muller?
3. How could this intern avoid a recurrence of this mistake?
4. How would you explain this type of spelling error to the students?
5. Do you feel that interns should be allowed to make mistakes of this nature? Explain your answer. ▼

CASE 4–5
▼

Sarah was in her fourth week as an intern in a sixth grade classroom, and her supervising teacher was very happy with her. Some of the other teachers in the building, however, were critical of her behavior during lunch period.

Parents were hired by the school district to supervise the lunchroom activities in order to give the teachers and students a short break from each other. The teachers had their lunch together in the workroom and enjoyed chatting. Some felt that it was rude that Sarah did not join them.

Sarah preferred to eat with her class and she felt that she could get to know the students better during an informal lunch period. To Sarah, this interaction was more important than joining the other teachers. One of the teachers, Mrs. Randolph, confronted Sarah in the hallway and told her that her omission at lunch was a sore point with a number of them. Sarah tried to explain her position but got a cold response.

1. How could this situation jeopardize Sarah's success in student teaching?
2. Do you think that her supervising teacher knows about the feeling of these teachers? If so, why did she not mention it to her?

3. In what ways was Sarah's feeling about eating with her class admirable?
4. What could Sarah and her supervising teacher do to ease this sore point among some of the teachers?
5. In what ways could the coordinator or principal help in this situation? ▼

CASE 4–6
▼

Luke had completed his sixth week in a junior high geography assignment. He felt uneasy because his supervising teacher had never said anything complimentary to him about his teaching. She had made some criticism about a few of his techniques but was never positive in her comments. Luke was particularly disappointed when he was marked only average on his mid-term evaluation. He thought he was surely doing something above average.

1. What could be some reasons that Luke's supervising teacher never offered any positive feedback to Luke?
2. Should Luke confront his supervising teacher about his concerns? If so, how?
3. How could the coordinator be of help to Luke?
4. What implications would self-evaluation have for Luke in this particular case?
5. How could a three-way conference (Luke, the supervising teacher, and the coordinator) on the mid-term evaluation be of help? ▼

REFERENCES

Charles, C. M. (1983). *Elementary classroom management: A handbook of excellence in teaching.* New York: Longman, Inc.

RECOMMENDED READING

Bey, Teresa M., & Holmes, C. Thomas. (Eds.). (1990). *Mentoring: Developing successful new teachers.* Reston, VA: Association of Teacher Educators. (I&S)
Mentoring can be a successful method for the supervising teacher to bring a student teaching intern into the profession. The material covered in this monograph is of interest to those who wish to review the research on mentoring in education and to look at the styles of mentoring the new professional.

Calderhead, James. (Ed.). (1988). *Teachers' professional learning.* New York: The Falmer Press. (I&S)
The supervising teacher may be interested in this entire text for discussion with the student teaching intern. These chapters are sequenced as development would be in the career of a teacher; the first five chapters deal with the professional development in student teaching relative to theory and

practice, reflective teaching, knowledge structures, and planning and post-lesson reflections. Case studies are included.

Geothals, M. Serra, & Howard, Rosa A. (1985). Introduction. General orientation: Assuming professional responsibility. In *Handbook of skills essential to beginning teachers* (pp. 1–7). New York: University Press of America. (I&S)
A discussion of the role of the student teacher is given, including diagrams of the functions involved in these roles. Responsibilities toward the supervising teacher, the coordinator, the rest of the faculty, and the school are listed.

Grambs, Jean D., & Carr, John C. (1979). Transition: Student teaching and success. In *Modern methods in secondary education* (4th ed.). New York: Holt, Rinehart and Winston. (I&S)
This material touches on many of the various roles the student teaching intern is expected to fill. Emphasis is placed on working successfully with both the college coordinator and the supervising teacher. Characteristics important for the intern to possess discussed here are a sense of humor, the ability to keep professional silence, and the ability to work with students in a humane and professional way.

Guyton, Edith, & McIntire, D. John. (1990). Student teaching and school experiences. In W. Robert Houston (Ed.), *Handbook of research on teacher education* (pp. 514–534). New York: Macmillan Publishing Company. (S) *The research base for field experiences is documented, including such aspects as curriculum models, structure, organization, and administration of student teaching. A paradigm for field experiences has been developed that fits such ethnographic needs better than does the paradigm for the methods used by the natural sciences.*

5 ROLE OF THE STUDENTS

The focal point of any educational program is, obviously, the student. A successful student teaching intern assists in meeting the educational needs of a given group of students.

Knowledge of pupils can benefit an intern enormously; therefore, interns who begin this assignment at the beginning of the year learn along with the teachers the needs of the students, their capabilities, and their learning levels. Interns who begin late in the year are at a disadvantage in knowing the level at which the students have been working. It is then more difficult for the interns to communicate with the students and to understand the structure of the classroom setting. It is up to the supervising teacher to fill these gaps.

One of the major concerns of the intern is classroom control. It is a shock for most interns to realize that they will soon be in charge of the discipline for an entire class. Often the intern cannot distinguish between teaching the students and making "friends" with the students, and many times does not have the knack of handling the entire group. Until the intern gains self-confidence and more knowledge about the group, it is necessary to begin by working with individual students and small groups. Most interns by this stage of their college work have had many practical experiences and will soon be able to prepare for entire-class teaching.

During the student teaching internship, ample opportunity to study and further develop skills and competencies that had been introduced earlier in the teacher education training program become available. Personal and professional qualities that the intern should attempt to refine during these weeks in the classroom include the following:

1. a desire for fairness to all students
2. a respect for all students regardless of ethnic, cultural, and economic background or state of health
3. the desire to be a good role model for the students and to help them in developing their own positive self-esteem

More and more, schools are becoming involved with children who may suffer from a health problem or a physical impairment. Each of these students deserves the very best in the way of emotional support and teaching skills. Frequently, instructional patterns must be altered to accommodate these students, and the intern should make every effort to serve these students well. Through cooperative learning strategies, the intern can show the other students the joys of assisting those who may have physical problems and cannot participate as everyone else does in the learning situations.

For those with health problems or physical impairment, the following two strategies are necessary:

1. Consider the safety of these students first.
2. Under no conditions should the student teaching intern administer medication. All medication should be administered by the school nurse. In the event there is no school nurse available, the office of the principal is the only entity that has the legal right to administer medication to a student.

All teachers and student teaching interns should be aware of the nature of Acquired Immune Deficiency Syndrome (AIDS). They should get the most recent statistical data from the local city, county, or parish health department. Students, teachers, administrators, or student teaching interns may be victims of AIDS, and should never be discriminated against because of this condition, just as one would not discriminate against a person because she had a broken arm. AIDS cases in schools are usually identified to the principal only; no one else in the school except for the school nurse has the legal right to know which students have AIDS. It is the responsibility of the principal to determine who, if anyone, in that school has a need to know such information.

Health department officials have indicated to classroom teachers that every individual with whom a person works in the public sector should be treated as if that individual has AIDS. This attitude avoids discrimination. With very young children who bite, or with injuries in the biology lab or in physical education class, the intern may question how to handle the flow of blood or other body fluids. This text cannot be completely prescriptive in this matter; however, it is important that student teaching interns be aware of the most current and realistic information available.

Family problems of students is another area of concern to the student teaching intern. Traumatic experiences in their family life affect the performance of students in the classroom to a great extent. The intern should be aware of such possibilities and develop special patience and consideration for those students whose home life is in upheaval. Frequently, special counseling is needed by such students. The intern should work very closely with the supervising teacher in such instances; care should be taken to remain objective but kind and supportive. Students have life-altering experiences and sometimes have no one but a teacher with whom to discuss their problems. Experiences such as a death or separation in the family, being witness to an accident or a crime, being a victim of crime, being a victim of abuse in the home, or poverty can permanently damage a student's self-image and ability to work successfully at school. Within the range recommended by the supervising teacher, the student teaching intern may effect a change for the positive in the life of a student.

Students often try to become personally involved with the intern. This is true at the secondary level as well as the elementary level. Everyone becomes involved to a degree, but the intern should avoid becoming too personally involved.

Younger students like to touch or pat their teacher on the arm or shoulder. There is a time and a place for this, but it is not during the middle of class. The supervising teacher can be very helpful in guiding these situations.

▼ GUIDELINES FOR THE SUPERVISING TEACHER

1. Prepare your students for the intern. Convince them that the intern is there to assume the role of the teacher.
2. Encourage the students to cooperate with the new person. The attitude of the students depends a great deal on your attitude.
3. Placing name tags on the desks of the students before the intern arrives is a good practice in the elementary schools. This is much appreciated by the intern, who is usually eager to learn names. In middle and high schools, the student teaching intern should be given a seating chart for each class.
4. Review the class rules with the students in the presence of the intern. Beginning interns are quite concerned about the status of their authority in the classroom; therefore, reviewing the rules should avoid misunderstandings at a later date.
5. Provide the intern with an opportunity to learn about the students who are in your classes. Cumulative records, individual conferences, open-ended questionnaires, or small group activities provide sources for this purpose.
6. Some supervising teachers prefer to avoid pointing out which pupils have been discipline problems. Therefore, interns have no preconceived ideas about pupils. Students often respond differently to interns. At times, interns see a side of the pupil overlooked by the supervising teacher, and the supervisor gets a new perspective on the child.
7. Assist interns in setting realistic standards of performance of themselves and the students. Encourage creative thinking and planning by students and intern. This means permitting the classroom routines to vary to provide for the special needs and abilities of the intern.

8. Update your intern on any real or threatened drug problem at your school. Caution the intern to be aware of certain areas and problem students. Review the current laws relating to drug use at school.

▼ GUIDELINES FOR THE INTERN

1. Think through a philosophy for working with students. Such a philosophy may include the following:
   a. Give students some freedom of choice and self-expression.
   b. Treat each student as an individual, and give the student opportunity to express ideas.
   c. Give opportunities for individuals to think for themselves.
   d. Try to avoid doing for the students what they can do for themselves.
   e. Try to have a positive approach, using a kind firmness.
   f. Make suggestions more frequently than you issue commands.
   g. Follow through when you have asked for a response. If you ask a question, give the students time to think about it. Do not just keep on talking.
   h. Try to give the students reasons for doing certain things required of them. Lead them to think through some of the reasons for themselves.
   i. Try to be consistent in your approach so the students know what is expected of them.
   j. Lead the students to finish the projects they begin.
   k. Talk in the language of the age group with which you are working. Avoid talking down to the students.
   l. Avoid having favorites.
   m. Plan ways students can accept responsibilities. Help them to follow through.
   n. Be alert to changing conditions and new needs.
   o. Remember that one does not have to be constantly talking to students in order for them to learn.
   p. Listen when students talk to you. Be alert to their ideas.
   q. Use questioning techniques to help students think through problems on their own.
   r. Study each student to learn the directions in which he or she needs to grow. Be aware of all students who do not participate.
2. Learn the names of the students quickly. This can be done by making a seating chart. Try to get to know the students individually. Your supervising teacher is your best resource in this respect.
3. Get to know your pupils as well as possible through observation, conferences, test scores, and examination of school records. During observations you might look for the following:
   a. How are the responsibility and initiative of the student promoted?
   b. How are pupil and pupil-teacher planning encouraged and carried out?
   c. What is the amount and quality of pupil participation?
   d. What is the evidence of pupil personality factors such as: excessive shyness, extremely critical attitudes, extreme sensitivity, day dreaming?
   e. What are the work habits of the pupils, such as the ability to work independently or cooperatively with other students and the willingness to ask for and use help from others?

4. Do your very best in working with the students. Regardless of age, students are quick to notice lack of preparation, uncertainty, and insincerity. They will try you at times, but they will want you to succeed if they feel you are sincerely interested in them.

5. Avoid the following common errors in working with students:
   a. calling on the better students too often
   b. failing to explain material at the level of the students
   c. taking for granted that students know certain facts
   d. punishing the entire class for misbehavior of one or two people
   e. punishing individual pupils before the entire class

6. Interns are not to touch or paddle a student in disciplinary action. Under no circumstances is the intern to inflict corporal punishment.

7. In the event you become aware of students administering medications to themselves or to others on the school site, report this immediately to your supervising teacher. Self-administered medications may be drugs. This is a serious responsibility.

CASE 5–1
▼

Sally is an intern in a fifth grade classroom. She has progressed satisfactorily but has been a bit ill at ease about the behavior of two or three of the boys. There were no major problems until today when one of her students, Don, refused to go to the office at her request. Don was larger than the intern and the supervising teacher was in the workroom. Sally decided to ignore the situation.

Shortly afterward she asked one of her other problem boys to quit bothering his neighbor. He yelled out: "I don't have to! You aren't my teacher!"

1. Was there a better way of handling Don after he refused to go to the office?
2. How should the supervising teacher deal with this situation?
3. How should Sally respond to the second situation?
4. What prior preventive measures could have been taken to avoid the development of such a situation?
5. How will these two incidents affect the self-esteem of the intern? ▼

CASE 5–2
▼

Teresa is a student in the biology class of Anthony, a new intern. She is very much attracted to this intern, who has been the star quarterback at the nearby university. Anthony asked her to sit down during a lesson, and she proceeded to run out of the classroom. Teresa's parents were contacted and the situation was explained to them during a conference. Teresa was counseled by the guidance counselor and she explained her deep attraction for Anthony. She felt that he was also interested in her and was crushed when he asked her to sit down.

1. What parties should have been included in the conference with the parents?
2. Was Anthony at fault in this situation? Explain your answer.
3. How would a good background in human growth and development help Anthony in understanding what was happening to Teresa?
4. How could Anthony avoid any indication that he was encouraging Teresa in her fantasy?
5. How will Teresa fit into Anthony's class after this? ▼

CASE 5–3
▼

Randy is an intern in an eighth grade science class. He has taken over three classes and appears to be doing a good job. Today Randy presented an activity project and became quite upset at the end of the lesson when his students went to the supervising teacher rather than to him for assistance on the worksheet. The supervising teacher noticed Randy's reaction and asked the students to go to Randy with their problems. The students continued to go to the supervising teacher.

1. Why do you feel that the students would not seek out the intern?
2. What would be the best way for Randy to solve this problem?
3. Could the supervising teacher be of assistance in this matter? In what ways?
4. What steps could Randy take to analyze the day's lesson to determine what went wrong?
5. How should Randy approach the next activity lesson? Under what conditions? ▼

CASE 5–4
▼

Betty is in her second week as an intern in a second grade classroom. Her supervising teacher runs a very relaxed classroom, which is a concern to Betty. As an intern, she is afraid that when she begins teaching she will not have control at all. The few times the supervisor has left the room, the students have gotten completely out of hand. Betty feels she has become overly friendly with two or three of the students and fears that this works against her. In fact, one of the students mentioned that he could hardly wait until she began teaching because he was "tired of working."

1. Do you feel that Betty's fears are justified?
2. Should Betty attempt to structure her classroom control according to the framework already set up by the supervising teacher? Explain.
3. What can be done by the supervising teacher to resolve this situation?
4. How should Betty prepare her coordinator for the initial observation?
5. What could Betty have done differently from the very beginning? ▼

CASE 5–5
▼

Jack has completed his fifth week in a seventh grade English assignment. His supervising teacher is concerned about his passive attitude toward the seventh-graders. Jack worked hard in preparing his lessons but never talked to the students individually or seemed interested in their affairs. He was primarily concerned with his lectures and treated his students as a group rather than as individuals.

1. Why is it necessary for an effective teacher to be interested in students as individuals?
2. What approach should Jack's supervising teacher take concerning this matter?
3. Should Jack be allowed to pass student teaching if he uses only the lecture approach to teaching?
4. In what way could the coordinator be of assistance to Jack?
5. What problems usually arise if the student teaching intern is more interested in the subject matter than in the students? ▼

CASE 5–6
▼

Marta was assigned to a senior high school internship. During the third week she discovered she was pregnant. Up until that time, Marta had shown little enthusiasm; from then on the situation got even worse. She seldom got out of her seat, which was located in the front of the room. During testing situations, the students began to copy from each other because there was so little supervision. Word got to the supervising teacher and she became furious. Cheating had not previously been a problem.

1. Should Marta be discouraged from student teaching because she was pregnant? Why or why not?
2. How could the cheating situation have been avoided?
3. In what way were the students at fault?
4. Can one teach effectively while sitting in front of the room most of the time? Explain?
5. How does the development of this situation present opportunities for teaching values? ▼

RECOMMENDED READING

George, Paul S., Stevenson, Chris, Thomason, Julia, & Beane, James. (1992). Teachers and students: Relationships and results. In *The middle school and beyond* (pp. 15–31). Alexandria, VA: Association for Supervision and Curriculum Development. (I&S)
These authors emphasize the needs and wants of both teachers and students in the classroom relationships. Healthy traits and desirable qualities are discussed.

Good, Thomas L., and Brophy, Jere E. (1991). Classroom complexity and teacher awareness. In *Looking in classrooms* (5th ed.) (pp. 23–46). New York: Harper Collins Publishers Inc. (I&S)
This chapter is a good review for the supervising teacher and a good introduction for the student teaching intern to the complexities of the classroom. Factors presented in this chapter include problems caused by a lack of teacher awareness of space, gender, time, and interaction difficulties.

Good, Thomas L., and Brophy, Jere E. (1991). Classroom life. In *Looking in classrooms* (5th ed.) (pp. 15–22). New York: Harper Collins Publishers Inc. (I)
Good and Brophy give the prospective student teaching intern a glimpse of the classroom. This chapter includes classroom narratives for both the elementary and the secondary schools.

Sorenson, Virginia M., & Veele, Mary L. (1978). You and your students. In *The student teacher's handbook* (pp. 23–29). Holmes Beach, FL: Learning Publications, Inc. (I)
Sorenson and Veele stress the importance of beginning the student teaching experience with the right relationship with your students. They give pointers in developing skills for initiating and maintaining those relationships.

Taylor, Barbara J. (1991). Guidance techniques for teachers and parents. In *A child goes forth* (pp. 263–276). New York: Macmillan Publishing Company. (I&S)
Taylor gives valuable realistic suggestions for working successfully with the young child. Although this chapter focuses on the preschool child, the information can be adapted for older children.

6 TEACHING COMPETENCIES

Required teacher competencies vary from state to state and from one university program to another. Most teacher competencies are lists of teacher abilities that revolve around the planning, implementation, and evaluation of student learning situations. These are based on a knowledge of student development, learning capabilities, and cultural, economic, and personality factors.

Sometimes in training programs, beginning teachers concentrate initially too heavily on teaching skills. It may be more helpful for these students to first become familiar with learner characteristics and motivation. Given such knowledge and a strong content background, students learning to be teachers may find that fitting their techniques to specific learning needs is relatively easy.

Implementing the competencies learned in methods classes is similar to that stage in putting together a jigsaw puzzle in which you begin to see the whole picture; you see where all the pieces fit in. A major thrill in the student teaching experience is actually using the competencies previously developed and having a successful experience in so doing. This is a moment supervising teachers can anticipate as eagerly as can the student teaching intern. This is the point at which the intern may exclaim, "Hey! This stuff all makes sense now!"

A good beginning activity for both the student teaching intern and the supervising teacher is to compare what the intern has learned in developmental psychology class about this age student. The supervising teacher can then add practical knowledge about the stages of physical, psychological, and social

development the students are going through. Once the range of levels of development has been ascertained, the intern begins to develop objectives for student learning. Based on those objectives, unit plans and lesson plans can be developed.

Ralph Tyler (Madaus & Stufflebeam, 1989) proposed a logical system of curriculum and instruction development. His rationale for such development has four major points:

1. Clarification of purpose
2. Selection of learning experiences
3. Organization of these experiences
4. Assessment of progress . . . (p. 200)

Tyler further suggested that a study of the learner be done. Although Tyler referred primarily to the development of programs, the supervising teacher can assist the student teaching intern in using this model in the development of unit and lesson plans (see Appendixes E through H).

Madeline Hunter (1976) has indicated that the most important factor for teachers is that of promoting learning in your students. Her book, *Teach More—Faster*, should be prescribed reading for every student who is becoming a teacher. The format of this text is refreshingly different. Much of what Hunter has written in her other books as well is immediately useful for the intern. When such materials are read and discussed by both the student teaching intern and the supervising teacher, both learn.

A good plan for success in student teaching is for the intern to begin classroom teaching in an area of strength with competencies that are better developed than others. This lends confidence so that when the student teaching intern moves into those less developed competencies, more self-confidence is there for the intern.

The primary competencies of teaching are planning, implementing instruction, and evaluating. How these are done are determined by preferences of the student teacher and the supervising teacher, unless the school district or the state department of education has specified other methods for so doing.

Beginning with setting objectives and establishing how those objectives are to be met, the student teacher can plan the most effective activities and materials to help the students reach those objectives.

Without seeming simplistic, this framework for developing teacher competence serves the intern well. The framework can easily be embellished as interests, abilities, and needs dictate.

▼ GUIDELINES FOR THE SUPERVISING TEACHER

1. Sometimes teachers who are effective in the classroom with their own students may not have articulated completely their position on teacher competencies. This is the time for you to review your thinking on these competencies. Decide on your priorities so that you can more clearly express them to your student teaching intern.
2. Being aware of your own priorities of competencies for teachers helps you be a better role model for your intern while at the same time sharpens your own teaching skills.

3. The review of research and current methodology in which you engage in order to be up to date in advising your intern pays double dividends. Observing, helping, and evaluating your intern throughout the student teaching process makes you more aware of your own level of competence in addition to helping you bring about positive critical development in your intern.

4. You should be aware that all your best intentions, suggestions, and help may be in vain. Although chances for such are minimal, it is possible that the intern assigned to you has insufficient preparation, motivation, or ability to become a successful teacher. Occasionally, psychological or addiction problems get in the way of the success of the intern. Your close association with the coordinator saves grief in such a situation. If the necessary level of competence in teaching skills does not become evident within a reasonable time, make appropriate arrangements with your university coordinator to have the intern reassigned at a later date after being cycled through additional methodology courses.

5. Help your student teaching intern organize a portfolio that documents her competence in particular areas. Such a portfolio could begin in an expandable folder and grow during the term to fit into a small file box. One method of documenting the portfolio contents is to label each file folder with a specific competency; in such a folder, place copies of all student teacher developed materials that pertain to that particular competency. By the end of the term, your intern will have a good collection that represents her ability in many areas of competence. Usually students are surprised at how well prepared they really are.

6. You will be more supportive of your intern if you unobtrusively remain in the classroom until you and he are both confident in lesson delivery competency. The beginning is not the time to leave the room and leave him on his own. The intern grows a great deal with your specific input and assistance at this critical stage of his student teaching assignment.

7. As you assist your student teaching intern in competency development, you will find that you will have been a major beneficiary yourself. Watching the student teaching intern begin the planning, implementation, and evaluation as a novice and helping the professional transformation occur will pay large dividends in your professional satisfaction.

8. During the time you are helping your intern in developing teacher competencies, consider a variety of methods of pinpointing difficulties. You may wish to come up with possible strategies such as the following:
   a. Insist upon a clear-cut lesson plan,
   b. If your intern uses nonstandard English while communicating information orally, make note of the mistakes for discussion at the next conference.
   c. Audiotape the lesson and during playback cooperatively evaluate as to whether the vocabulary was suitable to the topic and the audience.
   d. Also evaluate the audiotape as to suitability of volume and pace. If problems continue, give a demonstration lesson on how the volume and pace promote comprehension.
   e. Videotape a lesson of this type. The intern will probably see traits that worked against the purpose of the lesson as the videotape is reviewed.
   f. Present a resource person, a film, and/or a record as relevant examples.

9. Discuss all of the recommended competencies with your intern and together come up with practical ways of mastering them.

▼ GUIDELINES FOR THE INTERN

1. Keep in mind that the major purpose of student teaching is for you to demonstrate your teaching competence. You should realize, however, that this area is one in which you are continually growing. No one ever reaches the highest plateau of any teacher competency. Even experienced teachers of 20 years or more are working toward improving teaching techniques.

2. Realize that although you may have passed a written competency test, you are not assured that you will be effective in the classroom. Such abilities as classroom management, effective written and oral communication, as well as planning and teaching skills are difficult to measure adequately until you are assigned a group of students with whom to implement these skills.

3. As a beginning teacher, you may have developed idiosyncrasies of which you are unaware. These unique traits cannot be determined by competency tests. Encourage your supervising teacher to inform you of any problems of this nature.

4. Various economic and cultural factors in the particular school you are assigned influence the selection of competencies to be relied on. For example, a cutback in paper supplies in many schools may make it necessary for both the supervising teacher and intern to use the chalkboard more. To practice writing on the board is the only way to develop effective board handwriting skills.

5. Work very closely with the supervising teacher to make sure that you use the same system for testing and recording the minimum skills competencies. Parents must be notified if students are not developing these skills.

6. Discuss with your supervising teacher the competencies that you are expected to develop as a beginning professional. These discussions should take place often to provide for ongoing evaluation.

7. Develop your professional portfolio. Maintain samples of your professional work such as unit plans, lesson plans, tests, activities, and media materials. Set aside one section of your portfolio for evaluations from your supervising teacher and coordinator. Another section could contain notes and letters from students and parents recognizing your good work. An excellent method for documenting your teaching competence is to have someone videotape you as you are teaching a lesson.

CASE 6-1
▼

Bill is an intern in a fifth grade self-contained class. He is impressed with his supervising teacher, Mr. Randolph, who has made him feel welcome in the classroom. Bill was quite surprised at Mr. Randolph's attitude toward the recently adopted state minimum standards program; he resented spending the necessary time working on these minimum standards and was very hostile about it. Bill was embarrassed when his supervisor told the principal that he wanted a substitute teacher two or three days a week so he could keep up with the minimum standards. Needless to say, the principal did not appreciate the "humor" of Mr. Randolph's request.

1. How should Bill react in this situation?
2. How can he avoid getting caught up in the conflict?
3. In what ways could this situation affect his success as an intern?
4. What advice could the coordinator give Bill?
5. What opportunities could Bill use in helping Mr. Randolph accept the state minimum standards program? ▼

CASE 6–2 ▼

Betty is assigned as an intern in a third grade classroom. She is confident that she can be successful in student teaching except for one competency. She has always had difficulty with English grammar, especially verb tense. This is particularly true when she is nervous. Former teachers have been trying to help Betty resolve this problem for years.

1. Why should Betty discuss this matter with her supervising teacher at the very beginning of her student teaching?
2. How should Betty explain her difficulty with grammar to her coordinator?
3. How could a college student get this far in her program with such a weakness? Explain.
4. What steps can Betty take to improve her competence in grammar?
5. Under what conditions should Betty be allowed to successfully complete student teaching if this problem cannot be resolved? ▼

CASE 6–3 ▼

Chuck has begun his internship in a senior high English assignment. He was somewhat worried about his voice projection because he had been criticized in previous field experience assignments about speaking in a monotone. It came as a surprise when he realized that his supervising teacher also spoke in a monotone. Chuck was not going to be able to use his supervising teacher as a model in this area.

1. How could this problem be resolved?
2. Should Chuck discuss his feelings with his supervising teacher? How could this cause conflict?
3. In what way could the college coordinator be of assistance?
4. What other methods of presenting material to his class could Chuck use?
5. Which other high school faculty could help Chuck work on his vocal problem? ▼

CASE 6–4 ▼

Sally was in her fifth week of student teaching and assigned to an eighth grade classroom. She thought she was doing well but had received neither positive nor negative comments about her teaching from her supervisor. Sally was concerned that she may not be developing satisfactorily in the competencies necessary for successful teaching. The supervising teacher constantly changed the subject when Sally brought up the topic of evaluation. It was getting to the point that Sally was suspicious that she was not meeting the expectations of her supervisor.

1. How could Sally get this matter clarified?
2. Why do you think the supervising teacher always changed the subject?
3. What should the coordinator tell the supervising teacher about the importance of evaluation?
4. What methods of self-evaluation could Sally use?
5. What measures could be taken to make this a more profitable experience for Sally? ▼

CASE 6–5 ▼

Vito was in his sixth week of internship in an 11th grade mathematics class. He was disappointed when he received his mid-term evaluation report from his supervising teacher. He received high evaluations with the exception of the rating on his ability to keep adequate records, which was unsatisfactory.

The coordinator discussed this evaluation with the supervising teacher. She reported that Vito had taught effective lessons but was very careless in grading papers and recording grades. She said she had discussed this matter with Vito numerous times but no improvement had resulted.

1. What methods of feedback could the supervising teacher have used prior to the mid-term evaluation?
2. Should Vito have been content with only one unsatisfactory rating?
3. Why was he so careless in his record keeping?
4. What advice should Vito's coordinator give him?
5. If you were a principal interviewing Vito for a job, how would you express to him the importance of maintaining adequate records? ▼

REFERENCES

Hunter, Madeline. (1976). *Teach more—Faster* (p. 1). El Segundo, CA: TIP Publications.

Madaus, George F., & Stufflebeam, Daniel L. (Eds.). (1989). *Educational evaluation: Classic works of Ralph W. Tyler* (p. 200). Boston: Kluwer Academic Publishers.

RECOMMENDED READING

Barnes, Henrietta. (1989). Structuring knowledge for beginning teachers. In Maynard C. Reynolds (Ed.), *Knowledge base for the beginning teacher* (pp. 13–22). New York: Pergamon Press. (S)
This chapter reviews current research related to the necessary elements for teachers to develop meaningful frameworks for teaching. The data furnished by this author serves the supervising teacher well in guiding the student teaching intern.

Etheridge, Carol. (1989, Spring). Strategic adjustment: How teachers move from university learnings to school based practices. *Action in Teacher Education, XI* (1), 31–36. (I&S)
This article illustrates the translation of learnings from the university training to successful classroom practices. Examples of successful strategic adjustments are given.

Evertson, Carolyn M., Emmer, Edmund, Clements, Barbara S., Sanford, Julie P., & Worsham, Murray E. (1984). Organizing and conducting instruction. In *Classroom management for elementary teachers* (pp. 109–125). Englewood Cliffs, NJ: Prentice-Hall, Inc. (I&S)
This chapter is a good review of the implementation of instructional activities. The responsibilities of the student teaching intern to communicate directions clearly, to manage effective arrangement of activities, and to provide practice and feedback are among the many topics reviewed.

Gall, M. D., Gall, Joyce P., Jacobsen, Dennis R., & Bullock, Terry L. (1990). *Tools for learning: A guide to teaching study skills.* Alexandria, VA: Association for Supervision and Curriculum Development. (I&S)
Successful teaching/learning is based to a large degree on the successful study skills of the students. These authors have presented methods of identifying appropriate study skills and how to teach them in both the elementary and secondary classrooms.

Kim, Eugene C., and Kellough, Richard D. (1991). *A resource guide for secondary school teaching: Planning for competence* (5th ed.). New York: Macmillan Publishing Company. (I&S)
Part two in this text deals with instruction planning and part three deals with implementing instructional strategies. Although this focuses on the secondary level, adaptations can be made to use much of this material on the elementary level as well. Sample formats for teaching plans are given as well as directions for developing a self-instructional package.

7 GETTING TO KNOW FACULTY AND STAFF

Becoming acquainted with the total school faculty and staff is a wise move for the intern (see Appendix I for staff organization). Without seeming pushy, the intern should use every opportunity appropriate to meet and talk with other faculty members from the first observation day until the last day of the assignment. Professional relationships are likely to develop that both encourage and assist the intern. Additionally, knowing the name of the school secretary, the counselor, the nurse, and the custodian is a valuable professional procedure. It is also advantageous for the intern to become acquainted with the teacher aides and other paraprofessionals.

The number of people on the school faculty can determine the number and quality of interactions the intern shares with faculty. In a small school, the intern could get to know all the faculty and be known, at least on a speak-in-the-hall basis. The intern should speak to everyone, smile, and make some appropriate comment if possible. In a large school, there probably is faculty the intern will never meet. Every effort should be made by the intern to get to know and observe the teachers in the same grade level or in the same department.

During the initial visitations to the student teaching assignment, the intern should have the opportunity to meet a small circle of teachers. This group probably includes the supervising teacher, other teachers in the department or grade level, the department chairperson or grade level chairperson, the teachers across the hall and next door to the assigned classroom, the assistant principal, and the principal.

Although in many elementary schools the teacher eats with the class, some schools do offer a special dining area for faculty, which provides an excellent opportunity for the intern to get to know other faculty. Prudence dictates that the intern listen more than talk during such times. It is necessary to be friendly, listen courteously, and contribute to the conversation when appropriate. Just as this is an excellent opportunity for the intern to get to know the faculty, so is it a good opportunity for the faculty to get to know the intern. The intern should be careful to avoid seeming hostile even though hostility may exist toward some ideas discussed.

The intern should also avoid appearing to profess beliefs that run counter to those generally accepted by the community. By expressing unpopular ideas or by appearing to be discourteous, crude, or hostile, the intern will probably lose any opportunity of being offered a permanent position in that school or in any other school in the community. The host school always retains the right of having the intern removed from the student teaching situation. A lack of ability to get along with faculty is sufficient reason to request withdrawal.

The teachers' lounge is another good place to get to know faculty. The lounge offers a haven and refuge to tired teachers. Some teachers feel the lounge is a center to pick up on the latest news; others see it as a place to put their feet up and relax for five minutes before the next class with a cola or a cup of coffee.

Interns should recognize the teachers' lounge as a place to relax momentarily, to meet new people, to discover more about the profession of teaching, and even, if necessary, to discuss student-related problems that there may otherwise be no time to discuss, provided confidentiality is observed. Many times, teachers from a prior year may share ideas and concerns about students with interns that will greatly aid in developing individual programs for particular students. Usually the teachers' lounge contains a bulletin board, which should be checked frequently.

The intern should be careful about the impression being made on other teachers and should never criticize the supervising teacher, other teachers, or the administration, even though others in the group appear to criticize openly with no qualms. Remember that those teachers already have a job. Should the conversation become unprofessional, the intern can tactfully bring up a new topic, appear to be engrossed in the plan book, or generally ignore the situation.

During their college training, future teachers are often advised to beware of the teachers' lounge, to stay out of "that place." However, in the best professional and personal interest of the intern, appropriate use of the teachers' lounge may be suggested by the supervising teacher.

Even after eating lunch at the faculty table and spending the morning break (if there is one) in the teachers' lounge, there may be some teachers the intern will have failed to meet. At the first faculty meeting held after the beginning of the student teaching term, the principal will probably introduce the intern to the entire faculty group.

▼ GUIDELINES FOR THE SUPERVISING TEACHER

1. Prior to the arrival of the intern, discuss with your fellow teachers the fact that you will be having an intern in your classroom. Make a special point of discussing this with those faculty members and students who are also teaching the same subject.
2. If there are faculty members from the same home town or region, tell them about your intern.
3. Ask some of your fellow teachers for permission for your intern to visit in their classrooms to observe.
4. Before taking the intern with you to the first teachers' meeting, check with the principal for approval and give any information necessary for the introduction of the intern.
5. Find some congenial teachers who are in the teachers' lounge at the same time your intern is there and ask that they help make the intern feel comfortable at your school.
6. Location of the bathroom facilities in the teachers' lounge is part of the initial information the intern should have.
7. Share with your intern school customs involving use of student bathroom facilities and the teachers' lounge.
8. Names of teachers with similar interests would be appreciated by the intern.

▼ GUIDELINES FOR THE INTERN

1. The last thing a teacher needs is a permanent shadow, so do not become one for your supervising teacher. Stand on your own two feet.

2. Avoid following your supervising teacher around all day.
3. It is appropriate for the two of you to go to lunch together, but allow some other teachers to sit next to the supervising teacher.
4. Just as the supervising teacher needs a break from the students during the day, so do the intern and supervising teacher need a break from each other.

GET PLENTY OF REST. YOUR PATIENCE WILL NEED IT.

5. It is your responsibility to make of yourself a congenial, outgoing person that the other teachers enjoy being around.
6. Do your best to remember teachers' names when you are initially introduced.
7. If possible, remember something interesting about each teacher you meet, and as time progresses you may find you have developed friendships that will last for a long time.
8. Although shyness is often interpreted as aloofness, a safe general rule is to become acquainted with members of the faculty and have friendly conversation.
9. Indicate an interest in the activities of the school. If wisely and carefully used, this can be one of your best resources for information on school activities as well as on individual students.
10. Be extremely careful; do not gossip. Never let yourself be guilty of unflattering conversation about anyone—student or professional—either stated or implied.
11. Confidentiality is expected of any professional. In schools located near the college or university, the students taught by the intern may be children of faculty members at the school or college. In many cases parents and community residents are classroom volunteers; the intern should maintain professional discretion while also developing cordial relationships with all school employees.
12. You are a guest in the school and should not appear otherwise.
13. Remember that the teachers with whom you are associating already have contracts and you do not. You have to prove yourself; people are watching you and your reactions to practically everything to judge your professional development.
14. If there are several interns in your building, be careful not to cluster. Mix with the teachers, learn from them, and do not be afraid to ask their advice.
15. Use the teachers' lounge at appropriate times, during scheduled breaks, before and after school. This is where you have the opportunity to let the staff know that you are friendly.
16. When you go to the lounge, avoid exposing your educational philosophy to those teachers who are seeking a moment's rest.
17. Be aware of the time you are spending in the lounge.
18. Occasionally, particularly in the case of teachers with no homerooms, the lounge becomes a work room, a place to grade papers, make out tests, and check homework as well as develop lesson plans. Try to avoid disturbing these people at work.
19. If your lounge is used continuously during the day for relaxing, social-type activities, then find a corner in the library or the cafeteria (or some place your supervising teacher suggests) to work on your professional responsibilities. Trying to accomplish these tasks where others are relaxed tends to make you less productive.

20. The people you meet in the lounge may be good contacts for future job references, so behave accordingly.

CASE 7–1
▼

Mazie was the new intern in Mrs. Pollock's junior high math classes. Eager to become accepted as part of the school faculty, Mazie made a point of getting to know as many of the faculty as possible. A major part of her plan was for the faculty to get to know her. Early in the term, Mazie began to get to school a half hour earlier than the other teachers so she could get her work organized and begin visiting with the other teachers as they arrived at school. Lengthy visitations cut into the other teachers' work time, and they mentioned this to Mrs. Pollock.

1. What action should Mrs. Pollack take?
2. What responsibilities do the people who were being bothered have?
3. How might Mrs. Pollack help Mazie to accomplish her goal in more acceptable methods?
4. In what ways could the other teachers help resolve this situation?
5. What lessons can Mazie learn from this kind of behavior? ▼

CASE 7–2
▼

Manuel was assigned an intern in U.S. government with Ms. Soltice. Manuel held promise of becoming a good, strong teacher; however, his enthusiasm for his subject carried itself too far for some of his lunch table teacher friends. At times that enthusiasm would turn to aggression and hostility. As Manuel realized the situation had occurred, he would carefully apologize. Another teacher told Ms. Soltice that some of the lunch group were unhappy with his aggression and hostility and were trying to avoid him.

1. What actions should Ms. Soltice take to help Manuel with the other teachers?
2. How could Ms. Soltice help Manuel maintain his enthusiasm about his subject?
3. What help could other members of the lunch group contribute?
4. Are there other avenues toward which Ms. Soltice could help Manuel channel this enthusiasm?
5. How could the guidance counselor help ameliorate this situation? ▼

CASE 7–3
▼

The faculty at Meadowbrook Elementary were always happy to welcome interns, and their acceptance of Henry was no exception. Henry was to intern in Mrs. Lassiter's fourth grade classroom and he appeared to be eager to get to work. At first Mrs. Lassiter thought Henry was just shy about being new in the classroom because he never talked to the children. She further observed that when possible, Henry avoided talking with students and faculty although he did not seem nervous about working closely with her. After two weeks in his assignment, Henry still had not visited the teachers' lounge or the school cafeteria. Mrs. Lassiter felt immediate action was necessary.

1. What effect will Henry's aloofness have on his student teaching experience?
2. How could the college coordinator be involved with this problem prior to the next scheduled visit?
3. How could Mrs. Lassiter involve other supervising teachers in resolving this situation?
4. What kind of involvement with the children could Mrs. Lassiter prescribe?
5. How could a personality characteristic such as shyness be diagnosed prior to student teaching? ▼

CASE 7-4 ▼

James, the new intern in math at the high school, enjoys smoking cigarettes but the high school has a smoke-free environment rule. Having been accustomed to smoking between classes at the university, James felt that it would be impossible for him to live through the entire school day without smoking a cigarette. Because he felt that a nonsmoker would not understand his problem, he hesitated to mention it to his supervising teacher.

As his drive for a smoke grew during the first week of student teaching, James became inattentive and irritable.

1. Why would the supervising teacher assume that the problem with James was the student teaching assignment?
2. What should James do?
3. What clues should the supervising teacher watch for?
4. How could James resolve this situation?
5. How should he approach other teachers or interns to determine how they get through the day without smoking? ▼

CASE 7-5 ▼

Ella was thoroughly enjoying her student teaching. The faculty was happy with her and all aspects of her student teaching seemed progressive and appropriate. One day, one of the female teachers, who happened to be recently divorced and quite attractive, was alone with Ella in the teachers' lounge when the principal entered. Ella noticed innuendoes and began to feel uncomfortable in the presence of these two people who obviously would have liked a few minutes alone.

1. What should Ella do?
2. How could she have pretended to be oblivious of what was happening?
3. For what reasons should she confide in her supervising teacher?
4. What effect could a discussion of this situation with anyone have on her chances of being hired to teach in this school?
5. What future actions would you suggest? ▼

CASE 7-6 ▼

Bob is interning in a large high school that has a number of young teachers. As Bob began using the teachers' lounge, one of the young male teachers seemed to take Bob under his wing, trying to help in any situation, to be available to answer all questions, and generally be helpful. After a few weeks of such behavior, Bob sensed that this particular young male teacher had interests other than professional ones. Having realized that most of the faculty had seen them working together and talking to each other a great deal of the time, Bob knew that he was likely to be labeled in a way he considered inappropriate.

1. What are Bob's options?
2. How could he explain this to his supervising teacher (a female)?
3. Why should he go to the administration with this problem?
4. What is likely to happen if he decides to discuss this with any other male faculty member?
5. What advice would you give Bob? ▼

CASE 7–7
▼

Lu dearly loved working with the children in her first grade class and was excited about the prospects of a career in education. She considered her supervising teacher one of the very best and felt fortunate that she had this particular assignment. She was so impressed with her supervising teacher that she became her shadow. The supervising teacher began to feel confined. The intern, not wanting to miss a chance to learn from her supervisor, felt compelled to go with her to the lounge and continue dialogue there. The supervising teacher was at her wit's end.

1. How could the supervising teacher free herself of the student teacher periodically?
2. What should the supervising teacher do about this situation?
3. How could the university coordinator help?
4. Would the principal be the appropriate person to assist with the solution?
5. How could the supervising teacher enlist the help of other teachers with supervisory experience? ▼

RECOMMENDED READING

Conley, Sharon, & Cooper, Bruce. (Eds.). (1991). *The school as a work environment: Implications for reform.* Boston: Allyn and Bacon, Inc. (I&S)
This book is based on how teachers work in their schools and opportunities for future development related to their work. The student teaching intern can more easily understand the faculty and staff with whom he works by having a background knowledge in such topics as teachers' work cultures, in-school influence, and teacher commitment.

Drayer, Adam M. (1979). Problems of adjustment to school personnel. In *Problems in middle and high school teaching: A handbook for student teachers and beginning teachers* (pp. 211–242). Boston: Allyn and Bacon, Inc. (I&S)
The author lists practical, useful suggestions for developing good relationships with school personnel. Points for discussion are given and each is illustrated by a problem from student teaching experiences.

Gauss, John. (1985). Fellow employees. In *So you wanna teach, huh?* (pp. 25–36). Boston: University Press of America. (I&S)
The author gives practical advice with a touch of humor on how to succeed in school by knowing what happens behind the scenes. He recommends that the new teacher immediately get to know (in this order): the custodian, the school secretary, the principal, the vice principal, the school nurse, the counselor, the librarian, the cafeteria director, the groundspeople and fellow teachers.

Lovell, John T., & Wiles, Kimball. (1983). Organization and operation of the faculty. In *Supervision for better schools* (5th ed.) (pp. 248–268). Englewood Cliffs, NJ: Prentice-Hall, Inc. (I&S)
Although this material is written for the educator in a supervisory position, it benefits the student teaching intern and the supervising teacher to discuss how and if these concepts apply in their school. This chapter speaks to structuring the group and good uses of communication within the group.

Zimpher, Nancy L., & Grossman, John E. (1992). Collegial support by teacher mentors and peer consultants. In Carl D. Glickman (Ed.), *Supervision in transition: 1992 yearbook of the association for supervision and curriculum development* (pp. 141–154). Alexandria, VA: Association for Supervision and Curriculum Development. (I&S)
Zimpher and Grossman examine both the teacher mentor model and a new alternative approach to assisting students just beginning to teach. This alternative model is the peer assistance and review (PAR) model. Such a comparison of models highlights the decision of whether to have the same person responsible for both formative assistance and summative evaluation.

8 COMMUNICATION DURING THE STUDENT TEACHING INTERNSHIP

Communication is one of the most important elements in the success of the student teaching experience. It is a tool to be used both in the delivery of instruction and in the development of associations with all the various parties involved in the student teaching experience: the supervising teacher, the university coordinator, the students, the school administration and staff, other faculty, and parents and school patrons.

Clarity of expression is highly relevant to this situation. To be articulate in communication is to show a high quality of thinking, and, because thinking is a major tool of the classroom teacher, communication is a reflection of the kinds of thinking the professional is capable of doing.

Communication can be divided into writing, reading, speaking, and listening. During the student teaching assignment, all four of these areas of communication take on added meaning.

Although the student teaching intern has progressed through the university teacher education program with a heavy emphasis on reading ability, different aspects of that ability need attention during the intern assignment. Different kinds of materials are to be read.

Because the intern is attempting to adapt to a school setting, everything related to that school setting should be read carefully. The daily bulletin board usually located adjacent to the faculty mail boxes in the administrative office, notices from that office that are routinely delivered to the classroom, the bulletin board in the teachers' lounge, and notices from the district central office are all important for the intern to read carefully. Being a beginner in the school business means that an intern should maintain currency with what is being published in the daily newspaper relative to schools in the area and to all reports of school board meetings and activities. Maintaining an awareness of what is happening to students, faculty, and staff through reading the newspaper assists in having conversation topics with those individuals.

In an era of national and state reports on the condition of education and schools, the intern should try to at least skim such information to maintain current information. Much of what has been presented in theory in the university classroom begins to take form and meaning in the everyday life of the school.

A second area of reading that suddenly looms as very important to the intern is the content of material to be taught. This can be a major task and should be approached in a manner that streamlines the process and helps the intern use time more efficiently. The intern should find all the material possible; glance through everything; skim through those areas that seem most appropriate; and then make a plan as to exactly how much of the material actually needs careful reading. Knowing the total picture prior to beginning the intense reading helps save time and frustration. Because teachers are deluged with mountains of reading material, learning how to identify the necessary reading intensity for any material is a time saver for the student teaching intern.

Writing is another major form of communication for the student teaching intern. Writing is the basis of the development of unit and lesson plans, writing directions for students, and writing notes home to parents. Writing memos (see Appendix J), writing in the intern's journal for the supervising teacher and the coordinator, writing materials for student groups, and writing notices to other teachers are all important tasks that must be conducted with proper grammar and writing style.

Additional writing tasks that usually occur during the student teaching assignment are those of writing letters of application, letters of requests for materials, and composing resumes. In such materials the allowable margin of error is zero. Materials with misspelled words or errors in grammar automatically can cause applications to be cast in an unfavorable light.

Just because written materials must adhere to high standards is no reason to fail to use such methods of communication. The student teaching intern should quickly become immersed in successful writing so that no matter what the challenge, it can be met!

The chalkboard is one of the major methods of written communication with students. The supervising teacher has usually had years of experience to perfect such board writing; comparatively, the intern's writing on the board falls short. This can be remedied by practice, practice, practice, especially before or after school when no students are in the classroom. One of the things the university coordinator wants to see demonstrated is the ability of the intern to write legibly on the chalkboard.

Writing for overhead transparencies requires concentrated effort. It is important for the intern to observe how other teachers manage to stand beside the projector and yet avoid standing in front of the projected image on the screen. Handwriting and mathematics numbers and symbols must be readable. It is helpful for the student teaching intern to remember that such writing is meant to be read, not just written.

The importance of the spoken word in learning to teach cannot be over-emphasized. Getting involved in the classroom activity early and maintaining a comfortable relationship with the students and the supervising teacher contribute to a more pleasant speaking voice for the intern. The voice is an accurate indicator of the anxiety the intern may be experiencing, and although the students may not be aware of such clues, the supervising teacher will notice them. Vocal articulation is a most important competency for any teacher. Although teachers use their voices in different modes, for example drama coach, band director, or physical education teacher, clarity of meaning is basic to all. As the student teaching intern is observing other teachers during the early part of the assignment, being aware of how articulate various teachers are helps the intern to develop further personal articulation.

Vocal qualities such as tone, degrees of harshness, and volume require practice in order to perfect them in the classroom. It is important for the supervising teacher to stress that the differences in sophistication of presentations have a great deal to do with the differences in experience. The intern is there to learn how; it is okay not to know how to do everything perfectly at the beginning.

Classroom presentations take on a professional tone as the intern increases practice. That is why this kind of assignment used to be called "practice teaching." The intern's spoken communication with other faculty and staff and with the administration should be courteous, friendly, and professional.

The supervising teacher can model and show how other faculty model techniques of effective listening. Through listening to what students are saying, the intern can better plan instruction, can determine where the problems lie, and can actually manage better classroom control. The listening equivalent to eyes in the back of the head is to have ears of the heart: to hear what people are trying to say in addition to hearing what they are saying. It is especially important to listen to parents. Interns must be careful to avoid falling into the trap of feeling that they have the answers parents need if the parents would just listen! It is the intern who should listen. Frequently, in listening to parents, what is heard is what we are listening for, not what they are really trying to say.

During the student teaching assignment, it is critical for the intern to listen to the supervising teacher and to the university coordinator. Much of the student teaching experience is like mapping uncharted territory for the intern, and every square mile of the new terrain should be identified. Suggestions by either of these two individuals or by the school administrator should be considered imperative. As professionals, they should not have to say, "You must . . ." or "This has to be done this way . . ." The intern should understand the professional suggestion and implement it immediately.

Any discussion of communication would be incomplete without a mention of body language. The intern should be made aware of how body language indicates to students such things as control, sincerity to others when they are speaking, and levels of intensity to listeners. Posture, volume, and tone say as much as the words that are chosen to convey the oral message.

The degree to which the intern is assisted to learn and use appropriate communication techniques is to a large measure the degree to which the student teaching internship will be successful.

▼ GUIDELINES FOR THE SUPERVISING TEACHER

1. Try to anticipate the communication avenues in which your student teaching intern will be involved. Help him approach these with an appropriate mixture of caution and confidence.
2. Point out to your intern where the bulletin boards are and when notices are generally posted. Emphasize which types of notices should be given special attention.
3. Try to assist your intern to reach a balance between being comfortable but not too relaxed so that his voice is not strident and tense on the one hand or sleep inducing on the other hand.
4. Encourage your intern to read the local daily newspapers. This keeps her up to date with school and school district news and also gives her something to discuss with the other faculty and staff at school.
5. Point out to your intern that through listening to a variety of sources, he can stay more current in what is happening to the students.
6. Stress with your intern that student peer group jargon is changed as soon as adults learn it; it is advisable if she tried to avoid any use of it altogether.
7. Make appointments with some of your most articulate colleagues for the intern to observe them in teaching situations. Prior to the observations, review the kinds of things the intern should be looking for.
8. Share sample kinds of school memos with the intern. Point out the important elements of such documents.
9. Ask your intern to order free information or materials from organizations that offer such benefits. Prior to mailing the request, check to see if proper form has been followed and necessary information has been included.
10. Note any areas in reading, writing, speaking, or listening in which your intern needs additional development. Tactfully point out such needs; discuss these needs privately with the university coordinator because the university has resources that can assist in building up these areas of deficiency.
11. If the intern has difficulty with vocal articulation, help her gather her thoughts through writing and then expressing them. Some people think best through writing. This helps her develop a pattern for future use.

▼ GUIDELINES FOR THE INTERN

1. Become acutely aware of needed improvement in all of the areas of communication. Push yourself to improve and to try new schemes of enhancing your communication skills.
2. Particularly notice the body language of people who are listening to you. Are they saying through this language that they are not really hearing you? Are they indicating that they are listening intently?
3. Notice your own body language as you listen and speak to people. Is your body emphasizing what you are saying or is it discounting what you are saying? Do you look people straight in the eye when talking to them, or do you avoid eye contact? When you are seated with another and having a conversation, does your posture indicate that you have already turned off your hearing?
4. Listen with the ears of your heart as well as with the ears on your head. Note what parents and students are trying to tell you when maybe they do not know how to express themselves as well as you may.

5. Listen especially carefully to your supervising teacher and coordinator. Do not force them to be blatant about telling you such things as to wear pressed and clean clothes. Notice innuendoes. Notice suggestions. Make life more pleasant for them as well as for yourself by picking up on hints.

6. Talk with people, not to them. Even when you are teaching, maintain such channels of communication that students feel that you are discussing with them, not at them.

7. Be careful what you say, how you say it, and to whom you say it. You suddenly have access to information about students and the school that other people generally do not have. This is privileged information and it must be professionally guarded. The fact that you know should not pressure you into revealing such information to anyone.

8. If you are not comfortable with your occasional discussions with the school principal, you may want to role play such a discussion with a friend. This may help your self-confidence, and the next time you talk with the principal you may discover that you have reached new levels of successful articulation.

CASE 8-1 ▼

Jorge was happily assigned to Mr. Alonzo's sixth grade mathematics and science classroom. He felt that major contributions to the education of children could be made during the middle school years, and this was the level he had chosen to teach. He was excited about his students and their work. His preparation and presentation skills were good, and Mr. Alonzo felt that his students were getting positive benefits from Jorge being with him to do his student teaching.

The only problem was Jorge's handwriting. Although this would not seem to be a major problem, it was a critical one. Whenever Jorge wrote notes on student papers, to the school office, home to parents, or even on the chalkboard or overhead transparencies, his handwriting was illegible. As good as Jorge was in his other responsibilities, Mr. Alonzo was disappointed in the handwriting and discussed the problem several times with Jorge who agreed that it was a problem and that he would work on it right away. After 4 weeks and several reminders from Mr. Alonzo, no improvement was noticeable.

1. Recognition of the problem is a major step toward getting it resolved. What are the next steps that Jorge should take?
2. What kinds of limits about note writing could Mr. Alonzo insist on?
3. In what ways could a laptop computer help Jorge with this problem?
4. What activities could the university coordinator prescribe that would help improve Jorge's handwriting?
5. What kinds of screening processes in the teacher education program at the university could have remedied this situation earlier in his training? ▼

CASE 8-2 ▼

Hu was a young Asian student who was student teaching in mathematics in the local high school. Hu had come to the United States to attend college and become a teacher. He planned to return to his home country and teach mathematics there. In the student teaching assignment, Hu related well to the high school students, and his knowledge of mathematics was outstanding.

Hu's use of English in the delivery of mathematics instruction was acceptable, but outside the realm of mathematics, his English language speaking skills were relatively poor. He failed to understand what students were discussing in informal discussions and was frequently unable to respond to other teachers when in conversation with them. At faculty meetings, the supervising teacher felt that Hu was not understanding the information. Her concern was that although Hu was quite knowledgeable about mathematics, he was missing important training in how schools and classrooms are run and how students get along with teachers.

1. How important is it that Hu understand more than the language associated with mathematics?
2. How effective would it be for the supervising teacher to assign a student each period to serve as special interpreter? What problems would this pose?
3. Because Hu is going to return to his home country to teach, why should the supervising teacher be concerned about his English?
4. What benefit would extended observations of other teachers have in this situation? Teachers of which subjects would be of most value?
5. What level of fairness is involved in expecting Hu to speak two languages?
6. What opportunities may there be to find a middle school student who also speaks Hu's first language? ▼

CASE 8–3 ▼

Greta was enthusiastic about her work with the third graders in Mrs. Escalente's class. She prepared extensively and her instructional skills were good and continuing to improve. She related well to the students, was always cheerful, and was happy with her assignment.

The only problem that Mrs. Escalente could not resolve with Greta was her refusal to spend time reading the daily notices from the office and checking the bulletin board beside the teachers' mail boxes. This had caused several mix-ups with such things as changed schedules for art and physical education, a new library visitation policy, and an announced fire drill.

Mrs. Escalente felt that these notices were important and that Greta was not acting responsibly in ignoring them.

1. Learning to function as a member of the school faculty is an important component of student teaching. How could Mrs. Escalente impress on Greta the importance of staying up to date with what is happening at school?
2. In what cases could Greta's failure to read these notices cause her students to be in danger? How could she be guilty of negligence?
3. Why do you think there is a lack of balance between Greta's sense of responsibility for instructional delivery and her sense of responsibility for keeping closely attuned to school functioning?
4. What kinds of impressions is Greta making on a principal who she hopes will give her a job when she has completed her student teaching?
5. In what stage of her training in instructional methodology and teaching responsibilities should this topic have been covered? ▼

CASE 8–4 ▼

Erica was an enthusiastic, well-prepared student teaching intern in the computer lab. Her high energy level was infectious among the students and the other faculty. She knew her subject well and was more than eager to get to know everyone at the school. Her interest in conversations with other faculty and staff was high; she seemed to enjoy such conversations a great deal. She had a habit that began to turn people off, however, and fewer and fewer seemed interested in talking with her.

During conversations, Erica had a bad habit of interrupting while others were speaking. This characteristic also exhibited itself during class with students. Erica did not wait for them to finish talking before she jumped in with something she wanted to say.

Frequently, it was not directly related to what the other person was trying to say. It became apparent that Erica was not a good listener.

1. What listening skills are imperative for a teacher?
2. What do you think Erica saw as the reason that fewer and fewer people wanted to talk with her?
3. Why do some people feel that what they have to say is more important than what someone else is talking about?
4. How could the use of an audiotape recorder assist in demonstrating the problem to Erica?
5. How can the supervising teacher squelch the kinds of nonlistening interruptions that Erica is making without inhibiting her enthusiasm for her teaching? ▼

CASE 8–5
▼

Pia was a quiet, studious student teaching intern in Mr. Benson's geography class. She had a very high GPA and was intent on helping the students learn a great deal of geography, a subject in which she felt everyone should have high levels of interest.

Her planning was well done; her presentations were articulate; and her methods of evaluation were appropriate. However, students were becoming more and more restless. Mr. Benson had the feeling something was not clicking but he could not identify the precise problem.

At his request, Pia agreed to having a lesson videotaped. During his study of the videotape, Mr. Benson realized that Pia seldom looked at the students. She was always looking at the board, at her notes, out the window, at the floor, or the ceiling but seldom at the students. In other words, there was little eye contact with the students; she could just as easily have been teaching in an empty room. Her subject content was excellent but she was not relating to the students well at all.

1. How do you feel about people who look away when they are talking to you? How does that make you feel about yourself?
2. What points should Mr. Benson stress with Pia when studying the videotape with her?
3. With what psychological characteristics could the university coordinator help Pia in order for her to feel more comfortable with the students?
4. How could extracurricular activities help Pia to relate to students better?
5. What cultural background information would be most useful to the supervising teacher in helping to resolve this situation? ▼

RECOMMENDED READING

Carlson, Jon, & Thorpe, Casey. (1984). Communication: Learning to give and take. In *The growing teacher: How to become the teacher you've always wanted to be* (pp. 86–104). Englewood Cliffs, NJ: Prentice-Hall, Inc. (I&S) *Communication blocks, effective listening, kinds of responses, you-and-I messages, and open versus closed questions are discussed effectively. Exercises are included for reflective listening, I-messages, and open and closed responses.*

Conoley, Jane Close. (1989). Professional communication and collaboration among educators. In Maynard C. Reynolds (Ed.), *Knowledge base for the beginning teacher* (pp. 245–254). New York: Pergamon Press. (I&S) *This chapter discusses the need for effective communication on the part of the beginning teacher in such areas as collaboration, consultation, and problem solving. In addition to compiling current research, the author has included specific suggestions for improving communication within the educational setting.*

Gutek, Gerald L. (1992). The school system and staff. In *Education and schooling in America* (3rd ed.) (pp. 340–362). Boston: Allyn & Bacon. (I&S)

This chapter gives information that is usually understood after the teacher has been employed in a school setting. It is to the student teaching intern's advantage to discuss how the local school system varies from that described by Gutek. The school system hierarchy including line and staff relationships and the roles of teachers are explained.

Hevener, Fillmer, Jr. (1981). Relating to the students and parents. In *Successful student teaching: A handbook for elementary and secondary student teachers* (pp 62–69). Palo Alto, CA: R. & E. Research Associates, Inc. (I)
Building positive relationships with both students and parents is emphasized in this chapter. Hevener suggests a number of behaviors to assist the student teaching intern in developing and maintaining such relationships.

Machado, Jeanne M., & Meyer, Helen C. (1984). Developing interpersonal communication skills. In *Early childhood practicum guide: A sourcebook for beginning teachers of young children* (pp. 107–116). Albany, NY: Delmar Publishers, Inc. (I&S)
The authors have included material on how to understand what others are trying to communicate. They emphasize the value of caring, listening, and authenticity in communication.

9 BECOMING FAMILIAR WITH SCHOOL PROPERTY

Jamal, are you sure this is our fire drill route?

When an intern arrives at the student teaching assignment location, a great deal of time can be saved if she knows how to move quickly from one area of the school to another. A tour of the school building should be one of the first orders of business and should include the location of the library, teachers' lounge, physical education area, music room, general offices, guidance office, medical clinic, auditorium, gymnasium, cafeteria, and restrooms for students and for adults.

Knowing the whereabouts of the custodial and maintenance staff is another must. These important people can be valuable help in keeping a classroom running smoothly. Interns should know the necessary procedures for obtaining their assistance and, if possible, be introduced to them at the beginning of student teaching.

Classes in the elementary schools often have different procedures. It is necessary to know where to deliver or pick up students for physical education, music, art, and other special classes. When and where the pupils arrive and depart on the school buses must also be fixed well in mind; where pupils are to be delivered can often be different from where they are picked-up, based on school outdoor traffic flow patterns. Interns must also be informed about rainy or snow day schedules. Procedures for fire drills and other emergencies need to be studied as confusion can result if the recommended procedures are not followed.

Interns assigned to middle or high schools might easily be assigned hall duty during the term of their student teaching. Interns should expect to be assigned such duties that are normally given to classroom teachers.

The use of the media center or library in the assigned school could be a major factor in the success of the intern. Ample time should be given for a new intern to meet the people in charge of these sites and to look over what is available there. If the school district maintains a central media center or production lab, it is a good idea for the intern to arrange a visit.

The boundaries of school grounds are often not fenced. It is helpful to know these boundaries in order to participate in such activities as observation walks and recess periods. Off-limit areas in the middle and high schools should be explained to interns.

▼ GUIDELINES FOR THE SUPERVISING TEACHER

1. Arrange a tour of the school for the intern at the start of student teaching. This is an excellent initial contact between your principal and intern. Principals are usually proud of their buildings and appreciate the opportunity to show them off.

2. Try to get a map of the school for your intern; there is probably a fire drill map. If there is not one available, sketch one yourself. Fire drill and other emergency procedures should be explained as soon as possible. Your intern can be a big help during emergencies if properly trained.

3. Explain the pick-up and delivery system in operation for your class. Interns can be involved at the start in moving the pupils about the school; put them to work the first day.

4. If your school district has a central media center or production laboratory, make arrangements for your intern to spend some time there. In addition, make plans for your intern to spend at least part of a day in the school library or media center.

▼ GUIDELINES FOR THE INTERN

1. On your first visit to the school, report to the office of the principal. Teachers often have to sign in at this office at the start of the day. Someone will take or direct you to the classroom or office of your supervising teacher.

2. Take an early interest in touring the school building. This will probably be arranged for you by your supervising teacher. If not, suggest such a tour.

3. Study a floor plan of the building.

4. If you drive to school, inquire about the proper place to park. Schools often have restricted parking spaces for faculty and interns.

5. If you smoke, inquire from your supervising teacher as to where, when, or if this can be done. It might be permissible to smoke in the teachers' lounge, but ask your supervisor before smoking initially.

6. Find answers to the following questions:
   a. What are the school practices with regard to supervising corridors, group movement within the building, and space assignment on the playground?
   b. What are the responsibilities of the teacher before and after school?
   c. What are the duties of the teacher at lunch periods?
   d. What are the responsibilities of teachers for outdoor and indoor play periods?
   e. What are the other special duties of teachers in the building in which you teach?

7. Study the procedures for fire drill and tornado/hurricane alerts for your classroom. It might be that your supervising teacher is out of the room when the first fire drill takes place. It could be disastrous if there were a real fire and you were unprepared.

8. If you are an elementary intern, you should be eager to assist pupils getting to and from the buses. You should also show initiative in the supervision of restroom breaks for students. Line-up areas and methods should be noted.

9. Hold your phone calls to a minimum. Only emergency calls could be appropriate. Many phone calls are received by schools in a given day, and you should not be responsible for tying up the lines. Those calling you could ask to have a message placed in the mailbox of your supervising teacher.

CASE 9–1
▼

DeLos had been an intern for 3 weeks in a high school English assignment and appeared to have gotten off to a good start. There was only one concern that bothered his supervising teacher. DeLos was a heavy smoker who thought he must have a cigarette at each class break. His first pattern was to go into the rest room of the teachers' lounge to do his smoking because the lounge was near his classroom.

There was an unwritten law that the principal did not want any smoking on the school grounds—from students or teachers. After receiving complaints from other teachers about DeLos's smoking, his supervisor asked him to quit. DeLos continued to disappear a few minutes at each class break. It was evident that he was not going to the lounge; his supervisor suspected that he was going to the nearest pupils' restroom to smoke.

1. What action should the supervising teacher take?
2. How can DeLos justify his actions?
3. What responsibility does the supervisor have to the principal? To the college coordinator?
4. At what point should the coordinator be brought into the picture?
5. What options are open to DeLos? ▼

CASE 9–2
▼

argaret arrived at school the first day of student teaching and had difficulty finding a place to park. She thought she had lucked out when she found a space near the front entrance. She continued to park in the same spot for the first week of school. The next Monday morning the principal confronted Margaret and suggested that she find another space to park because she had been parking in a space that had customarily been taken by one of the regular teachers. Margaret was embarrassed and upset.

1. How important an issue is this?
2. Should a student intern be given all of the privileges of the regular teachers? Explain.
3. Why would it have been wise for Margaret to have inquired about where interns were to park?
4. In what way could Margaret appease the teacher whose parking space she had taken?
5. How could the supervising teacher help Margaret with this embarrassing situation? ▼

CASE 9–3

Gerry was an intern assigned to a seventh grade social studies class. All middle school interns were asked to visit the school district's central media center on the second day of student teaching. At a group meeting held on campus registration day, the interns were given precise directions on how to get to the media center. Gerry decided to drive alone to the center. He did not give himself enough time, got lost, and missed more than half of the session.

The next day, Gerry's supervising teacher asked about his experiences at the media center. She was noticeably upset when he explained what had happened. She asked him if this episode was indicative of how he would perform in her classroom. Her lecture concerning the importance of promptness was long and to the point.
Gerry was upset. What a way to begin student teaching!

1. How could this have been prevented?
2. Why does his supervising teacher make such a big deal out of this matter?
3. What chances do you think Gerry has in being successful in this assignment?
4. What do you think Gerry should do now?
5. In what ways could the coordinator assist Gerry? ▼

CASE 9-4
▼

Marty was in her third week as an intern in an eighth grade English assignment. She was in the middle of her third period class when the fire drill bell rang. Marty did not know what to do with her class; she did have the insight, however, to ask her students because the supervising teacher was out of the classroom. They were able to get out of the building in a reasonable time so they were not conspicuous. Marty thought about the possibilities of a real fire, however, and was upset with herself for not knowing the fire drill routes.

1. Why was it inexcusable for an intern not to know fire drill procedures?
2. Whose responsibility was it to inform Marty of the fire drill routes?
3. How should Marty react to comments of her students about her lack of information?
4. What can Marty do to show that she has learned a lesson from this event?
5. What could have resulted if this had been a real fire? ▼

CASE 9-5
▼

Rocky met his ninth grade physical education class in the gymnasium for his first lesson. His supervising teacher was called to the office, causing Rocky to feel pressured and anxious. As planned, he was to take this class to the athletic field for a game of soccer. There was a busy four-lane highway to be crossed to get to this field; what Rocky did not know was that there was an overpass to be used. Instead, he led the students across the busy highway causing frustrations to the passing motorists. Rocky was quite embarrassed when he found out about the overpass.

1. In what ways would Rocky have been liable in case of an injury to a student while crossing the highway?
2. What responsibility should the supervising teacher accept for Rocky's failure to use the overpass?
3. How could this dangerous situation have been avoided?
4. What can Rocky do to regain the confidence of his supervising teacher and students?
5. How could this experience be of value to Rocky in years to come? ▼

RECOMMENDED READING

Cohen, Louis, & Manion, Lawrence. (1983). Extra-curricular activities. In *A guide to teaching practice* (pp. 237–242). New York: Methuen & Company. (I&S)
The authors include good suggestions for planning and implementing extracurricular activities. Responsibility, safety, and travel activities are highlighted.

Cohen, Louis, & Manion, Lawrence. (1983). The school as an organization. In *A guide to teaching practice* (pp. 9–13). New York: Methuen & Company. (I&S)
Both formal and informal school structure are explained in this material. Methods of organizing activities and the use of time for successful classroom experiences are also included.

Lovell, John T., & Wiles, Kimball. (1983). The supervisory team at the local school. In *Supervision for better schools* (5th ed.) (pp. 232–247). Englewood Cliffs, NJ: Prentice-Hall, Inc. (I&S)
This chapter may help the student teaching intern to more readily understand that the supervisory structure serves as an instructional support team. These authors review the responsibilities of this team in assisting with planning and resources.

Machado, Jeanne M., and Meyer, Helen C. (1984). Understanding home and school interactions. In *Early childhood practicum guide: A sourcebook for beginning teachers of young children* (pp. 175–182). Albany, NY: Delmar Publishers, Inc. (I)

HOOL PROPERTY

The authors discuss the procedure for planning and making a home visit. Other home/school interactions discussed include parent conferences (formal and informal) and written communication.

Tracey, Katherine. (1980). Affiliation. In Donald R. Cruickshank (Ed.), *Teaching is tough* (pp. 75–111). Englewood Cliffs, NJ: Prentice-Hall, Inc. (I&S)

This material has probably already been experienced by the supervising teacher. The in-depth explanation of these topics is excellent for discussions. Affiliation usually is perceived only peripherally by student teaching interns, but having access to Tracey's work will assist in the process of assimilating the intern into the social and academic structure of the school. Activities and checklists are included.

10 BECOMING FAMILIAR WITH SCHOOL POLICIES

Dealing with students in a school without being familiar with school policy is rather difficult. The student teaching intern should obtain from the supervising teacher or the school secretary a copy of school and district policies and should read both thoroughly.

The administration expects all personnel to be aware of school policies and usually is happy to discuss policies with the intern, provided sufficient time is available. If the intern feels there are too many rules to remember, she should discuss this with the supervising teacher and time should be spent on those needs that appear to be most pressing and that arise most often. Any rule or policy covering emergency situations or actions should be committed to memory immediately.

Early awareness of school and district rules pays huge dividends for the student teaching intern during the student teaching assignment. Frequently, interns see such rules as an encumbrance on them just for the sake of having a rule. It is helpful to understand that state laws pertaining to education are translated into rules by the state department of education. Each school district within the state must abide by these rules. Accordingly, each school within a district must abide by the district rules (which must include the state rules and may include additional district rules). By the time these rules get passed along to the individual school, the original laws have been enhanced by additions at the state department level and the district level. Most schools also add rules that apply specifically to their situations. Therefore, by the time the original law gets interpreted and translated through the various levels of school government, a great deal of encumbrance may have been added.

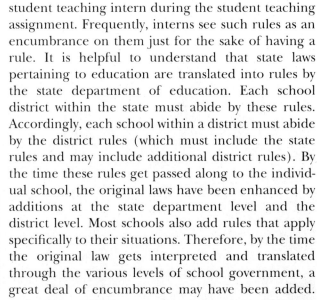

An urban district may have some rules different from those of a rural district because of the needs of the area. The intern can feel confident that a strong familiarity with the policies of the assigned school is a good foundation for the knowledge of any set of school policies in the region.

▼ GUIDELINES FOR THE SUPERVISING TEACHER

1. Most school administrators keep a copy of the district handbook in the school and, in addition, give each teacher a copy of the new school handbook at the beginning of the school year. If possible, obtain a copy of

the district handbook for the intern as well as a copy of the school handbook. If extra copies are not available, share your copies with the student teaching intern for use during the term.

2. As early in the student teaching assignment as possible, discuss at length with the intern those school policies that are most critical, such as those concerning questions of legality and the health and safety of the individual students.

3. If it appears the policy manuals have not been studied, impress on the intern the need to do so.

4. You may have the intern prepare a notebook with copies of procedures such as those for fire drill, checking out students, parents as visitors, caring for sick children, and escorting children off school grounds.

5. Test and double test your student teaching intern on knowledge of emergency procedures; this may save a life.

▼ GUIDELINES FOR THE INTERN

1. Probably some of the most important materials to be read at the beginning of your student teaching assignment are policy handbooks, both those of the individual school and of the school district.

2. You should be aware that most elementary and secondary schools have developed school policy handbooks and student handbooks. These are distributed to each student the first day of school. Most students know the school rules and they expect the intern to know them as well.

3. As you read, make notes for future reference.

4. Prioritize for your own use those policies most applicable to you and your students.

5. Ask your supervising teacher about those policies that seem strange, unnecessary, or impractical.

6. Policies may be a topic of conversation for the teachers' lounge, and the intern can profit from this provided neutrality is maintained. Specific examples of situations offered by other teachers may cause the policies to be more easily remembered.

7. Interviews with the dean and the guidance counselor are profitable in terms of helping the intern apply policies and rules to particular situations. This knowledge also assists the intern to see the practicality and usefulness of many of the policies.

8. Take care of district and school handbooks and return them to the right people at the appropriate time. Your principal may have an extra copy of the school handbook so that you can have a personal permanent copy.

9. Situations may arise during the term in which the supervising teacher and the intern must explain school policy to parents. In some areas, the district and school dress code is routinely challenged by some parents and students, particularly in secondary school. It is important that you know the rules.

10. You will have opportunities to reinforce school regulations during discussions with students; this is another reason to be thoroughly familiar with the policies.

11. If you visit with the supervising teacher prior to the beginning of the term, try to read all available policy materials before student teaching begins.

CASE 10–1 ▼

Edward, the new intern in Mrs. Smith's classroom, had appeared well dressed each day for the first week of his student teaching assignment. Mrs. Smith had observed that Edward had begun associating with two of the male teachers who were usually not well dressed and she was aware of their growing influence on him.

As Mrs. Smith expected, Edward appeared at school the second week wearing clothes that were more casual and looking less well groomed.

1. What kinds of advice about this type of problem could Mrs. Smith have given Edward at the beginning of his first week of the assignment?
2. What action could Mrs. Smith take at this point?
3. How could her suggestions be seen as jealousy by Edward?
4. In what ways could Mrs. Smith enlist the help of the two male teachers?
5. Because this was not a breach of a particular school policy, should Mrs. Smith mention it to Edward at all?
6. To what extent should Mrs. Smith feel a responsibility for Edward's success after completing his work in her classroom? ▼

CASE 10–2 ▼

Denise, a first grade student, suddenly became ill during the day and Cashay, the intern, called her mother to ask her to come get Denise and take her home. This occurred while the supervising teacher was in the library working on a resource unit. The intern had suggested that Denise's mother drive her car right up to the door and Cashay would take Denise out to the car. The supervising teacher arrived on the scene as Cashay was re-entering the building and Denise and her mother were driving away.

1. What action should the supervising teacher take?
2. What were the legal responsibilities of the supervising teacher? Of Cashay?
3. How should the supervising teacher discuss with Cashay the problem caused when she had allowed Denise to leave school without her mother's signature on the sign-out pad and without a note?
4. Should the supervising teacher bring this to the attention of the principal? Are there legal requirements that she do so? If so, what?
5. How effective would it be to have the mother return the following day and document the sign-out sheet? ▼

CASE 10–3 ▼

Beverly, the new English intern, was working with the yearbook staff and discovered that ad sales were not completed. She invited four seniors on the yearbook advertisement sales staff to work on ad sales during her planning period, accompanying her in her automobile. She had excused herself from the supervising teacher by saying she had some work that needed to be done that period. Her trip with the students did pay off in five ad sales but the supervising teacher discovered that all four students had left school without permission.

1. How should the supervising teacher approach Beverly?
2. How severe is this infraction of school policy?
3. Should the college coordinator be called?
4. Should the parents of the four students be involved?
5. What action do you think the principal will take? ▼

CASE 10–4
▼

During the 10-minute break following lunch for his students, Russell rested in the faculty lounge before reporting to his newly assigned student teaching classroom. As he listened to other teachers discuss school policies relative to teachers' hours, he became aware that a number of the teachers did not observe school regulations but instead seemed to come and go from the campus at their leisure during their planning period and immediately after school was out.

It seemed to Russell as if some of these faculty members arrived barely in time to get to their classrooms ahead of the students. Russell realized that he must have had a puzzled look on his face because one of the teachers leaned over to him and said quietly, "They just use the east entrance and don't go through the front door."

Rest time over, Russell returned to his class of 10th grade biology students. During class, he began thinking of errands he might be able to take care of during the school day by leaving school for only a few minutes each day or immediately after school.

1. What responsibility does Russell have to stay at school during school hours?
2. What options does he have if he wants to run those errands during the school day?
3. As a student teacher, how would he be expected to maintain school policy?
4. How should the supervising teacher handle this situation?
5. What are the best sources of advice relative to school policy during the student teaching internship? ▼

CASE 10–5
▼

Bobby enjoyed student teaching in Mrs. Hargroves's chemistry class. He was an intelligent young man and the college was proud of his record. He felt that every problem could be handled in a logical, rational method. As Bobby became more and more acquainted with school policy, he felt some of the policies were outdated or inappropriate and his expressions of his opinion were not always to people who understood that he was a developing professional and had not yet learned levels of discretion.

1. How should Mrs. Hargroves approach this situation?
2. How can Bobby be led to understand the need for established school policy and his responsibility to the school board?
3. To what extent should the administration of the school be involved in this situation with Bobby?
4. Could an informational discussion with the assistant principal be of any help to Bobby? What kinds of things should the assistant principal discuss?
5. What assistance can the college coordinator give to the supervising teacher? To Bobby? ▼

RECOMMENDED READING

Glasser, William. (1990). Building a friendly workplace. In *The quality school: Managing students without coercion* (pp. 122–133). New York: Harper & Row, Publishers. (I&S) *Glasser discusses control theory in terms of rules. He advocates few rules, nonadversarial rules, and the use of student-developed rules. This is helpful reading for the student teaching intern.*

Greene, Maxine. (1989). Social and political contexts. In Maynard C. Reynolds (Ed.), *Knowledge base for the beginning teacher* (pp. 143–154). New York: Pergamon Press. (I&S) *Supervising teachers find this material valuable to share with the student teaching intern in view of understanding the social and political contexts of schooling and the policies and rules thereof. This material is helpful for the advanced intern or the graduate student with an in-depth background in the sociological foundations of education.*

Hevener, Fillmer, Jr. (1981). Learning the community and school. In *Successful student teaching: A handbook for elementary and secondary student teachers* (pp. 18–23). Palo Alto, CA: R. & E. Research Associates, Inc. (I) *In this chapter, Hevener stresses the importance of getting to the student teaching placement site early by arranging a preteaching conference with the supervising teacher. He emphasizes such details as learning the bell schedule, referral procedures, the nonteaching responsibilities, and information about the faculty and department meetings.*

Lunenburg, Fred, and Ornstein, Allan C. (1991). Local school districts. In *Educational administration: Concepts and practices.* Belmont, CA: Wadsworth Publishing Company. (I&S) *The authors give a good overview of state and local policy and the implementation of school policy by the local school superintendents and school boards. Although this text is written for those pursuing administrative careers, it gives the supervising teacher and the intern an opportunity to discuss the implications of local school district activities.*

McCarty, Donald J. (1989). The school district: A unique setting. In Maynard C. Reynolds (Ed.), *Knowledge base for the beginning teacher* (pp. 155–162). New York: Pergamon Press. (I) *This material carefully explains the power structure in typical school districts, the governance and management of schooling within the district, and the impact of the school district itself on what happens in the classroom. The rules and policies under which an intern works are developed through the community power structures, political pressures, administrators, and unions.*

11 AVAILABILITY OF MATERIALS

Today's economic problems also exist within the classroom. Budgetary priorities and other economic factors result in classrooms that need additional materials and supplies. Each teacher is faced with the necessity of developing curricular materials to supplement those provided by the schools. Interns can be of immeasurable help in locating these necessary supplementary materials.

A task of student teaching interns is to find or develop available materials. These materials should be examined thoroughly. Excellent teachers' manuals accompany many texts and should be supplied to the intern for study and use.

One of the first places interns can look for added supplementary materials is the school library or media center. They should check textbooks, teaching kits, games, trade books, books on learning centers, films, filmstrips, picture files, tape recordings, slides, maps, globes, charts, models, and lists of community resources. Catalogs listing these materials may be available in the school media center or the university curriculum library. Because teachers often have very little time to devote to investigating new materials, interns can be very helpful in finding new resources for both the teachers and for themselves.

Wonder where he learned to use AV equipment?

Procedures for letting teachers and students use the library vary from school to school. Some are quite flexible and allow students to come in for research and study during those precious "teachable moments." It is necessary to make prior arrangements with the librarian so that the students' time can be used wisely. The librarian can be one of the main resources for your classroom; public and university libraries may also provide needed resources.

Some school districts have a book room or central depository for books. These books are many times outdated but can be quite beneficial for additional reading, for making games, and for use in learning centers. Teachers sometimes trade books with other teachers; this helps in locating books at different reading levels. Interns should become familiar with all of these aids in finding materials.

Interns are encouraged to take advantage of the opportunity to visit any central media center that is available for the entire school district. Professional libraries in various schools should be accessible to interns. Interns should consult subject area specialists and supervisors in the district office.

Interns should become familiar with the operation of the major types of audiovisual equipment in the building. They should have prior knowledge about threading and operating such equipment but may need some special instructions. There are many different types of machines with their own unique characteristics, such as film and filmstrip projectors, overhead and opaque projectors, audio- and videotape recorders and playback devices, and computer software.

It is important for interns to know the procedures to follow for scheduling the audiovisual equipment. Where is the equipment stored? Can this equipment be checked out to the classroom, or is there a special place for viewing? How much advance notice is necessary to make such arrangements? Are there spare bulbs available for the projectors? Who can assist with repairs in case of emergencies? Who is financially responsible for the equipment when it is checked out to the intern?

Interns should consider the possibility of enriching the classroom with resource persons from the community. Before such persons are invited to the classroom, however, they should be cleared by the supervising teacher. If carefully selected, individuals can be found who have a specialized knowledge that will fit in with the current instruction. It is helpful if the school and/or district has a list of persons who have been used successfully. Student teaching interns will probably be aware of resource persons from the college community. Bringing in appropriate examples from the community can do much in promoting positive public relations. The resource persons have proved to be an added asset to the "real life" interests of students. Some resource persons' presentations may not be as relevant for classroom use as others; therefore, it is wise to prepare and plan with the resource persons prior to their arrival at school.

Attractively arranged bulletin boards can do a great deal in both elementary and secondary classrooms to improve the atmosphere of the classroom. Displays of student work and teacher-made bulletin boards all have their place. Interns are often assigned to create bulletin boards on certain timely topics.

Field trips can be valuable learning resources. Teachers and interns considering field trips must get approval and support from the principal. If the intern is encouraged to participate in field trips, certain points should be understood:

1. A successful field trip requires a great deal of planning, a major element of which is the inclusion of a sufficient number of reliable, experienced chaperons.
2. The school policies concerning field trips should be studied. Check with the principal and supervising teacher concerning legal responsibilities involved, the need for medical authorization slips, and insurance that is available.
3. It is imperative to get parental consent of your students for such a trip.
4. Students should know the purpose of a field trip and be involved in the planning.
5. Thorough arrangements for transportation should be made.
6. These trips should be well supervised with careful planning for the movement of students to and from school.
7. Beneficial evaluation and follow-up techniques should be included in the planning.

There is great variation from school to school and classroom to classroom in the amount and types of resource materials and equipment available. Interns are quite fortunate if they are assigned a school with a wealth of such resources. Criteria for judging materials and resources for use in the classroom should be jointly developed by supervising teachers and student teaching interns.

▼ GUIDELINES FOR THE SUPERVISING TEACHER

1. Explain the overall organization of materials to your intern. You are able to keep many teaching techniques in your mind due to past experiences, but your intern does not have that advantage.
2. Encourage the multi-media approach if this does not go against your philosophy. Interns are usually very cautious about bringing additional resources into the classroom unless they are encouraged to do so.
3. Give your interns ample time to visit the library and central media center. Take them down yourself and introduce them to the media center staff. The team approach to the selection of materials is recommended.
4. Care of equipment should be discussed; this is usually a new set of tasks for the student teaching intern. Such things as courtesy in returning materials on time and in good condition should be stressed.
5. Discuss with your intern the importance of previewing audiovisual materials before using them in class.
6. Encourage your interns to bring in resource persons if they desire. Make sure that anyone you allow the intern to bring into the classroom knows exactly what is expected.
7. Assign your interns the responsibility for certain bulletin boards early in the student teaching assignment. This will show them that you have confidence in them and respect their ideas. It might be necessary to make a few suggestions the first time around.

▼ GUIDELINES FOR THE INTERN

1. Discover how much emphasis is placed on the use of textbooks in the classroom to which you are assigned. Are only textbooks at grade level allowed? Does your supervising teacher favor a multi-media approach?
2. Examine the materials available in your classroom. Teachers' manuals should be made available to you; these manuals are to be used as guides and not as the only sources of material and ideas. After you survey the range of materials, you will have a general idea of the curriculum being stressed.
3. Bring in materials from outside the school. You have attended methods classes and should be able to bring in worthwhile supplementary materials.
4. Take time to visit the school library and district media center prior to your teaching assignments. Use your time wisely; there is no excuse for not having your resources well in mind.
5. Be certain to follow the advice of your supervising teacher concerning the use of materials. Be a good listener and note the advice given to you.
6. Learn how to operate the audiovisual equipment. Ask for instructions if you do not know how to operate a piece of equipment. It is not a weakness to request aid; a person who asks shows a desire to learn.
7. Be certain to preview any material you decide to use. Titles alone can be misleading. You must decide if the material is appropriate and determine how it is to be used.
8. If you are assigned a bulletin board to prepare, make sure you get the job done as well as possible and on time. Take initiative and anticipate changing bulletin boards. Always get a preliminary sketch of your new bulletin board approved by your supervising teacher prior to putting one up.
9. Survey the school for possible locations for group activities, committee work, and games. Adequate space for such activities is often at a premium. Initially discuss the merits of these types of activities with your supervising teacher.

CASE 11-1 ▼

P hil, an intern in a sixth grade classroom, was quite excited about taking a field trip to the Naval Air Station Museum, which was 50 miles away. His supervisor had explained the importance of overplanning and Phil had taken his advice. All of the suggested precautions had been followed. One week before the field trip, Phil decided to invite the other two sixth grades to go along. The principal and supervising teacher approved because Phil had been so well organized up to this point. They left all the details up to Phil.

When the 90 sixth-graders boarded the buses to leave for the NAS Museum, it should have been evident that planning had not been completed. There were very few adults for supervision and some of the students lacked permission slips. When they arrived at the museum, they learned that they had not been expected at that particular time and tours for them had not been planned. Arrangements had not even been made for all 90 students to eat lunch. To make matters worse, one of the frisky sixth graders was lost on the Navy base for a few hours. They arrived late back at school at 5 P.M. to find a group of angry parents.

1. Who should be held responsible for these mishaps?
   a. principal?
   b. coordinator?
   c. Phil?
   d. supervising teacher?
2. What effect would this field trip have on the home-school relations in this community?
3. What could be done immediately to ease the situation with the parents?
4. How could new policies on implementing field trips avoid this predicament in the future? What kind of policy would you recommend?
5. How could the supervising teacher salvage Phil's enthusiasm for continuing in his internship? ▼

CASE 11-2 ▼

S ally was interning in an eighth grade science class. She planned to show a videotape on sea animals when her coordinator arrived for his first observation. The day finally came, and Sally was quite nervous. The coordinator arrived on time and took a seat in the back of the room.

It was evident that Sally had not made the necessary preparations. Not only was the VCR not set up, but she also had to go the library for the videotape. The class became very restless. After about 15 minutes into the period, Sally turned on the monitor and began to show the videotape. There was no introduction to the film and no discussion afterward. Sally asked the students to complete a worksheet about the film, thereby ending the lesson.

To say the least, the coordinator was upset. The fact that the supervising teacher was not in the room also disturbed the coordinator.

1. Why would an intern be so negligent about having materials and equipment available?
2. What do you imagine the coordinator had to say during the conference with Sally and her supervising teacher?
3. Should the supervising teacher be in the classroom during the coordinator's first observation? Why or why not?
4. How could careful planning by Sally have made this into an interesting and exciting lesson?
5. What kinds of personal problems may have been affecting Sally to have caused such a poor performance? ▼

CASE 11–3 ▼

Jean's supervising teacher asked her to prepare a bulletin board in her fourth grade classroom. She suggested that Jean come up with an idea that would motivate the students to read some science fiction. She asked that the bulletin board be prepared prior to the open house which was to be held in 2 weeks.

A week prior to the open house, no progress had taken place on the bulletin board. Jean's supervisor asked her about the matter, and she said she had some good ideas. The coordinator had been invited to the open house and planned to attend. The supervisor would be quite embarrassed if the bulletin board was not prepared.

The day of the open house arrived and still no bulletin board. Jean's supervisor finally prepared a display herself. Jean later explained that she was very much opposed to teacher-made bulletin boards, preferring displays of students' work.

1. What action should the supervising teacher take concerning this matter?
2. How should the coordinator react to Jean's difficulties?
3. Why should Jean have mentioned earlier her objections to teacher-made bulletin boards?
4. How would Jean's failure to produce the bulletin board affect the rapport she and her supervising teacher may have previously established?
5. Could Jean's failure to prepare a bulletin board be just cause to withdraw her from student teaching? Explain your answer.
6. What follow-through would be effective the next time the supervising teacher gave Jean a responsibility? ▼

CASE 11–4 ▼

Kathryn, an intern in a third grade class, had been a straight A student in college and was an avid reader. Her supervisor asked her to take a group of students to the school library to do research on their projects. Kathryn and her group left for the library and were asked to return in 30 minutes.

After Kathryn helped the students initiate their work, she became "lost in the stacks." She found a historical novel and became completely absorbed in it. Her group of students became noisy and unruly. Kathryn was so engrossed in the novel that she ignored completely her third-graders. After an hour of tolerating the misbehaving students, the librarian finally went searching for the supervising teacher to retrieve the students.

Finally, Kathryn came to her senses and returned alone to her classroom. Her supervisor was very disturbed over the matter.

1. Do you feel that Kathryn will ever make it as an elementary teacher?
2. Should she be pulled out of her student teaching assignment because of this failure?
3. How should the supervising teacher handle this situation?
4. How would the college coordinator react to Kathryn's problem?
5. What steps should the supervising teacher take to ensure that this will not develop into a pattern of behavior in Kathryn's professional life? ▼

CASE 11–5 ▼

Andy was in his fourth week in a ninth grade English assignment. He had an intense interest in mythology and obtained permission from his supervising teacher to do a unit in this area, which had not previously been covered. After surveying the school library, he found very few resources on this topic.

1. Where could Andy go to find such resources?
2. How could he adapt his own collection for classroom use? Would it be demolished or worn out by the students?

3. What cautions will he have to take in teaching this unit? What community traditions and opinions might cause people to object?
4. What were the possibilities of bringing in resource people in this unit on mythology?
5. What care must Andy use in defining whose mythology he was teaching? How would this affect the multicultural school population? ▼

CASE 11-6
▼

Rudolph surprised his supervising teacher by bringing in a guest speaker in his fourth period American history class. To make matters worse, the guest talked in a monotone and was very ill at ease in front of the class. The students were considerate but also were very bored and restless. The supervising teacher told Rudolph that he wanted a conference scheduled at the end of the day.

1. What did Rudolph expect from his supervising teacher?
2. Do you think that Rudolph's supervising teacher will be critical of his bringing in the guest speaker? Why or why not?
3. How could this situation have been avoided?
4. Should the use of resource persons be a matter that an intern should decide on alone?
5. How should Rudolph express his apology to the class for bringing in a boring speaker? ▼

RECOMMENDED READINGS

Cawthorne, Barbara. (1982). *Instant success: For classroom teachers, new and substitute teachers in grades K through 8.* Scottsdale, AZ: Greenfield Publications. (I)
Materials in this book have been developed and teacher tested for success. Although suggested for new and substitute teachers, the activities are useful for the student teaching intern to keep on standby. Activities are coded for grade level and permission is given for individual teachers to reproduce the worksheets.

Hensen, Kenneth T. (1988). Using media. In *Methods and strategies for teaching in secondary and middle schools* (pp. 223–240). New York: Longman, Inc. (I&S)
This chapter can be a self-taught lesson by the intern because it furnishes both a pretest and a posttest. A discussion of the variety of media available in most schools is given. This reminds the student teaching intern of possibilities for using such media.

Kemp, Jerrold E., & Dayton, Deane K. (1985). *Planning and producing instructional media* (5th ed.). New York: Harper & Row Publishers. (I&S)
This text gives explicit, step-by-step directions for producing media for teaching from photography to computer-assisted instruction. Background reviews of learning theory and managing the media production activities are included.

Morlan, John E., & Espinosa, Leonard J. (1989). *Preparation of inexpensive teaching materials* (3rd ed.). Belmont, CA: Davis S. Lake Publishers. (I&S)
This book offers a brief, useful review of the design of instruction and an extensive presentation of methods of preparing materials for teaching. Because of the explicit instructions and the day-to-day usefulness, this book is one the student teaching intern could well add to his professional library.

Schurr, Sandra L. (1989). *Dynamite in the classroom: A how-to book for teachers.* Columbus, OH: National Middle School Association. (I&S)
This text was developed to demonstrate how concepts could be demonstrated through instructional materials. Given a solid background in instructional theory, this author includes the uses of many aids and materials in the classroom, including learning centers, gaming and simulation, investigation task cards, shoebox learning, and study kits.

12 DISCOVERING SCHOOL REFERRAL SERVICES

T he size of the school district, not the size of the school, normally determines the number and kinds of referral services available to students. Most referral services fall within the categories of physical and mental health support, although social services (family and economic) are usually available also. School policy frequently dictates that actual referrals are made by only one school official, usually the principal, on recommendation of the guidance counselor. It is critical for the intern to be aware of what is available so that as indications of need become apparent, these needs can be relayed to the appropriate school authority after discussion with the supervising teacher.

The guidance departments of various schools offer a variety of services to children and youth. The intern should be informed of the services available through this department.

Although the variety of services available depends on the financial capability of the school district and the cooperativeness of local public health officials, most students can receive help when needed. Sometimes such help is the result of the action of the individual teacher searching for free services available for the student when parents are unable to pay.

In addition to services offered by the school district, communities frequently

offer assistance through Community Mental Health, Pregnancy Consultation Services, and the Division of Youth Services. Some schools have school nurses, and the intern, with the consent of the supervising teacher, can make an immediate referral when needed. When students are aware of the availability of a school nurse, the students themselves sometimes ask for a pass to see the nurse. If a student frequently requests this service, the intern should consult with the school nurse regarding the nature of the student's problem. Follow-up evaluation sheets also provide this information.

Smaller schools may share a school nurse, and some schools have the services of only a county or parish health department nurse. Schools may maintain an infirmary, usually consisting of a cot or two where students who are ill can be made comfortable with some isolation while waiting for someone to pick them up from school.

Under no conditions should an intern administer medication to a student. If it is necessary for a student to take medication during school hours, the school nurse or the person legally designated by the principal is the appropriate person to dispense medication. This ruling applies to all medication, including aspirin, as some students are allergic to aspirin.

For those chronic cases needing medical attention but not sufficiently acute to send immediately to the school nurse, the intern should discuss the history of the case and the current situation with the supervising teacher and with the school nurse. The nurse may make the appropriate referral to a doctor.

Referrals for dental needs are sometimes more difficult to discover. Unexplained changes in behavior, a droopy head, unusual grouchiness, and general inattentiveness may indicate some otherwise hidden dental-related pain or any number of illnesses.

Mental health problems are usually handled differently. The intern should discuss the situation with the supervising teacher and with the guidance counselor. If the school has no guidance counselor, the situation should be discussed with the principal or the designated faculty member in charge of student services. That person will help the teacher deal with the problem and may aid in referring the situation to a district psychologist or area psychiatrist. Keeping a daily log of the behavior of the student helps in explaining the problem to the referral professional. Such a record is frequently required to initiate a referral to a psychologist.

Children with special needs are often dependent on the skill of the regular classroom teacher in identifying their problems, developing the necessary remediation, and initiating a referral for assistance.

Another important topic that should be discussed with the student teaching intern is that of child abuse and how to recognize it. Some have a broad knowledge about signs of such abuse; others know very little about such things. Suspected abuse victims must be referred to the proper authorities.

Students with economic need frequently appear in some schools and almost never appear in others. The intern should discuss with the supervising teacher such cases. In one school, a second-grader never wore shoes to school and claimed that he had none. Arrangements were made to purchase a pair of shoes for the boy. Faithfully, he thereafter carried his shoes to school in his arms every morning and took them home again in the afternoon, all the while remaining barefoot. Such a case is an illustration of the need for follow-through by the referral agency.

Some students are irritable and disgruntled in class because they are hungry. Free lunch programs and food stamps for the families of such students should be investigated. Frequently local churches maintain clothes closets, and the student who has insufficient clothes can go or be taken there for fitting. Interns must sometimes deal with family pride, and when suggesting referrals for economic services, this family pride as well as the pride of the student must be handled carefully and discreetly.

▼ GUIDELINES FOR THE SUPERVISING TEACHER

1. Use wisdom and experience in deciding just how much information you wish to disclose immediately to your intern about your students and their needs. The intern will be concerned with those cases occurring during the student teaching term.
2. If the intern is not sufficiently perceptive to notice situations as they develop in the classroom among the students, point out those situations. The student in the class is the top priority in student teaching, and occasionally the supervising teacher must intervene to avoid problems for the students.
3. Help the intern to understand that teachers are patient and should not become discouraged over the amount of paperwork and "red tape" involved in obtaining services for a child.
4. Explain to your intern the backgrounds of the children with special needs in your classroom. Your intern might have had a course or courses dealing with special needs students but some are completely unaware of this element (see Chapter 13).
5. Introduce your intern to the workings of the guidance department including contact with a guidance counselor.
6. Discuss with your intern your experiences with abused children, a topic that is very much on the minds of interns today.

▼ GUIDELINES FOR THE INTERN

1. Read all school and district policies concerning referrals of any kind. Discuss these with your supervising teacher. You may remember cases from your own school days and how critical such needs can be to students.
2. Discussing problems with other professionals helps place these problems in the right perspective.
3. Any classroom management problems or any changes in student behavior should be investigated as potential health or economic needs.
4. Be especially alert to the needs of the students who are sleepy and lethargic, quiet and afraid to speak, suddenly exhibiting erratic behavior, and those who seem to find concentration difficult.
5. Discretion is paramount. The intern should never discuss any referral in the presence of other students and uninvolved faculty.
6. Be aware of information of health or learning problems available in the students' cumulative folders.
7. The school nurse can offer materials that would help you recognize particular symptoms and needs including those related to prescribed medication as well as covert drug usage.
8. Discuss with the school nurse the appropriate first aid measures expected of you in the classroom.
9. Although you may have no need during the student teaching term, find from your supervising teacher the appropriate referral action for child abuse and similar advocate agencies.

10. One of the best resources in developing this facet of professional training, discovering school referral services, can be the supervising teacher.

CASE 12-1
▼

Eloise, a 10th-grader, has missed English class for 4 days with alleged health problems. On checking with Eloise's other teachers, the English intern discovers that Eloise has reported to other classes with no problems.

1. What could cause the student to miss this class so frequently?
2. What action should the intern take?
3. What should be the advice and actions of the supervising teacher?
4. Whose responsibility is it to contact the parents?
5. How could a 10th grader miss these classes undetected? ▼

CASE 12-2
▼

George is a high school senior who appears to mix well with his peers. He is rather quiet and seldom speaks. His grades are barely average, although his written work is consistently turned in on time. He is a clean, well-groomed student who listens attentively and appears to understand. The intern is warned by the supervising teacher not to call on George in class because of his stuttering.

1. Should the intern do nothing and just concentrate on getting written answers from George?
2. In what way can the guidance counselor help the intern?
3. What would be the advantage or disadvantage of bringing up the subject of George in the teachers' lounge?
4. What are some appropriate actions for the intern?
5. How do you think George feels about never being called on? ▼

CASE 12-3
▼

Donnie, a fourth-grader, is smaller than most of his classmates and he never seems to have much energy. Mornings he seems cranky and weak and watches the clock until lunch time. He receives free lunches which he devours immediately and gets large second helpings from the cafeteria staff. After lunch he is sleepy in class and seems to get revived about the time school is out.

1. Have you observed similar situations in your previous experiences? Explain.
2. How should the intern approach Donnie's problem?
3. What role should the supervising teacher play, considering the fact that this situation existed prior to the arrival of the intern?
4. What other individuals should be involved in the solution to Donnie's problem?
5. Who should be involved in a home visit in this case? ▼

CASE 12-4
▼

Carol, a first grade girl from a middle class home, was always vivacious and alert to classroom happenings until the morning she came in and confided to the intern that she was afraid to go home that day because her stepfather had threatened "to beat her up the next time he laid eyes on her." The intern discreetly mentioned this to the supervising teacher who replied that Carol had told her about such threats before.

Because the stepfather was on the school board, she had not mentioned it for fear of making him upset with the school and of losing her job.

1. Would it be wise or unwise to ignore the supervising teacher's advice? Explain.
2. Should the college coordinator be involved?
3. What actions should the intern take to protect Carol from violence and further threats?
4. How could the supervising teacher be more professional in this case?
5. The fact that Carol brought this matter to the intern tells us what about this situation? ▼

CASE 12–5
▼

Student teaching in middle school geography was a happy experience for Molly. She enjoyed her students, her subject, and even working with her supervising teacher. She was floored one day when one of the girls in her eighth grade class came up to her privately and asked for help. Assuring the student that she would try to help, Molly prepared to listen patiently. The student proceeded to explain that she thought she might be pregnant and did not know what to do, where to go, or with whom to talk. This was not a situation Molly had been trained to cope with and she was at a loss for a response momentarily.

1. What should be Molly's first response to the student?
2. How much of the conversation with the student should Molly share with the supervising teacher?
3. What recommendations should Molly make to the student?
4. How should Molly implement a school referral? Through whom? To what agency?
5. Should Molly attempt any type of follow-up of this situation? Why?
6. In what way do you think Molly's university experience prepared her for this situation? ▼

CASE 12–6
▼

Sally was the new student teacher in tenth grade typing. Her supervising teacher, Ms. Joseph, was an outstanding teacher and a good professional role model. Sally felt fortunate to be student teaching with her. Ms. Joseph's son, Calvin, was a senior in the same school and had friends who were also friends of Sally's. Sally was aware of Calvin's increasing involvement in a drug ring within the school; however, she did not want to broach the subject with Ms. Joseph for fear of ruining her student teaching situation. She was aware that in the past Ms. Joseph had refused to believe reports of Calvin's activities in such matters.

1. As a professional person, what was Sally's responsibility in this situation?
2. Should she wait until her student teaching was completed and then try to discuss this with Ms. Joseph?
3. Should she discuss the alleged situation with the administration? With the dean?
4. How productive would a conversation with Calvin probably be?
5. How could the college coordinator be instrumental in assisting Sally? ▼

RECOMMENDED READING

Ballast, Daniel L., & Shoemaker, Ronald L. (1978). Getting started: An action approach. In *Guidance program development*. Springfield, IL: Charles C. Thomas, Publisher. (I)

This material speaks to the special needs that students may have and how they may be served through the guidance office. In the cases in which students have needs that extend beyond the school, it is the guidance office that makes referrals to the community agencies.

Fennimore, Beatrice S. (1989). *Child advocacy for early childhood educators.* New York: Teachers College Press. (I&S)
The early childhood student teaching intern is beginning a career closely related to child advocacy. Through reading Fennimore's work, the intern can become more attuned to the possibilities for the need for and location of referral services for students in the classroom.

Foster, Charles R., Fitzgerald, Paul W., & Beal, Rubye M. (1980). Collaboration of teachers and counselors. In *Modern guidance practices in teaching* (pp. 110–131). Springfield, IL: Charles C. Thomas, Publisher. (I&S)
The role of the counselor and the potential for collaboration by the counselor and the teacher are stressed. Of special appeal to the student teaching intern is the list of ways and the discussion about ways in which the counselor can help with student problems in addition to the counselor services to teachers and staff.

Maher, Charles A., & Zins, Joseph E. (Eds.). (1987). *Psychoeducational interventions in the schools: Methods and procedures for enhancing student competence.* New York: Pergamon Press. (I&S)
This material gives an in-depth look at some of the intervention techniques now in use and assists the student teaching intern in understanding the current alternatives.

Sandoval, Jonathan. (Ed.). (1988). *Crises counseling, intervention, and prevention in the schools.* Hillsdale, NJ: Lawrence Erlbaum Associates, Publishers. (I&S)
This book is not to be totally digested by the student teaching intern because of its in-depth treatment of the subject. However, a review of the kinds of problems that exist aids in recognizing them and discussing referral with the supervising teacher. Childhood and adolescence crises that are discussed include maltreatment, illness, death, parenthood, homosexuality, and suicide.

13 SPECIAL NEEDS

Mainstreaming students with special learning needs into the regular classrooms is a present-day common occurrence. When the trend changed from placing special needs children in special classrooms to mainstreaming them, there were numerous anxieties among classroom teachers who were not familiar with the problems and joys of working with special needs students. Today, most beginning teachers have had at least some training in educating these students.

Lewis and Doorlag (1991) state that in order for these students to learn successfully, they require instructional adaptations. These authors classify the variety of special students into four groups: handicapped, gifted and talented, culturally diverse, and at-risk for school failure. The divisions within categories are as follows:

Handicapped students:

Learning disabilities
Mental retardation
Behavior disorders
Speech and language disorders
Vision and hearing disabilities
Physical and health handicaps

Gifted students:

Unusually bright
Creatively gifted
Gifted in special areas:
  Art
  Music
  Drama
  Leadership

Culturally diverse students:

Home culture at variance with school
Some also differ from peers in language
Most typically members of minority cultures:
  Asian Americans
  Black Americans (largest minority group)
  Hispanic Americans (second largest cultural group and largest bilingual group)
  Native Americans

Students at risk:

Threatened by complex societal problems:
  Poverty
  Homelessness

81

Child abuse
    Drug and alcohol abuse
Potential dropouts
Potential and actual delinquents
Runaways
Teenage parents
Suicide risks

Regular classroom teachers are usually given assistance by special educators who help in planning the educational programs of these mainstreamed students, providing suggestions for modification of regular classroom activities, and helping to supply specific materials and equipment.

Interns should become familiar with the educational plan devised by the mainstreaming team, which includes the classroom teacher. This Individual Education Plan (IEP) is required before special students can receive special assistance. Some special students remain in the regular classroom at all times; most of them can succeed in the mainstream. Others are released for part of the day to work with the special teachers. Placement outside of the regular class occurs only when deemed necessary by the mainstreaming teacher, the special educator, and the administration.

Some interns have the opportunity to work with special students during student teaching, presenting a wealth of experiences that should be valuable for these future teachers.

Experienced teachers may very well tell interns that the special needs students are most likely to cause confusion and concern if provisions are not made for them. If interns feel some anxiety about their knowledge in the area, the resources listed at the end of this chapter should be helpful. The more the intern knows about these students, the better job of teaching can be done.

The attitude of the teachers who are working with special needs students is most important. Most of their needs are the same as those of all children and youth. The best strategy is to be flexible and make modifications for these special students. The arrival of an intern should make additional time and attention available to work with them. If the supervising teacher and intern consider *each* student in the class as a unique individual who could become a worthy citizen, all should go well.

▼ GUIDELINES FOR THE SUPERVISING TEACHER

1. You have undoubtedly identified the learning disabled students in your classroom. Their difficulty in processing information might be quite perplexing to the intern. Unless properly oriented concerning these students and their needs, the intern might be at a loss as to how to plan for their achievement.

2. Point out to the intern any gifted and talented students you might have in the classroom. It is hoped your intern can be helpful in assisting with their special learning projects and assignments. Gifted students can work on and accomplish amazing projects if given a chance to "beat their own drums."

3. Get the intern involved early with assisting the culturally diverse students, thereby giving him an opportunity to develop a respect for each culture represented in your classroom.

4. At risk students will probably make themselves known to the intern in a short time. It is most important to discuss these unique students prior to the time the intern begins teaching. There is a good chance that interns have had little experience in working with such students; they need much guidance. Students who use or abuse alcohol or other drugs, victims of child or substance abuse or neglect, and delinquents who are potential dropouts are particularly challenging for the intern.

5. Acquaint your intern with the various special educators who assist you with the special needs students, letting her spend some time with them if possible.

6. You and your intern should have some challenging conference sessions working out plans to best use your time and activities to meet the needs of these special needs students. Your intern will have valuable experiences as a result of your efforts.

▼ GUIDELINES FOR THE INTERN

1. Keep in mind that all students can learn.

2. Depend on your supervising teacher for advice in working with these students. Your supervisor is a master teacher and probably has worked previously with a large number of special needs students. You may be involved with other members of the mainstreaming team.

3. If you can incorporate ethnic studies into the curriculum, it would give a big boost to the self-concept of the ethnically diverse students. Of course, this would have to meet the approval of your supervising teacher.

4. Be a good listener when working with these students. Whether the students are gifted, mildly retarded, physically disabled, or otherwise, they can sense whether you are truly interested in them as worthwhile persons.

5. Make sure you are familiar with Public Law 94–142. The needs of children and youths with disabilities are addressed by this law, which is called the Individuals with Disabilities Education Act. It guarantees educational services to all students with disabilities including the development of Individual Educational Programs (IEPs) for each child and education in the least restrictive environment.

6. Do not expect students to perform beyond their capacities. Students cannot be expected to perform tasks just because they are intellectually bright. Some individuals have specific learning problems even though they are generally quite intelligent (Patton, Kauffman, Blackbourn, & Brown, 1991).

7. Remember that individuals with mental retardation are people who are much more like than unlike the rest of us. It is important to treat them, as well as persons with physical impairment or health problems, in ways that are as normal as possible. Do not underestimate their abilities (Patton et al., 1991).

8. Be conscious of appropriate seating arrangements of your special needs students. For example, seat persons with hearing impairments near the speaker or interpreter.

9. Respect the worth of every student in your class including all of the special needs students. If you do not understand the background and needs of special needs students, do additional research.

CASE 13–1

William, a gifted 10th grade student, is in Mrs. Smith's homeroom class. He has become a special concern of Mrs. Smith's new intern, Norma. William has a knack of stirring up trouble in the classroom. His bluntness has a tendency to irritate his classmates as well as several of his teachers.

Today Norma tried to encourage William to attend the upcoming career fair where she told him he might gain some insights concerning various careers. He was very huffy to Norma, telling her that he intended to become a medical doctor and did not want to consider any other careers. Norma was trying to be helpful to William and felt very bad about his response.

1. Why do you think William was so blunt?
2. How could attendance at a career fair benefit a student like William?
3: What could Norma and Mrs. Smith do that might help William become better accepted by his classmates?
4. Is bluntness a characteristic of gifted students? What characteristics do they usually exhibit?
5. Many gifted students drop out of school. How could this talent loss be prevented? ▼

CASE 13–2
▼

Part of Fred's student teaching assignment was hall duty every Monday and Wednesday. As a new intern, he was very eager to do a good job. All went very well the first week of duty. Then Ramon, a senior student with muscular dystrophy who was confined to a wheelchair, entered the picture. Ramon was disgruntled because of his condition and his outlook for the future. He barrelled through the halls with his motorized wheelchair at top speed. Fred did not want to hurt his feelings but finally reprimanded Ramon for his dangerous maneuvers. Ramon was quite disrespectful to Fred and told him to "bug off"!

1. Why was Fred justified in attempting to discipline Ramon?
2. What measures should be taken with Ramon because he was disrespectful to Fred?
3. How should Fred have reacted to Ramon's discourteous response?
4. What should Fred's supervising teacher do about this matter?
5. Why is it important for interns to be assigned to duties typically given to classroom teachers? ▼

CASE 13-3 ▼

Gordon has been assigned to Mrs. Breams, a 10th and 11th grade social studies teacher. Mary, a deaf student who is relatively new to the school, is in the fifth period history class.

Mary has an interpreter assigned to her but seldom looks at him during lessons. Gordon is in his sixth week and is teaching three of his five assigned classes including fifth period. He asks Mary, through the interpreter, why she ignores help, and she indicates that she has little interest in social studies. Gordon is in a quandary!

1. Why should this matter be taken to the teacher of the hearing impaired?
2. How should Gordon respond to Mary's noted lack of interest in social studies?
3. What can Mrs. Breams do to assist Gordon?
4. How could Mary's attitude affect the other students in her class?
5. If Mary does not change her attitude, should she be allowed to continue to be mainstreamed? Explain your answer. ▼

CASE 13-4 ▼

Charles's assignment is a fourth grade classroom with Mrs. Green as supervising teacher. He is in his seventh week of student teaching and has thoroughly enjoyed the experience.

On Wednesday, as he was having lunch in the cafeteria, Charles was a bit startled at what he saw. Billy, one of the boys in his class, appeared to have a small gun in his pocket. Charles, thinking it was a water gun, confronted Billy and asked for the gun. To his surprise, Billy handed him a loaded pistol. Charles was in shock!

1. Should Charles have been more cautious in approaching Billy? Explain your answer.
2. What measures should be taken by Charles and Mrs. Green now that the gun has been found?
3. How should this be handled with Billy's classmates?
4. What can an elementary school do to avoid such happenings?
5. How should the parents of the other students in Charles's class be informed of this occurrence? ▼

CASE 13-5 ▼

Janey was shocked at how fast her student teaching assignment was flying by. She was already in her fifth week and was presently teaching half of her seventh grade classes.

Janey felt that for the most part, she had been successful in her teaching. As she took over her third class, however, she was confronted by her first major problem: Rebecca. Rebecca had serious problems that, according to her supervising teacher, were reflected in temper tantrums, imitations of animal noises, and complete rejection of the people around her.

Janey felt her first lesson was a disaster. Rebecca paid no attention whatsoever and delighted in periodically neighing like a horse. Janey ignored her and completed her lesson; however, she was completely drained of energy. She wondered if Rebecca was going to keep her from becoming a teacher.

1. Should Janey have ignored Rebecca's misbehavior? Explain your answer.
2. How could the supervising teacher have prepared Janey better for this class?
3. Why is it important to let students such as Rebecca know what is expected of them?
4. Why would a student like Rebecca be mainstreamed into a regular classroom?
5. Janey had observed Rebecca for more than 4 weeks. Why do you think she was shocked at her behavior? ▼

REFERENCES

Lewis, Rena B., and Doorlag, Donald H. (1991). *Teaching special students in the mainstream* (3rd ed.) (p. 411). New York: Merrill/Macmillan Publishing Company.

Patton, James R., Kauffman, James M., Blackbourn, J. M., & Brown, Gweneth B. (1991). *Exceptional children in focus* (5th ed.) (p. 25). New York: Merrill/Macmillan Publishing Company.

RECOMMENDED READING

Evans, William H., Evans, Susan S., Gable, Robert A., & Schmid, Rex E. (1991). *Instructional management: For detecting and correcting special problems.* Boston: Allyn & Bacon. (I&S)
This book focuses on the classroom needs of special students. A comprehensive analysis of instructional environments is provided. Practical examples of instructional problems in the form of vignettes may be of particular interest to the intern.

Lewis, Rena B., & Doorlag, Donald H. (1991). *Teaching special students in the mainstream* (3rd ed.). New York: Merrill/Macmillan Publishing Company. (I&S)
The practical strategies in this book suggested to meet the needs of mainstreamed students are particularly good. Specific information about students with special needs is informative and clear-cut. The tips for the teacher sections presented in each chapter are helpful.

Office of Educational Research and Improvement, Urban Superintendents Network. (1987). *Dealing with dropouts: The urban superintendents' call to action.* Washington, D. C.: Author. (I&S)
One of the categories of special needs students is the at-risk students who may be on a collision course with further schooling. This monograph is a collective request for concerted community effort to save these students and keep them in school.

Patton, James R., Kauffman, James M., Blackbourn, J. M., & Brown, Gweneth B. (1991). *Exceptional children in focus* (5th ed.). New York: Merrill/Macmillan Publishing Company. (I&S)
These authors present a very practical easy-to-read book that is quite effective in describing exceptional children. Particularly helpful are the suggestions for working with the children of special needs.

Reynolds, Maynard C. (1989). Students with special needs. In *Knowledge base for the beginning teacher* (pp. 129–142). New York: Pergamon Press. (I&S)
Reynolds gives a succinct review of various groups labeled special needs (SN) students. His review of some strategies for instructing SN students includes the recommendations that we should put our greatest teaching strengths with these children and youth.

Robinson, Phil C., & Huene, Gail Von. (1982). Meeting students' special needs. In *Helping teachers manage classrooms* (pp. 70–76). Alexandria, VA: Association for Supervision and Curriculum Development. (I&S)
This chapter focuses on the services becoming more and more available to the special needs students. Understanding teachers and community resources combine to help these students stay in school and succeed.

Shepard, Lorrie A. (1989). Identification of mild handicaps. In Robert L. Linn (Ed.), *Educational measurement* (3rd ed.) (pp. 445–472). New York: Macmillan Publishing Company. (S)
This article contains a variety of issues relating to the schooling of mildly handicapped individuals, including the bias of assessment and issues related to early identification. The definition, assessment, and school placement of mild mental retardation, learning disabilities, and emotional disturbance are discussed fully.

Westling, David L., & Koorland, Mark A. (1988). *The special educator's handbook.* Boston: Allyn & Bacon. (I&S)
This book contains helpful information for student teaching interns in exceptional student education and for interns who are working with special needs students. The Suggestion Boxes make the material immediately useful.

14 MULTICULTURAL STUDENTS

If student teaching interns can visualize a matrix of potential psychological characteristics among the students in any given class, and see the diversity of such psychological characteristics, it is much easier for them to see a similar matrix of the characteristics possessed by the students from culturally diverse backgrounds in the assigned classes. Such a matrix could look something like a honeycomb with the same labels across the horizontal axis as across the vertical axis. These characteristics include such things as sex, race, country of family origin, handicapping condition, age, language preference, and economic status.

At a minimum, interns in most schools have students of different sexes from various economic levels. Some of these students also have handicapping conditions. Most schools have a population variety from several races, ethnic groups, and countries of family origin. A picture of most classrooms shows a rich cross section of different skin tones, different hair and facial characteristics, and different styles of dressing, just as classrooms have always exhibited a wide variety of psychological characteristics.

Although some teachers feel they must learn a great deal more in order to function effectively with different kinds of individuals, it is important to remember that the most important element and the key to success with each of these students is to relate to them individually. All other differences matter little if a real desire to work together for the benefit of the student is expressed by the intern to each individual student. This expression takes the form of patience, body language, use of the eyes in communicating, and facial expressions. A teacher's smile can go a long way when even the languages are incompatible.

It is important to keep in mind the purpose of the school and the intern's relationship to that purpose: to help educate children, to take them where they are and move them forward in the skills of living, working, studying, and getting along with others in order to make their lives better according to their own definitions of what is better.

Many times teachers are frustrated because students from culturally diverse backgrounds are not making the same progress as other students. In fact, those students may be making far more progress because of their point of beginning, the amount of translation they must use, and the kinds of feelings they must deal with as they work on their school assignments.

It is important for the supervising teacher and the student teaching intern to discuss characteristics of students from culturally diverse backgrounds in the classroom. What assists them in learning? What different instructional techniques can be used to help them succeed? It is very helpful for the intern to observe in as many classrooms as possible in which there are students from culturally diverse backgrounds in order to note how the teachers and how other students successfully relate to these students.

Most contemporary schools have a good mix of students. If a third grade Asian child is having difficulty, one source of assistance is a successful fifth grade Asian student. Most often, students do not have the problems relating to other students that adults anticipate. Peer acceptance and involvement are very important, however, prior to the successful classroom achievement. Occasionally, the teacher can assist peer acceptance through purposefully directing classroom activity combining specific students in small group work. Most classrooms have students who want to help others with their work; use these students to assist with students from culturally diverse backgrounds.

Some handicapping conditions among students are temporary; such conditions are truly educational. Once the student is out of the wheelchair or off the crutches, she is more understanding and tolerant of other students who may have similar problems adjusting to the classroom situation.

A concept that should receive major emphasis during the student teaching internship is that of the likenesses of students. Emphasizing the ways in which all students are alike, for example, enjoying play activities, enjoying food, liking friends, needing rest and sleep, helps them to understand that people have more likenesses than differences.

Differences among students can be used as instructional enhancement. The music, art, customs, foods, dances, types of clothing, and folklore of the different cultures within a class can generate many approaches to learning. Using information about these exciting differences, the subjects in the curriculum can be more exciting for all the students. Language arts is a natural subject for examining cultures; writing, storytelling, listening, reading, library research, and even spelling can be involved in studying different cultures. Any subject in the curriculum can be related in this way; all it requires is creativity and appreciation of differences.

The differences of cultures tend to stimulate classroom students into their own research, whether that takes the form of interviewing older people or spending time in the library looking up specific topics. These differences are a vast resource of rich, available educational activity. With the help of the supervising teacher, the student teaching intern can enlist the parents and other family members of students from culturally diverse backgrounds to come to the school for presentations, interviews, and cultural reviews.

▼ GUIDELINES FOR THE SUPERVISING TEACHER

1. Give your student teaching intern optimum exposure to students from as many cultures as possible. This is a time for the intern to learn to interact with students of all kinds.
2. Set the role model of patience and caring in helping students from culturally diverse backgrounds find their niche in your classroom.
3. Encourage your intern to find and read as much material as possible about the nature of cultures other than her own. This is excellent discussion material for the two of you; you will find that this research on the part of the intern benefits your own learning.
4. It is possible that you and your intern are of different cultures, sexes, or economic strata. Learning to work together will benefit both of you and helps her to adapt to other cultures more readily.

5. Help your intern to understand that whatever traditions and customs other cultures have is really just their way of coping with the processes of life. These processes may be very different from each other from culture to culture, but the purpose is the same: to maintain life and improve it. This kind of understanding assists the intern in realizing that likenesses among different cultures are much greater than are their differences.

6. As your intern prepares special materials on various cultures, request that two sets of everything be produced. This allows him to take a set with him when he completes the student teaching position, and it means that you have a set to keep for permanent use. These can be time-consuming to develop and keeping copies is important.

7. A notebook with a section for each culture represented in your classroom is a gold mine for your intern to use. Depending on the ages of your students, they could produce the entries for such a notebook including food, dress, customs, music, dance, drama, history, and geography. Such a collection, beginning as a notebook, could become a cardboard file drawer with appropriate culturally diverse art work decorating it.

8. People love exciting things, and interns are no different from your classroom students in this regard. They enjoy studying the various cultures in the class as much as the students do.

9. Demonstrate the effects of positive body language and smiles. This may be the initial opportunity for the intern to see such measures demonstrated effectively.

▼ GUIDELINES FOR THE INTERN

1. Put on your adventurer's hat and be ready for some exciting study. By using the information represented by the various cultures in your student teaching classroom, your students have, firsthand, exciting topics to study and learn about. Their living data are more exciting to them and probably more accurate than your library research, although it is necessary, also. This is a part of your student teaching internship that can be fun and be a learning experience for you as well as for the students in your classroom.

2. Practice deliberately smiling and caring. Frequently, students from different cultures tend to isolate themselves either alone or within small groups. Break through these walls; let them know that you are there to help them learn and that being comfortable in their classroom is a prerequisite for such learning.

3. Read everything you can find in the university library; have your students do research in the school library. Develop a game of verifying information about cultures represented in your class. Assign students to library projects on what writers think customs of those groups are, and compare that with the reality of the customs of the children in your classroom. This is live, exciting research for the students.

4. Emphasize the foods of different cultures. Where possible, prepare some of these foods in your classroom so that students know the ingredients and tastes for themselves. Research on why certain ingredients are used by some cultures and not by others helps students understand more of our physical world and its flora and fauna.

5. Plan for students to write and act in their own drama depicting certain cultural customs. Students enjoy this and remember these lessons.

6. Use the music and art of the various cultures as subjects through which to

study history as well as contemporary society. Some music and art is quite different from what you or the children have been exposed to previously. Students can learn to appreciate it or even just to accept it as being representative of another culture's efforts toward entertainment and personal expression.

7. You may wish to plan your multicultural studies around a "Culture of the Month" organization. If so, plan an initial outline of activities and research and use that as a template for each month so that each culture receives equal treatment and support.

8. Visualize each different student in your classroom as an opportunity for you to learn. Your culturally diverse learning under the direction of the supervising teacher is priceless. Observe how other teachers in the school celebrate cultural diversity. Take notes. Keep records of all ideas. Such materials and ideas will enrich your own teaching for your professional life.

9. You will find that as you accept students of other cultures, they learn from you to a similar degree. Care for each student; let the students know that you have a real concern for their learning experiences to be successful and that you are working toward that objective. Keep in mind that to the student of another culture, you are from a different culture yourself!

CASE 14-1 ▼

Lee was a new Asian student who had just transferred into the eighth grade class where Ester was student teaching. He seemed to be a loner, was quiet, and did not mix with the others. Although initially he had done very well on the mathematics work and tests, he had recently just barely passed. The supervising teacher encouraged Ester to have a talk with Lee as soon as possible without having a scheduled conference (which could cause Lee anxiety). Ester found the right moment for a brief talk with Lee and discovered that some of the larger boys in the class had taunted him for his good grades in mathematics. So that they would not continue to bother him, Lee had decided the mathematics grades were not worth it and deliberately did poorly on his papers.

1. What kinds of emotions do you think Lee was experiencing?
2. How could Ester cause better acceptance of Lee's mathematics ability by using cooperative learning within the group?
3. What would be the outcome if Ester openly scolded the larger boys for threatening Lee?
4. What would happen if Ester and her supervising teacher left the matter alone and did nothing?
5. What would be the ideal resolution of this problem? ▼

CASE 14-2 ▼

In developing a research project in seventh grade social studies, the student teaching intern assigned the students to talk with their parents and grandparents and to develop a family tree that they could bring back to class and share with the group to illustrate the wide variety of cultural backgrounds within the group. The project had been cleared earlier with the supervising teacher.

The next morning when the student teaching intern arrived at school, a parent of one of her students was waiting for her in the classroom. The supervising teacher had not yet arrived. As the intern walked into the room, she was greeted with a hostile "What in this world do you mean, nosing into my family background? You and your students have no business whatsoever knowing anything about my family. That was a crazy assignment you gave my son yesterday, and I have told him that he doesn't have to do it!"

1. What do you think was the immediate reaction of the student teaching intern? How would you have responded?
2. What are some of the statements the intern may have made to the angry parent?
3. What kinds of alternate assignments could the intern have suggested?
4. How do you feel the intern treated this person's son after this meeting?
5. What kinds of psychological preparation should interns make prior to their internship in order to survive such a meeting intact? ▼

CASE 14–3
▼

Sammy Runningbear enjoyed being at his new school. The family had just moved to town and his sixth grade class had accepted him because he had helped them win the baseball game against the other sixth grade class. As sixth grade peer groups will, the boys became buddies with each other.

The intern in Sammy's classroom was about to initiate a short unit on rhythm in dance, music, and poetry. When she discovered that Mr. Runningbear was an accomplished Native American drummer, she invited him to perform with his drums for the class. Mr. Runningbear accepted the invitation; he visited the class, played his drums, and explained some of his Native American customs.

The visit appeared to be a success until the following day when the boys in class began drumming on their desks, singing "I am Runningbear; I am Runningbear." Sammy was very embarrassed and ashamed.

1. What immediate action should the intern and the supervising teacher take?
2. What steps could have been taken prior to Mr. Runningbear's visit to have avoided such a demonstration?
3. What is happening to sixth-graders physiologically and psychologically to make them particularly susceptible to this type of behavior?
4. How could Sammy's embarrassment and shame be turned to pride in his ancestry? Is there need for this? Why?
5. How could the intern involve the parents of the demonstrating students to share their cultural heritage with the class? ▼

CASE 14–4
▼

Harriet was interning in the 11th grade history class and received a request for a conference from the mother of one of her students. The conference time was set and the mother appeared. It seems that she objected to Harriet's use of terms such as *forefathers, the common man,* and *founding fathers.* The mother suggested that she use, instead, such words as *ancestors, the average person,* and *founders.*

1. How should Harriet respond to the student's mother?
2. Which terms are most appropriate? Why?
3. If there was a problem with these terms Harriet was using, why had they been used in her classes at the university?
4. What other terms would be considered sexist language and should be avoided by teachers?
5. Why had no one ever told her before that these kinds of terms cause problems for some people? ▼

CASE 14-5
▼

Cecelia was an African American student teaching intern in Mr. Piner's senior class in English literature. She enjoyed her students and the professional association with the faculty at the high school. Cecelia was very proud of her African American heritage, including the fabric art prints that had been made into beautiful clothing. She liked to wear such clothing to her student teaching assignment, and the students appeared to appreciate the relief from the rather conservative clothing that most of the other teachers wore. Mr. Piner had a personal dislike for such clothing and told her that she should not wear it to school again. This represented a part of Cecelia's heritage and she was hurt.

1. How could Mr. Piner say such a thing? Did he have the right to do so?
2. What feelings would have prompted him to forbid her to wear such clothes?
3. How could the university coordinator convince Mr. Piner that his decision was very narrow?
4. If you had been Cecelia, what would you have done?
5. In what ways should the opinions of the students be considered?
6. What options were available to Cecelia? ▼

RECOMMENDED READING

Adler, Mortimer, & McKenzie, Floretta Dukes. (1985). Must all students be given the same kind of schooling? In James William Noll (Ed.), *Taking sides: Clashing views on controversial educational issues* (pp. 150–163). Guilford, CN: Dushkin Publishing Group, Inc. (I&S)
Mortimer Adler and Floretta Dukes McKenzie debate the nature of current reform in education. This very interesting discussion gives a basis for thought-provoking professional conversations.

Amodeo, Luiza, & Martin, Jeanette. (1988). A neglected educational issue: Rural, minority women. In John Sikula (Ed.), *Action in Teacher Education, The Journal of the Association of Teacher Educators, tenth-year anniversary issue, commemorative edition* (pp. 99–102). Reston, VA: Association of Teacher Educators. (I&S)
Rural, minority women seem to have compounded problems in employment, education, and other job related factors. Eight recommendations are given indicating areas of priority for improving conditions for these women.

Baptiste, H. Prentice, Jr., Waxman, Hersholdt C., deFelix, Judith Walker, & Anderson, James E. (Eds.). (1990). *Leadership, equity, and school effectiveness.* Newbury Park, CA: Sage Publications. (S)
This book contains material on equity in schooling written by 22 outstanding educational professionals. Of particular interest to the supervising teacher is "Teacher Effectiveness Research and Equity Issues" by Jane Stallings & Jane McCarthy and "Teacher Education That Enhances Equity" by James B. Boyer.

Franklin, John Hope. (1990). The desperate need for black teachers. In Marcella L. Kysilka (Ed.), *Honor in teaching: Reflections* (pp. 95–97). West Lafayette, IN: Kappa Delta Pi. (I&S)
The author briefly describes the need for African American teachers in America, particularly for the role models children need. A suggestion offered is the redevelopment of education as a profession that is again attractive to young African American students.

Garcia, Ricardo. (1991). *Teaching in a pluralistic society: Concepts, models, strategies.* New York: Harper Collins Publishers. (S)
This book contains much useful information that the supervising teacher may be able to share with the student teaching intern. The author includes material relative to teaching and learning in a pluralistic society in addition to instructional models and strategies for successful educational practices in such a society.

Hall, Edward T. (1989, Fall). Unstated features of the cultural context of learning. *The Educational Forum, 54*(1), 21–34.
This professor emeritus of Northwestern University gives an anthropological perspective on learning.

Differences among cultures and assumptions related to context, information, and meaning are clearly explained.

Pai, Young. (1990). *Cultural foundations of education.* New York: Merrill/Macmillan Publishing Company. (I&S)
This book examines education as a cultural phenomenon and considers the process of teaching, learning, and counseling within such a perspective. Case studies are included that involve African American, Asian American, Hispanic American, Native American, and White American groups.

Whitehurst, Winston, Witty, Elaine, & Wiggins, Sam. (1988). Racial equity: Teaching excellence. In John Sikula (Ed.), *Action in Teacher Education, The Journal of the Association of Teacher Educators, tenth-year anniversary issue, commemorative edition* (pp. 159–167). Reston, VA: Association of Teacher Educators. (I&S)

This article discusses the shortage of minority teachers in the work force and two major efforts to improve this situation. One effort is a predominately African American institution that is trying to maintain its teacher education program, and the other effort is a Virginia school district of over 25,000 students.

Zeichner, Kenneth M. (1989, Spring). Preparing teachers for democratic schools. *Action in Teacher Education, 11* (1), 5–10. (S)
Zeichner looks at the demand for reform and crisis in inequality in schools as well as the need for beginning teachers to experience community-based teacher education. He indicates the need to broaden school empowerment to include parents. This contains good reference material for the supervising teacher.

15 OBSERVATIONS

Students have been observing in their own classrooms since kindergarten days. Now, in student teaching, classroom observations take on more significance.

In most student teaching situations, the intern is required to observe for a time in the teaching assignment as well as in the classrooms of other teachers. It is inappropriate for the intern to expect to be ushered into the "best" teacher's classroom to observe; all teachers have some strong points and as many teachers as possible should be included in the observations.

Arrangement can be made by the supervising teacher for the intern to observe in classrooms throughout the school. It is not necessary for interns to observe only those subjects they are prepared to teach, but it is advantageous for the intern to observe in classrooms of different subjects and different ages in order to maintain an objective assessment of the classroom situation. A physical education teacher, for example, can certainly profit from observing English, history, or music classes.

An elementary intern can easily observe a number of elementary teachers in their classrooms. A secondary intern can follow the daily schedule of a single student, noting interpersonal interactions.

There are two primary things to keep in mind in planning observations. One is the schedule of observations; the intern should arrange this with the supervising teacher. The second is plans for the observation, deciding ahead of time what to look for.

The supervising teacher can indicate beforehand strong points of the person being observed to make the observation more effective. Interns should be aware of a great deal that is going on in the classroom they may not be actually watching.

Students sometimes think that teachers have eyes in the back of their heads. This is a trait that teachers must learn. Through peripheral vision or through sound cues learned from various students, they can know what is happening in the back of the room even when they are not looking in that direction. Observing other teachers aids in developing this trait.

Other kinds of information that the intern wants to glean from observation include the kind of interaction that goes on in the classroom. There are student-student interaction, student-teacher interaction, and probably teacher–other person interaction. If there is a teacher aide in the classroom, there is another set of configurations of interactions. Communication patterns among people in the classroom are also worth noting, although they vary with each teacher.

The intern should be aware that these are not just person-to-person interactions but are a different configuration each time. Interns should be able to adjust to the intensity of the interaction both on the part of the student and

95

of the teacher, or both involved parties. Most interns are relatively new at dealing directly with students. They dealt with students when they were students, but this assignment is a different relationship.

Another important awareness is the physical logistics of a classroom, such as the management of the physical objects in the classroom. This refers to such things as the arrangement of the desks, the seating of the students, and the lighting in the room. The intern should be aware of such things as the teacher's movement throughout the room. If the teacher stands back against a window, students have to look into a glare, and all they can see is the silhouette of the teacher. The intern should be aware of such things as:

the location of the pencil sharpener
the order that the teacher has for the students to go sharpen their pencils (Is there any order?)
the location of the trash basket (Is it located so that it is in full view for students to pitch toward? Or is it located in some less accessible place where a student cannot make a display?)
the location of the teacher's desk in relation to the students' desks
the location of the teacher's desk in relation to the doorway
the kind of ventilating system (Is the room too hot or too cold?)
the mechanics of opening and closing the windows
methods of adjusting blinds, etc.
adjustment of the lighting
free movement allowed in the room

The observer should be intent on finding how these things are regulated. Does the teacher come in first thing in the morning and adjust everything and put it out of mind until the end of the day? Minor details are important.

Because the students expect routine to remain the same when the intern takes over, classroom detail is important to observe and remember. An activity to note is the method used for turning in papers. Does each student bring papers up to the teacher's desk individually so that on the return trip an opportunity exists for visiting other students at their desks? Or, are all the papers passed up at one time in an orderly fashion either directly to the front or directly to the side and then to the front? Is there a pattern? Are there patterns throughout the classroom activity that students know and can depend on, or does it appear to you as an observer that the students are confused as to which way to turn? In other words, are there established procedures in the classroom?

Another major area in classroom management that the intern should be aware of during observations is the emotional climate and styles of rapport in the classroom. How is this managed? How much stress is evident? Are the students hostile toward the teacher? Is the teacher hostile toward the students? Is either irate with the other? Is either frustrated? Do the students seem to help each other in terms of calming each other? Are the students calmed by the teacher? Does the teacher seem to be trusting the students to behave? Is there an air of tranquility or an air of tenseness? How does the teacher calm an upset student? What methods does the teacher use to quiet the class? Presence of a positive emotional climate is all evidence of good classroom management, of trust on the part of the students, and frequently a great deal of faith on the part of the teacher. The supervising teacher and the intern should discuss this in detail.

The intern should note the routine maintenance of the room (cleaning of chalkboard, the erasers, the floor). It is important for the novice teacher to realize that students feel a sense of belonging in the room they help maintain, decorate, and care for.

▼ GUIDELINES FOR THE SUPERVISING TEACHER

1. It gives your intern a great deal of self-confidence to see that teachers really have many of the same questions the intern has. At times, interns may feel that they alone face classroom problems. They may think that "these are problems only to me. I'm the only person in the world faced with these anxieties. How am I going to get this material across? How will I plan? How will I evaluate? How will I live with all of these people in this classroom?" When interns know that all teachers have faced these questions and periodically face most of them again and again throughout their teaching careers, they gain self-confidence. They see how other teachers deal with such questions even if they cannot answer them all.

2. It is the responsibility of the supervising teacher to establish an observation schedule. It is wise to plan no more than 1 hour, or in the secondary school, one period at a time. It might be beneficial for the intern to observe Mrs. X at one time today and at a different period tomorrow, not two periods the same day.

3. If the intern is observing subjects such as English or math, try to develop a schedule that has variety.

4. If the intern is observing in the elementary grades and if there is a junior high or middle school nearby, it is beneficial if there could be some observation in those levels, not of extended length but enough to know what these students are like after leaving your classes. The intern may have observed in such classes during his college training.

5. Planning for observations should be done with specific purposes in the minds of both the supervising teacher and the student teaching intern. Arrangements should be made by the supervising teacher ahead of time so that the intern does not appear in Mrs. X's classroom unannounced and say to Mrs. X: "Oh, I'm here." Although Mrs. X and the supervising teacher may be very good friends, this type of situation is not imposed on friendship.

▼ GUIDELINES FOR THE INTERN

1. Observation in the classrooms of other teachers should be planned for maximum benefit to you and minimum concern and bother to your host teachers.

2. One of the things that most interns are concerned with is that of getting along with students. As you go from one classroom to another, observe how one teacher gets along with students and mentally compare this with how other teachers get along with students.

3. Try to develop a list of qualities that seem to make one teacher able to appropriately manage the classroom or an individual student; notice those qualities that may not be positive. You should mentally file these qualities and never discuss them in terms of personalities.

4. The intern should not discuss with the supervising teacher the fact that Mrs. Z, the next door teacher, does certain activities that really bomb; the supervising teacher may be teaching next door to Mrs. Z for a number of years and such discussions are not appropriate. It is acceptable to discuss particular qualities but do not identify them with any personality.

5. When appropriate, take detailed notes during your observations and record questions. There may be some activities that you discover while observing that you wish to pursue further, and this is an excellent time to expand your general teaching repertory.

6. Be careful during observations to avoid disturbing those classes you have been allowed to observe. If you have questions, ask them later, not during the class time of your host teacher. Melt into the classroom environment. Slip into a chair by the door. Avoid moving about if the students are not doing so.

7. For optimal benefit from the observations, a list of objectives of the observation should be discussed with the supervising teacher, both before and after the observations.

8. Of major importance in your developing professional reputation is your gratitude. After the observation, leave the room without disturbing the lesson but make a point of seeing that teacher before leaving school at the end of the day and thank him for allowing you to observe in his classroom. Interpersonal relations are very important. You may wish to comment favorably about something you observed.

CASE 15-1 ▼

Steve was the new intern in Coach Mills's ninth grade physical education class. Prior to the beginning of the term, Coach Mills had made arrangements for Steve to observe in several classes taught by the other three physical education teachers. The third day of the term, Coach Mills was in his office when in stormed his fellow teacher Mrs. Batley with: "Get that brat out of my class!"

As Coach attempted to calm Mrs. Batley, she explained that as Steve was observing her class just now in basketball exercises, she had her back to the class for a moment and the next thing she knew, Steve was on the court demonstrating trick shots and pretending to be a big league basketball star. She had requested that he get off the court and he had responded with: "In just a minute. They need to see this one super shot."

As Mrs. Batley seethed, Coach Mills's mind raced:

1. Had he done the wrong thing in accepting an intern?
2. Why had the college not warned him about Steve?
3. What could he do?
   a. immediately
   b. during the next several days
4. What other arrangements for observations, if any, should he make for Steve?
5. What specific recommendations should Coach Mills give Steve prior to any future observations? ▼

CASE 15-2 ▼

Rose had been scheduled by her supervising teacher to observe in one classroom for reading from 8:30 until 9:15 and in another classroom for math from 9:25 until 10:00. The second teacher approached the supervising teacher at lunch and asked about Rose. The supervising teacher investigated and found that Rose had made the first scheduled observation but had then gone to the teachers' lounge and had become engrossed in conversation and did not realize the passage of time. At 9:45 she had suddenly remembered her second appointment but decided not to go into that teacher's classroom late. She had remained in the lounge until 10:10 and then returned to the classroom of her supervising teacher, not telling her what had happened. The supervising teacher felt disappointed and perplexed.

1. How could she explain to the intern exactly how she felt?
2. Should she trust the intern a second time?
3. How would she know it would be safe to trust her?

4. How should this be explained to the teacher whose observation was missed?
5. What points should the college coordinator make in his discussion with Rose about the importance of keeping professional appointments? ▼

CASE 15-3
▼

Mary was interning with Ms. Ness, the senior English teacher. Mary gave an impression of being very professional and very interested in every teacher she observed. She took notes during her observations and commented to each teacher that she wanted to teach just the same way. She seemed sincere in her compliments but when Mr. Scott and Ms. Jones, two English teachers with methods diametrically opposed, accosted each other in the teachers' lounge with the statement Mary had made during her visit with each of them, both they and the other teachers in the lounge were able to see the artificiality in Mary's compliments. This was called to the attention of the department chairman who in turn talked with Ms. Ness.

1. How could Ms. Ness help Mary to repair her professional reputation in the school?
2. What was Mary's responsibility in resolving the problem?
3. How could the English teachers as a group turn this situation around to help Mary develop as a better teacher and more professional person?
4. Because of the psychological nature of this behavior, how could the college counseling service be of assistance to Mary?
5. On what basis should Mary continue with her scheduled observations? ▼

CASE 15-4
▼

Bert, the new kindergarten intern, was completing his fifth day at school when he was approached by one of the teachers he had observed 2 days prior. Somehow, he knew immediately from the gleam and squint of her eyes what had happened.

The events of the previous afternoon in the grocery store raced through his mind. Yes, he had run into a friend of his older sister and he had discussed this particular teacher and what, in his opinion, was inappropriate handling of the friend's child. Bert gulped and gathered his courage as the teacher approached.

1. How could Bert have avoided this?
2. What will the content of this conversation likely be?
3. What options does Bert have to regain the respect of this teacher?
4. How would you react if you were Bert's supervising teacher and had arranged the observation?
5. What is a good rule to remember relative to discussing student problems in public? ▼

CASE 15-5
▼

Alice happily anticipated her teaching career and was excited about student teaching. Her supervising teacher had established an observation schedule in other teachers' classrooms at the beginning of the term. Although she was to be working with high school students as a career, she had not gotten over being a shy young woman. Her supervising teacher recognized this difficulty but had failed to communicate it to those teachers with whom she had set up the observation schedule.

As Alice visited her scheduled observations, she became more and more aware that her host teachers were expecting more reaction from her than she was exhibiting. She was quite embarrassed when one of the teachers asked her a question during his class. Not wanting to speak out, she sat there and just shook her head from side to side. The teacher went on with the class and in a few moments, Alice rose quietly and slipped out of the room.

1. Was it inappropriate for the teacher to ask Alice questions?
2. What do you think Alice did when she returned to her own classroom?
3. In the discussion later between the supervising teacher and the teacher Alice was visiting, what might have been said?
4. What effect does Alice's shyness have on the students she will be teaching?
5. What positive approach should the supervising teacher take?▼

CASE 15–6
▼

Middle school home economics students welcomed Jan to observe their class as she began her student teaching assignment in another classroom in their school. Jan's eagerness was almost overwhelming to the teacher whose class was being observed. During the lecture portion of the period, Jan had furiously taken notes. Later, during the lab time, Jan had proceeded individually to discuss their projects with several students. This hindered the class somewhat, but the teacher had agreed for Jan to observe.

1. Should the teacher allow this procedure to continue?
2. What steps should the teacher take?
3. Should the supervising teacher be told how disruptive Jan had become in class? How could this be remedied?
4. How could the supervising teacher assist Jan in becoming more discreet in her data gathering?
5. What steps could the college coordinator take to give Jan positive assistance in this situation? ▼

RECOMMENDED READING

Balch, Pamela M., & Balch, Patrick E. (1987). Becoming an effective observer. In *The cooperating teacher: A practical approach for the supervision of student teachers* (pp. 85–106). New York: University Press of America. (I&S)
Guidelines to help the student teaching intern focus observation activity and recognize effective teaching are given; checklists are provided. Flander's Interaction Analysis and a set of questioning skills using Bloom's taxonomy are illustrated.

Cohen, Louis, & Manion, Lawrence. (1983). Watching how others make lessons "happen." In *A guide to teaching practice* (pp. 106–112). New York: Methuen & Company. (I)
This brief reading assists the student teaching intern in learning how to observe effectively. Relating the contents of the classroom and their relationship to the lesson are sometimes overlooked in an observation design. Twelve questions form a good review for observing motivation.

Duke, Daniel Linden. (1990). Making sense of the teacher's world. *Teaching: An introduction*

(pp. 37–61) New York: McGraw-Hill Publishing Company. (I&S)
This chapter is an important one for the new student teacher in that it assists in learning how to identify by observation good teaching practices in the classroom. Hints on conducting an observation, what to look for, how to pinpoint the identification of classroom activity, and potential assistance from theory and research in the other social sciences are included in this material.

Good, Thomas L., & Brophy, Jere E. (1991). Observing in classrooms. In *Looking in classrooms* (5th ed.) (pp. 47–109). New York: Harper Collins Publishers, Inc. (S)
The authors present an extensive survey of coding methods for classroom observations. Information is provided on the Brophy-Good Dyadic Interaction System, the Emmer Observation System, the coding vocabulary of Blumenfeld and Miller, and educational ethnography. Although advanced, this material can be introduced to the student teacher by the supervising teacher at useful times.

Wiggins, Sam P. (1957). Observing, assisting, and teaching. In *The student teacher in action*

(pp. 119–138). Boston: Allyn & Bacon. (I&S)
Although this material was printed a number of years ago, the content remains important and timely. Wiggins discusses what and how the stu- *dent teaching intern should observe; he uses lists and specific steps as the intern proceeds through the stages of increasing involvement in the assignment.*

16 CLASSROOM ORGANIZATION

As the supervising teacher and the student teaching intern prepare to work together, one of the main areas of concern is classroom organization. Interns are usually concerned over whether they will be able to develop an effective plan for classroom organization. The supervising teacher is usually concerned with the quality of classroom organization the intern will maintain. For most interns, the student teaching experience is the first opportunity to put together all the components of teaching experienced during their training.

Frequently field experiences prior to student teaching give the student only a portion of the responsibility and, although the assignment may be well done, there may be difficulty with trying to meld the entire program for a classroom into one picture.

This melding process is one of the most anxiety-laden experiences for the novice teacher. Prior to developing a comprehensive and realistic "feel" for teaching, the intern must experience this synthesis of the many theories and the relatively small amount of practice experienced in the training program. While working with this synthesis, the meaning of teaching changes for the intern.

Student teaching interns must operate within the organizational framework of the classrooms to which they are assigned. Dr. Gordon Eade, Assistant Dean of the College of Education at the University of West Florida and long-time student teaching coordinator, compares the student teaching assignment to operating "within a balloon." Interns should be able to push out here and there but must stay within the confines of the balloon. When the intern pushes out in a certain direction, other parts of the balloon have to make adjustments, thereby changing shapes. Keeping fresh air in the balloon and not breaking through are cautions to keep in mind by both the intern and the supervising teacher.

Well-organized classrooms have rules and principles set up concerning use of facilities, space, materials, and time. If organized properly, the use of these principles diminish problems in student conduct and promote learning.

Although the supervising teacher can suggest, advise, and warn, only experience can bring reality to the intern concerning the many facets of classroom activity labeled teaching. The value of such advice depends on the receptivity of the intern.

As the intern divides teaching into such components as planning, delivering the lesson, evaluating, and re-teaching, there is a vague realization that something is missing. That difficult-to-pin-down element is classroom organization, not a separate component of teaching, but rather a pattern or matrix that falls across the entire teaching spectrum from the first day of kindergarten until graduation.

Classroom organization is not something that is to be done in a classroom;

it is not an end unto itself. It is, rather, an approach given to those activities involved in the learning process.

An intern does not "do" classroom organization. Use of the best efforts of the students, school materials and their effects, the training of the intern, background, resources, and current time usage contribute to classroom organization. When these resources are well utilized, the teacher is acclaimed for having "good" classroom organization. When they are ill used, the teacher is said to have poor classroom organization.

The attitude that forms the basis for effective classroom organization is one in which the teacher-to-be likes herself, likes people in general, and enjoys working with them in a helping relationship. The teacher who loves subject matter and does not like students will be a poor teacher and may have many organizational problems. A liking and helping attitude exerts positive forces in the classroom. A positive action on the part of the beginning teacher is more likely to produce a positive action on the part of the students in the classroom.

Once the attitude has been analyzed, then the supervising teacher and the intern can consider applying that attitude throughout the learning activities in the classroom. This is the "rule" stage. In considering what activities to do in the classroom, this positive, personal attitude should be applied in an objective way to facilitate the highest quality of learning possible in the classroom. The intern and the supervising teacher can break down the classroom activities into academic processes and physical activities, carefully maintaining the attitude that is to be infused into the teaching process.

Specificity begins at this point. The physical classroom can be divided into those properties of the classroom itself (desks, windows, heat, light) and those properties of the students (physical distance between students, pathways in the room, behavior patterns based on the seating arrangement, access to materials, books, learning centers, and pencil sharpeners).

The appearance of the classroom gives an indication about the extent to which the teacher cares for the environment in which the class operates. It is evident that no two classes are alike. Each one has its own environment (Eby, 1992).

The academic processes involve those nontangible actions in the classroom through which students encourage or discourage each other. The development of internal motivation can be considered a product of effective classroom organization. The teacher who can successfully develop internal motivation within students has few classroom organization problems. This again reflects the basic attitude of the teacher whose class is responding.

Considerations that should be discussed by the intern and the supervising teachers are organizing the interaction and the art of questioning. The use of praise and feedback, when necessary and appropriate, should also be discussed.

▼ GUIDELINES FOR THE SUPERVISING TEACHER

1. As a beginning teacher launches into the world of the classroom in the internship, the supervising teacher can be of great service by helping to identify the various composite parts of the totality of teaching. Being able to see the total picture helps many interns find confidence and thereby perform better, both in planning and in presentation.

2. The intern must understand that effective classroom organization is imperative and profitable in the teaching/learning process.

3. Throughout the term, as you share with the intern the major components of classroom organization, bits and pieces of information and advice should be shared; this information is more than a list of things to do to get the classroom ready or a list of things for students to do or to avoid doing.

4. Encourage your interns to use those methods that work best for them as long as they operate within "your balloon."

5. If there is time in the schedule, arrange for the intern to observe other selected teachers' classrooms for directed observation and later visit them for a discussion of effective classroom organization.

6. Offer the intern a wide variety of experiences in seeing how classrooms are run, discussing the variations between classes, pointing out social, economic, cultural, and maturational differences and social patterns, and you will be of immeasurable value to the intern.

7. One of the most important factors in a student teaching program is your modeling. Interns are watching for you to do the right thing at the right time.

8. Tell your intern to pick up clues from your students. For example, if a student refuses to do work assigned, the intern must learn to seek solutions to the problem.

▼ GUIDELINES FOR THE INTERN

1. Carefully observe your supervising teacher during the early part of your assignment. Inquire about anything you do not understand. Your supervising teacher is your model.

2. Remember that the best organization requires rules. You should know when to do what with what. Also, keep in mind that no set of rules fits all circumstances. The needs of students must have priority over organization.

3. Interns should be flexible and experimental in nature. Be sure to stay "within the balloon."

4. Provided that you have examined your professional attitudes, and this has led to a discussion with as many teachers as you can interview and/or observe, you are probably now ready for the specificity mentioned earlier in this chapter.

5. Make as many physical classroom arrangements as possible prior to the arrival of the students. Never suggest that students rearrange their own chairs; bedlam may result.

6. Adjust the lights, window shades or blinds, air or heat prior to the arrival of the students. This necessitates that you arrive at the school sufficiently early so that you do not appear rushed. You may have to make additional adjustments as your lessons progress.

7. Have work ready for students to begin immediately on entering the room and being seated. Develop within the group a desire to come in and get to work on materials that serve in an ongoing way. When all are in the room, that particular work can be put away for a time as other class work begins. Having a few self-directing assignments on the board helps the early arrivals and those students finishing early.

8. Develop a plan for pencil sharpening and other routines. This should include an emphasis on courtesy and expediency. Do not allow students to leave their seats at just any time to sharpen a pencil. Warn them ahead of time, so they may plan ahead and bring a spare pencil. Have extra pencils ready and trimmed in a mug on your desk so that a student may silently borrow and return them without interrupting the class by announcing the lack of a pencil.

9. Classes have been known to become disorderly while waiting for audiovisual equipment to begin. Prepare videotapes, projectors, and filmstrips prior to time to use them. Set them up while students are working on something else.

10. Be sure the students know what is to be done when their work is finished, where to put their work, and what to do next.

11. Be specific in your own plans for record keeping and student procedures such as going to the restroom, lining up for lunch, and distributing materials.

12. Have the desks spaced so that natural pathways through the room assist traffic to flow easily and not cause crowded areas. Be sure there is a wastebasket in the classroom.

CASE 16–1
▼

After Shelley began her full-time teaching in the fourth grade, her supervising teacher breathed a sigh of relief that the classroom was proceeding normally. She liked Shelley's approach to planning and her methods with the students. Something kept nagging at the back of her mind and as she completely reviewed Shelley's progress, she became aware of the problem.

Shelley had allowed the children to keep their desks in a sloppy manner. Some books and materials were scattered on the floor under the desks; books inside the desks were disheveled. Prior to Shelley's arrival, the students had been required to keep their desks clean and neat with no books or materials on the floor. The supervising teacher knew something must be done before the children's habits got worse.

1. Should the supervising teacher speak to the children about their desks?
2. How could the supervising teacher approach the situation without hurting Shelley?
3. What reaction do you think Shelley would have to the supervising teacher's suggestions?
4. Is it important that fourth-graders keep their desks neat? Why?
5. What is the connection between the organizational abilities of a teacher and sloppy desks of the students? ▼

CASE 16–2
▼

When the college coordinator first visited the classroom where Wendy was student teaching, he realized that trouble might be brewing. Wendy had been placed with Miss Grimlet, notorious for her organization and neatness. Wendy, however, seemed to thrive on the lack of such qualities. Although Wendy had a number of qualities that could easily help her become a good teacher, she would have difficulty fitting into a classroom situation with Miss Grimlet.

Overnight he pondered the situation. Then he called Wendy and set up a conference with her in his office on campus after school.

1. What do you think the coordinator told Wendy?
2. What hope is there for compromise in this situation? Why?
3. How would Wendy discover the supervising teacher's tolerance level?

4. Would you consider the supervising teacher's neat habits a good professional role model? Why?
5. What are Wendy's chances of being successful in this assignment? ▼

CASE 16–3
▼

Bill greeted the students in his new student teaching placement as they arrived the first morning. When the bell rang, his supervising teacher began the day's assignment in high school geography. Later in the first class, the supervising teacher introduced Bill to the class and asked him if he would like to say a few words.

Bill seized the opportunity and told the class some things about himself as an introduction. He proceeded to tell them that "some things" would change around the classroom, that he had plans for re-arranging the desks, that the trash basket should be moved to another more accessible location in the room, and that the teacher's desk would be better nearer the door.

The class members looked at Bill as if they could not believe what they were hearing. The supervising teacher interrupted Bill, thanked him, and proceeded with the geography lesson.

1. If you were the supervising teacher, how would you introduce Bill to your other classes during the day?
2. How should the supervising teacher react? What should she say to Bill?
3. In what way could the coordinator be of help in this situation?
4. Should Bill be allowed to continue his student teaching in this classroom? Why?
5. What could have been done prior to this introduction to avoid this development? By whom? ▼

CASE 16–4
▼

Margie was student teaching in 11th grade history with a supervising teacher who did not share her philosophy of getting the students involved in the material. The supervising teacher primarily used lecture and drill as teaching methods. Margie wondered why she had been placed with such a teacher. She realized that maybe she could have a good influence on her supervising teacher as well as learn from her.

At one point, Margie wanted the students to become involved in group work. When she discussed her plans with the supervising teacher, she was told that there was to be no group work in that classroom and that the desks were never to be moved for such foolishness. Margie was bewildered and frustrated.

1. What were Margie's options?
2. Should Margie involve the coordinator with her problem? The principal?
3. What would result from going against the supervising teacher's wishes and using the group process?
4. What skills in diplomacy could Margie develop while at the same time getting to use her own methods of teaching? How?
5. Discuss the possibility of Margie requesting a different placement for student teaching. ▼

CASE 16–5
▼

Charlie, a young aggressive intern, was assigned to a fifth grade classroom. His supervising teacher, Ms. Doyle, was delighted to have an intern and told Charlie on his first day that anything he wanted to do was fine with her. She said she would stay out of his way.

Within the first 2 weeks, Charlie completely overhauled the reading program in his classroom. He started by giving every student an interest inventory and proceeded to locate a wide variety of books at different reading levels to match those interests.

One of the first steps Charlie took was to discontinue working in the basal readers. He endeavored to individualize the reading program, which included developing a listening and reading center and building individual study carrels. Parents donated comfortable furniture, which added an informal atmosphere. The fifth grade students were enthralled with their new reading program. Ms. Doyle was also very excited about Charlie's work and invited other teachers in the building to visit.

1. Do you feel that Charlie was out of line in this situation? Why or why not?
2. Was Ms. Doyle wrong in allowing Charlie to completely revamp this program without her assistance? Explain your answer.
3. Can you think of any circumstances that would make it permissible for an intern to make so many changes in such a short period of time?
4. Do you feel that the students benefited from Charlie's project? In what ways?
5. Would you prefer to have an intern like Charlie or one who would sit back and want to be told what to do? Explain your preference. ▼

REFERENCE

Eby, Judy W. (1992). *Reflective planning, teaching, and evaluation for the elementary school.* New York: Merrill/Macmillan Publishing Company.

RECOMMENDED READING

Bauer, Anne M., & Sapona, Regina H. (1991). *Managing classrooms to facilitate learning.* Englewood Cliffs, NJ: Prentice-Hall, Inc. (I&S) *This book presents a thorough coverage of classroom organization that would facilitate learning. Interns and supervising teachers can benefit from reflections on this information.*

Charles, C. M. (1983). *Elementary classroom management: A handbook of excellence in teaching.* New York: Longman, Inc. (I&S) *This book thoroughly covers the basics of classroom organization. It is quite evident that the author has had an extensive background in classroom teaching. The information is clear and the suggestions presented are beneficial for both elementary supervising teachers and interns.*

Eby, Judy W. (1992). *Reflective planning, teaching, and evaluation for the elementary school.* New York: Merrill/Macmillan Publishing Company. (I&S)

The chapter "Planning for a Healthy Classroom Environment" describes what reflective teachers consider to be a healthy classroom climate. Interns could profit from reading about and discussing the experiences of elementary students on their first day of school in four hypothetical classrooms.

Emmer, Edmund T., Evertson, Carolyn M., Sanford, Julie P., Clements, Barbara S., & Worsham, Murray E. (1984). *Classroom management for secondary teachers.* Englewood Cliffs, NJ: Prentice-Hall, Inc. (I&S) *This book discusses what a teacher can do to create a well-organized classroom. Checklists to help teachers organize planning activities in key areas and case studies illustrating how important concepts can be applied in classrooms should be of interest to secondary teachers and interns.*

Evertson, Carolyn M., Emmer, Edmund T., Clements, Barbara S., Sanford, Julie P., & Worsham, Murray E. (1984). Organizing your classroom and supplies. In *Classroom management for elementary teachers.* Englewood Cliffs, NJ: Prentice-Hall, Inc. (I&S) *Excellent advice is offered to student teaching interns and beginning teachers relative to the physical organization of classroom furniture, supplies, equipment, and student belongings. Classroom diagrams are included with suggestions. An effective set of activities and a checklist are included.*

17 CLASSROOM MANAGEMENT

Uppermost in the minds of many interns is the topic of classroom management. Some have heard horror stories and have seen examples of poor as well as good management techniques during their own schooling and during field experiences at the university. They are correct in assuming that truly effective teaching can seldom take place without effective classroom management.

Appropriate classroom management begins with a positive attitude and varies from individual to individual. Frequently, student teaching interns attempt to model after their supervising teacher or some other idealized teacher, and they discover painfully that what works for one usually does not work for all.

Students in training to become teachers often ask such questions as: "What rules do you have for running a classroom?" and "Where do I find the answer to fill my bag of teaching tricks?" Many interns mistakenly use a list of rules in lieu of an attitude. This does not imply that the use of rules in classroom control is inappropriate; rules are necessary. However, rules must have a base and that base is attitudinal, derives from the personality and characteristics of the teacher, and is unique in each classroom.

As beginning teachers realize that the development of appropriate classroom management must first of all be an internal matter holistically seen, they are on their first steps toward developing into competent professionals. Piecemeal rules may last a few weeks or occasionally a school year, but there is always anxiety lurking in the beginner's mind that something is missing. When it is realized that the missing element is to teaching as the foundation is to a building, steps are usually retraced and new beginnings are made with the help of fellow teachers or instructors.

Interns should definitely operate "within the balloon" mentioned in Chapter 16. They can reach out but must stay within the framework that exists in their assigned classrooms.

More than we like to admit, much of the misconduct exhibited by students in the classroom is caused by inappropriate behavior of the teachers. This possibility should be considered and behavior should be reviewed.

After interns reflect on their own classroom behavior, it is advantageous for them to look at various models. During student teaching, interns accept any model being used in their particular classrooms. It is important, however, that they continue to reflect on which model or combination of models they incorporate as they move into their own classrooms. They should develop their discipline plan, which will be determined by their own philosophy and personality. Studying the models and ideas presented by such writers as Glasser, Dreikers, and Canter (mentioned in the Recommended Reading at the end of this chapter) would certainly be worthwhile.

All disciplining skill emanates from the teacher. A teacher, experienced or

new, must be confident and positive of attitudes toward students before he can be an effective disciplinarian. A disciplined classroom is a well-ordered, systematic setting in which all who enter can sense the outcome of the planning and yet not necessarily see the minute details of management.

Interns could also profit by reviewing the developmental characteristics of the students assigned to them. Are they typical or atypical? What are the specific causes of noted behavior problems? Supervising teachers should discuss such issues with their interns.

Specific instructions should be given to interns prior to their observing other classes. For example, an intern could be asked to observe how a certain teacher deals with the transition between one task and another. It is possible for interns to observe other classes but see very little if specific goals are not determined.

Student conduct is related to rules. A few specific rules are usually appreciated by both students and teachers. Few classrooms can operate successfully in a situation where there is no control. No behavior management system is 100% effective for every teacher. We cannot eliminate all misconduct no matter how we try; we can only minimize the causes and occurrences.

Some teachers believe that punishment is negatively correlated to learning. Misbehavior usually spreads if punishment continues. Very little can be accomplished by threats. However, effective use of praise for good conduct is important. We live in a "rewards" system; everyone wants to feel worthy and important and to be rewarded.

Use all human resources possible to help solve behavior problems. This includes guidance personnel, district office personnel, the principal, supervisors, parents, and, probably most important of all, the students themselves.

A positive attitude and enthusiasm are important ingredients for teachers to have in establishing positive classroom management. Bad days are surely to occur but it is hoped these days are few and far between if the proper preparations are made.

▼ GUIDELINES FOR THE SUPERVISING TEACHER

1. You serve as a model for your intern concerning the formulation of solutions of behavior problems that inevitably occur.

2. Arrange to have your intern observe other teachers who are strong in certain aspects of management and instruct her to look for certain things.
3. Your intern may also be able to discern that those teachers who continually have difficulty with students and the classroom activities are usually people who have some personal hang-ups that the students intuitively know or people who are weak-willed, wishing only to be liked by students.
4. Explain thoroughly the makeup of your students to your intern. The more the intern knows about them the easier the internship will be. Advise your intern to pick up clues from the students and attempt to get to know them as individuals.
5. Turn over your class only when you feel that your intern is ready to handle the situation. It is a must that interns thoroughly understand your organization and discipline plan.
6. Expect some mistakes from your intern. Remember that she is a beginner in this business of teaching. Interrupt only when life and limb are threatened.
7. Invite your intern to sit in on parent conferences. It is most important that they realize the importance of listening closely to what parents have to say.
8. Through visitation the intern will begin to understand that those teachers who like students, who like teaching, and who know how to express it are more readily accepted by their students and have fewer student-related problems.

▼ GUIDELINES FOR THE INTERN

1. Remember that you will not be fully in control until you get your own class. Be patient; your day will come.
2. As an intern in a student teaching assignment, it is appropriate that you maintain the method of classroom control developed by your supervising teacher. Do not try to change any of the established routine. Learn from it, build on it, and when you have your own classroom, you will be better able to manage effectively from the very beginning.
3. Attempt to anticipate as many of the problems ahead of time as you can and plan accordingly. Think through what you would do if specific things were to happen. Discuss this with your supervisor.
4. You cannot operate without rules. This would not be fair to the students or yourself. It is easier to start with rigid and strict rules in the beginning of the year. As you get to know the students, it is easy to add other less rigid rules. The reverse can make life more hectic for you.
5. Be aware of the social patterns with your students and assign seating accordingly. Do not allow any student to seclude himself; seat the loner with someone who is friendly. Be aware that those students who sit near the doorway may talk with students who walk up and down the hall. Those students who sit near windows may daydream easily.
6. Never let yourself be caught off guard in responding to actions among your students. Plan for all contingencies, and if you miss any in your planning, never let the students know.
7. React calmly in all situations, remembering that most of the behaviors in your classroom are normal and merely need some reshaping and control.
8. Be sure that you know what comes next so that there is no lull nor time for trouble. Have every minute planned, but be flexible. Move easily from activity to activity.
9. Use your supervisor! Discuss your lesson plans prior to teaching to avoid any difficulties.

10. Prepare to make a few mistakes. Remember that some of your students are not receptive to academic pursuits no matter how hard you try.
11. While you are student teaching, think through the discipline plan you hope to use when you get your own class.

CASE 17–1
▼

Jessica happily anticipated her student teaching in middle school science. However, her supervising teacher's class seemed to have several potential troublemakers. During her initial visits to the classroom and during observations at the beginning of the term, the supervising teacher noted that Jessica seemed to try to appease the troublemakers in an attempt to make them like her. Mrs. Lewt, the supervising teacher, realized that Jessica would have difficulty with these particular students if she did not use a rather formal approach with them.

1. How should Mrs. Lewt counsel Jessica?
2. What difficulties might arise if the supervising teacher did nothing?
3. What effects on Jessica's student teaching would such friendliness have?
4. How could Jessica successfully remedy the situation, assuming that she wishes to do so?
5. In what ways could the use of a formal approach affect the students? ▼

CASE 17–2
▼

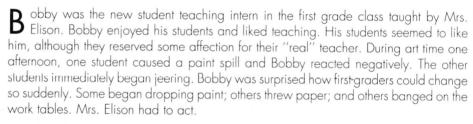

Bobby was the new student teaching intern in the first grade class taught by Mrs. Elison. Bobby enjoyed his students and liked teaching. His students seemed to like him, although they reserved some affection for their "real" teacher. During art time one afternoon, one student caused a paint spill and Bobby reacted negatively. The other students immediately began jeering. Bobby was surprised how first-graders could change so suddenly. Some began dropping paint; others threw paper; and others banged on the work tables. Mrs. Elison had to act.

1. What should be the immediate reaction of Bobby to the students?
2. What should the supervising teacher do at this moment?
3. How could Bobby develop appropriate relations with this class?
4. What could have been said or planned by the supervising teacher to avoid such a situation?
5. What do you think about male interns being assigned to kindergarten or first grade classrooms? ▼

CASE 17–3
▼

Sara was assigned to a third grade class for student teaching. Her supervising teacher, Ms. King, had been teaching many years and was close to retirement. Her control of the classroom was quite lax and this was a big concern to Sara. When she questioned Ms. King about the rules of the classroom, she was told that there were no specific rules but some were put in place as the need developed. Sara was perplexed as to how she could possibly control the class with this type of organization.

1. What do you think of Ms. King's plan for handling discipline?
2. What could Sara do to enhance her success in the classroom?
3. Would it be inappropriate for Sara to ask Ms. King for permission to add specific rules for the classroom? Explain your answer.

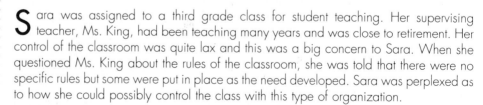

4. How could this situation have been avoided?
5. In what ways could Ms. King make Sara feel more comfortable about this situation? ▼

CASE 17–4
▼

Sheryl has been working 3 weeks as an intern assigned to Mrs. Bennett's fifth grade class. Everything appeared to be going well except for one problem. One of the students, Barbara, evidently had little respect for Sheryl or Mrs. Bennett. She pouted most of the time and frequently refused to do assigned tasks. The matter seemed to be getting worse as the days went by. Barbara is becoming quite sassy and belligerent.

1. What could Mrs. Bennett do to help matters?
2. How could Sheryl's strengths be used?
3. What assistance could be obtained from outside the classroom?
4. One student can sometimes set the tone for a classroom. If Barbara is permitted to continue her pouting tantrums, what could be the effect?
5. Should a student be permitted to disrupt a class in this way? Explain your answer. ▼

CASE 17–5
▼

Anne was getting along very well in her science classes at the high school. Students had accepted her and her first 4 weeks had gone very smoothly. A new student, Amos, was assigned to her second period American History class and troubles began. Amos had the habit of whistling during the major part of the fourth period. Both Anne and her supervising teacher, Mrs. Gamble, constantly told Amos to stop his whistling as this was bothering both of them and the other students. Amos did not realize he was whistling, appearing to do it subconsciously. The other teachers who had Amos in classes reported the same problem.

1. What could cause Amos to whistle subconsciously?
2. How could such a small matter cause so much confusion?
3. What could Anne and the other teachers do to resolve this problem?
4. In what ways could class members help?
5. How could Amos's whistling be put to constructive use? ▼

RECOMMENDED READING

Albert, Linda. (1989). *A teacher's guide to cooperative discipline: How to manage your classroom and promote self-esteem.* Circle Pines, MN: American Guidance Service. (I&S)
The theoretical base of Cooperative Discipline has developed around the ideas of Rudolph Dreikurs and his teacher, Alfred Adler. This positive program shows teachers how to work hand-in-hand with students, parents, and colleagues. The self-esteem gained by the students is one of the major goals of this program. This is good reading for the intern and the supervising teacher.

Cangelosi, James S. (1986). *Cooperation in the classroom: Students and teachers together.* Washington, DC: National Education Association. (I&S)
This book presents numerous suggestions for obtaining effective behavior management. The ideas presented are drawn from a variety of classroom discipline approaches. This is good reading for interns and supervising teachers who are in the process of developing a discipline plan.

Charles, C. M. (1989). *Building classroom discipline: From models to practice.* New York: Longman, Inc. (I&S)

This book presents comprehensive coverage on the following eight models of discipline: Redl and Wattenberg, Kounin, Neo-Skinnerian, Ginott, Dreikurs, Jones, Carter, and Glasser. Implementation for classroom practice helps make this book practical. This is beneficial information for pre- or inservice teachers who are attempting to formulate a discipline plan of their own.

Duke, Daniel Linden, & Meckel, Adrienne Maravich. (1984). *Teacher's guide to classroom management.* New York: Random House, Inc. (I&S)
This book recommends that teachers be given the opportunity to select their own approach to classroom management. A number of strategies for encouraging productive student behavior are presented and are worthwhile reading for interns.

Glasser, William. (1990). *The quality school: Managing students without coercion.* New York: Harper & Row Publishers, Inc. (I&S)
Glasser contends that no more than half of our secondary students are willing to make an effort to learn and therefore cannot be taught. He goes on to recommend a Learner-Team Model, which is described in detail. This is challenging reading for secondary interns and supervising teachers.

Jones, Fredric H. (1987). *Positive classroom discipline.* New York: McGraw-Hill Book Company. (I&S)
This book contains a concentration on teaching strategies that encourage positive behaviors from students. The author's realistic experiences in classroom discipline are reflected. Both interns and supervising teachers could benefit from discussing ideas presented here.

Jones, Vernon F., and Jones, Louise S. (1990). *Comprehensive classroom management: Motivating and managing students.* Boston: Allyn & Bacon. (I&S)
This book presents a wide variety of research-supported methods used in managing classes. Ideas for dealing with disruptive students and the focus on methods that work with at-risk students are included in this third edition. Interns and supervising teachers could benefit by reading and discussing pertinent material presented in this book.

National School Safety Center. (1986). *School discipline notebook.* Sacramento, CA: Pepperdine University Press and the National School Safety Center. (I&S)
This brief 61-page book presents a realistic approach to school discipline. Much of the information is drawn from various junior and senior high school handbooks from many states.

Skinner, B. F., & Rogers, Carl. (1985). Does behavioral control provide the best learning environment? In James William Noll (Ed.), *Taking sides: Clashing views on controversial educational issues* (pp. 83–97). Guilford, CN: Dushkin Publishing Group, Inc. (I&S)
Interns are most interested in the topics of classroom control and could profit from reading the opposing views presented by B. F. Skinner and Carl Rogers. Skinner links learning and motivation to the influence of external forces; Rogers insists on the reality of subjective forces in human motivation.

•18 PLANNING

Successful teaching is a result of effective planning. Planning enables one to predict the future course of events. Although planning involves a knowledge of many elements of the educational picture, for example, scope and sequence and taxonomies of development and learning, many candidates for the student teaching internship identify planning with the immediate activity. It is important for the beginning teacher to realize that effective planning for a particular class is rooted in a realistic plan for the total school year. Without long-range planning, short-range planning is ineffective, inefficient, and frequently a waste of time.

The student teaching intern should be knowledgeable about the philosophy of the school. A copy of such a document is usually available in the administrative office; the supervising teacher can tell the intern where to locate such a document. As schools prepare for visits by visiting accreditation teams, such documentation is updated for the current student population of the school.

Given the philosophy of the school, the student teaching intern can integrate the statewide scope and sequence plan for the particular discipline and grade level. For instance, the state plan may indicate that eighth grade English is to include particular elements of thought processing, grammar, composition, and literature. However, state guidelines are much more explicit. Merging the state plan with needs of the school population gives the student teaching intern a baseline for beginning specific planning.

Writing course goals for the year and dividing such goals into objectives for units for each grading period (6 weeks or 9 weeks) gives the intern a readily available starting point for writing unit plans. All units need not be of the same time frame; however, the total of the time for all the units should total the weeks available in the school year. A functional approach is to develop units that end simultaneously with the grading period. Such planning gives both the student teaching intern and the students a feeling of closure and relief as well as the opportunity for a fresh new start with the beginning of the new grading period and the new unit.

Each unit should be developed by setting the goals for the unit and then writing the objectives to be met by the end of the unit. Daily lesson topics and objectives naturally develop from such unit planning. The sequencing of activities to meet the unit objectives causes the daily lesson plans to fit together. Compare this planning to a fence, with the daily lesson plan being the fence post and the unit theme being the wire of the fence. Without the daily lesson plan (the fence post), the unit theme (the fence wire) loses its support and direction and leads nowhere.

The planning of an effective lesson is an essential skill of teaching very much in the mind of the supervising teacher. Concern always exists about the level of readiness the student teaching intern has developed in the area of planning before reporting to the student teaching assignment.

During the early stages of student teaching there must be extensive cooperative planning between the supervising teacher and intern. As planning skills improve, however, the intern depends less and less on the supervising teacher, who in turn has much more confidence in the intern. Of course, the supervising teacher must continuously evaluate the lesson plans of the intern and provide necessary guidance.

A specific lesson does not develop in a vacuum; it must fit into a sequential and relevant pattern of development. This concept is often difficult for some inexperienced teachers to realize and requires assistance from the supervising teacher. Such items as planning classroom activities, the scope and sequence, the subject matter to be used, the units to be taught, and methods of evaluation are primarily the responsibilities of the supervising teacher, but they are shared to a greater extent with the intern as the term progresses.

Interns should have been trained to write unit and lesson objectives prior to their student teaching internship. Such objectives may take a number of formats, but they should include the knowledge, skills, or attitudes to be learned, the activities that enhance that learning, the degree to which the learning should occur, and how the extent and quality of the learning is evaluated.

Interns should show a great deal of professional growth as lesson plans are evaluated by themselves and by supervising teachers. The college coordinator can be most helpful in the planning of instruction. Some colleges and universities require a student teaching seminar concurrently with the internship, and topics such as unit and lesson planning are high priority topics for such seminars.

Most plans may need some last minute revisions on the basis of the previous class. In order for the effective organization of teaching to be ensured, plans should be ready far in advance. By total year planning, the intern has the entire picture in mind. If the need arises, the lesson plan for the day can move forward or can include alternate activities that were planned for the future.

The future plans can easily be revised. A good guide to use with a lesson plan is to consider if, with adaptation, it could be used with another group of students.

Although the student teaching intern is not in the school for the total year, the involvement in such extensive planning enhances planning skills for future years and gives a surprising amount of self-confidence in the actual classroom teaching performance. Few things contribute to a person's self-confidence as much as knowing the total picture.

▼ GUIDELINES FOR THE SUPERVISING TEACHER

1. Make it clear to your intern at the beginning that you have high expectations in the area of planning. Under no circumstances should the intern be permitted to teach without having the unit plans and daily lesson plans approved by you.

2. At the beginning of student teaching, you should assist your intern in making and using unit and daily lesson plans. You may help best by asking questions and assisting the student teaching intern to focus more clearly on precisely what is to be done.

3. Assist in making materials accessible to the intern. Interns cannot be completely responsible for the materials they use and need guidance from you and other school personnel. Inform the intern about additional materials and resources that may be used with specific units and daily lessons.

4. Timing may be one problem area for your interns; they may spend too much time with a specific lesson or group. Most need guidance in this area. Suggest that they overplan rather than fail to plan enough. Interns can always delete material, but it is difficult to add material and activities on the spur on the moment. Few experiences are more horrifying to a student teaching intern than to be in front of a class and use up all the material with 20 minutes still remaining in the class period. Help your intern plan alternatives for such an occasion.

5. Give your intern guidance in judging how much can be taught within a specified time and how much time should be spent on a particular skill or area.

6. A conversation concerning the learning levels of your students is valuable for your intern in preparation for planning. It may be difficult for some interns to realize that, for various reasons, all students are not eager to learn. Help them to remember their own school career and feelings about some of their classes in retrospect.

7. Interns must learn to be flexible when it comes to planning because there are many interruptions. Provide a schedule listing coming activities not included on lesson plans, plus classes that rotate on various days. Help the intern to see the total picture; the learning strand does continue even though some students are excused for one reason or another. Sometimes interns feel that their classrooms are just revolving doors for their students. Help them remain centered in what they are doing.

8. It is helpful if both you and the intern jot down notes during the day on concerns and questions to be discussed during the next conference. Many important points are forgotten if there is not an organized method of recording these concerns as they arise (see Appendix B for suggested format).

▼ GUIDELINES FOR THE INTERN

1. Determine prior to student teaching which grade levels and general topics you are expected to teach. Preparation of the necessary ground work prior to the development of a teaching unit or special project is helpful. Of course, your supervising teacher expects to approve all of your plans prior to your teaching.

2. What works for the supervising teacher does not necessarily work for you. In fact, your plans should be more detailed. Your teaching style may differ from that of the supervising teacher, also. This is to be expected; however, learn as many effective teaching techniques and strategies as you possibly can from your supervising teacher. Keep a notebook on this topic. As important as this material seems at the moment, you may forget by next year when you are in your own classroom and need to remember these techniques and strategies.

3. As you become more experienced, the detail required in lesson plans may decrease. However, the thoroughness of planning should not decrease.

4. Obtain and organize your materials before executing your lesson. Students become very restless if this has not been done. Your lack of strong organization plays into their mischievous nature.

5. You need to make sure that you are "on task" and teaching the material required. This is particularly important because of local and state minimum skills, which many students are required to show mastery on tests.

6. You need to budget your activities and materials to meet your time allocation. It is probable that you will have difficulty with the timing of your lessons. Most of the time you will probably have more plans than you can complete, but there will also be times when you run out of materials. As you gain experience, you achieve skill in budgeting your time considering the activities to be completed.

7. Your teaching environment must be given consideration. For example, if you are going to need a listening center, it must be established prior to the lesson. If you are planning to do research in the library, you should check with the librarian or media specialist and schedule this while you are still in the planning stages. Large art, science, and technology projects need to be located in an area where they will be protected.

CASE 18–1
▼

Jan, a fifth grade intern, wanted to teach a unit on poetry because this was her favorite subject. Her supervising teacher encouraged her and suggested that she teach this unit but only for 15 minutes per day. She explained that the unit would have to be limited because of work on the state minimum skills that needed to be covered at this time. The supervisor was out of the room during the 40-minute language arts period; Jan spent all of this time on her poetry unit. Later, when the test was administered for the minimum skills, the supervisor discovered that certain skills had not been taught.

1. Should Jan have been aware of the importance of minimum skills at this stage in her career?
2. How should the supervising teacher handle Jan's failure to follow instructions?
3. Would a conversation concerning the importance of minimum skills be helpful?
4. How serious is this mistake of Jan's?
5. Should the coordinator be informed of this situation? What could he do to help Jan? ▼

CASE 18–2 ▼

Mike was enjoying his internship in a seventh grade social studies class and was teaching full time. His major problem was that he could never remember to watch the clock. Every day his class was late going to lunch, and he could never get them to physical education class on time. Mike was warned by the supervising teacher that this was creating serious problems with the other teachers and the principal.

1. What could cause an intern to be negligent in this way?
2. Why would this negligence be considered a serious problem?
3. What could be done to make sure Mike got the class to the right areas on time?
4. Is there any way that the students could help?
5. What suggestions would you give Mike to avoid having problems of this nature as he begins his career as a permanent teacher? What personality characteristics could he develop that would help this kind of situation? ▼

CASE 18–3 ▼

Mary had greater expectations for her sixth grade students than her supervising teacher had. She always included more activities than were necessary in her lesson plan and rushed to complete them. The supervising teacher noted that certain students were becoming quite tense about Mary's lessons. When she discussed the matter with the intern, Mary explained that she was afraid she would run out of materials within a specified time block. She also indicated that she wanted to be certain that the students were challenged.

1. What level of tension needs to be present for a lesson to be challenging?
2. How could the supervising teacher make Mary feel more at ease?
3. In what way could the supervising teacher help Mary to see that her behavior is being reflected in the student stress?
4. How could this conflict be resolved to the benefit of both Mary and her students?
5. How could the personality characteristics such as the ones causing Mary's difficulty be dealt with in teacher education methods classes prior to the student teaching internship? ▼

CASE 18–4 ▼

Jean is a creative intern assigned to a high school English class. Her supervising teacher was quite impressed with her ideas and encouraged her to incorporate them into her teaching. She was scheduled to take over her first English class on Monday of the third week and planned to initiate some creative dramatics. Jean's supervisor wanted to see her first lesson plan a week before delivery and expected a very creative plan. Four days before the lesson, Jean still had not handed in a lesson plan. It appeared that she did not begin planning sufficiently early and, according to another intern, had the reputation of not carrying her tasks to completion.

1. What should the supervising teacher do at this point?
2. Would it be unfair not to allow Jean to teach without a prior lesson plan? Explain.
3. Under what conditions would it be appropriate for the supervising teacher to discuss his intern with another intern in the building?
4. What kinds of time lines should the supervising teacher set for Jean?
5. At what point should the coordinator be called in? ▼

CASE 18–5
▼

John was completing his third week as an intern in an eighth grade science class. He had taken over the science class and thought he was doing a good job. According to his supervising teacher, however, John had one major problem. His lesson plans were much too general. Because he was just teaching one class at this time, his supervising teacher expected much more detailed plans. John's attitude was that he did not feel it was necessary to write detailed plans because he had noticed that his supervisor's plans were quite brief.

1. Which part is wrong in this situation? Explain.
2. Was it unfair to expect John to produce detailed plans? Explain.
3. How could this problem be resolved?
4. Why would it be permissible for a supervising teacher to have only brief plans?
5. How can the coordinator and the supervising teacher assist John in understanding the difference between his stage in professional development and that of his supervising teacher? ▼

CASE 18–6
▼

Rudolph had completed his seventh week in a 10th grade social studies assignment. His major weakness appeared to be in the area of planning. He had five consumer economics classes but prepared only one lesson plan to take care of all five classes. His supervising teacher insisted on one lesson plan with modifications for each class, but Rudolph continued along the same pattern. In disgust, the supervising teacher called the college coordinator.

1. Why did the supervising teacher insist on modifications for each class?
2. Why do you think that Rudolph thought he was doing a satisfactory job of planning?
3. What should be the coordinator's plan of action to help resolve this situation?
4. What are some of the major difficulties in teaching several sections of the same course simultaneously?
5. What options for teaching classes with other teachers in the building would be available? Would this be professionally advisable for Rudolph? ▼

CASE 18–7
▼

Ashley has completed her fourth week of student teaching. She has the feeling that her teaching is going well and has been told so by her supervising teacher. Ashley is concerned, however, because she has not had any feedback concerning the lesson plans. She was told by her supervising teacher during the first week that he would leave the planning up to her. He said that he did not want to see her plans but would tell her if the lessons were not going well.

Ashley had prepared detailed plans for every day that she had taught and kept them in a notebook. She was happy that she had done this, especially when her college coordinator asked to see her plans before his first observation. When she told him about the attitude of her supervising teacher toward her plans, he was very disturbed.

1. Why would the college coordinator react this way?
2. Was Ashley wise in preparing thorough plans even though they were not requested? Explain.
3. Was she justified in wanting feedback on her lesson plans? Why or why not?
4. In what way should the format of an intern's lesson plans change as the number of lessons to be taught increases?
5. The coordinator realizes that Ashley may have a stronger professional commitment than her supervising teacher. To what extent should she confide this in Ashley? What professional guidelines should the coordinator use in this situation? ▼

RECOMMENDED READING

DeLandsheere, V. (1988). Taxonomies of educational objectives. In John P. Keeves (Ed.), *Educational research methodology and measurement: An international handbook* (pp. 345–354). New York: Pergamon Press. (I&S)
This article presents the taxonomies of Bloom, Gagne-Merrill, Gerlach and Sullivan, Krathwohl, and others. Also included is Guilford's model of the structure of the intellect.

Doll, Ronald C. (1992). The planning process. In *Curriculum improvement: Decision making and process.* Boston: Allyn & Bacon. (I&S)
Doll presents a thorough review of appropriate strategies for curriculum planning. He offers problems, trends, and suggested steps in curriculum planning, extending this to planning for restructuring. This material is useful background information to share with the student teaching intern.

Keeves, J. P. (1988). Sex differences in ability and achievement. In John P. Keeves (Ed.), *Educational research methodology and measurement: An international handbook* (pp. 482–487). New York: Pergamon Press. (I&S)
Keeves gives a historical overview of the research in sex differences in ability and achievement including a reference indicating that differences between sexes are not large when compared with differences within sexes. Current developments in this area of research are included.

Marzano, Robert J., Brandt, Ronald S., Hughes, Carolyn Sue, Jones, Beau Fly, Presseisen, Barbara Z., Rankin, Stuart C., & Suhor, Charles. (1988). *Dimensions of thinking: A framework for curriculum and instruction.* Alexandria, VA: Association for Supervision and Curriculum Development. (I&S)
This book discusses in depth the kinds of thinking skills to be developed and used in the teaching/learning process. The relationship of various levels of thinking skills to content area knowledge is discussed giving examples and models. A glossary and summary outline in the appendixes is most helpful in the instructional planning process.

Mosston, Muska, & Ashworth, Sara. (1990). *The spectrum of teaching styles: From command to discovery.* White Plains, NY: Longman, Inc. (I&S)
This text can assist the student teaching intern to understand how the teaching process fits into a pattern of a chain of decision making. The spectrum model is very detailed; however, an awareness of this model helps the student teaching intern in understanding how the fragmented parts of the process of teaching fit together.

19 IMPLEMENTATION OF THE CLASSROOM PROCESS

Implementation! This is where it is for teachers! As student teaching interns approach the first attempts at putting it all together, they experience a number of emotions that characterize the implementation of the actual classroom teaching process.

First, the intern probably experiences a deep interest in the class of the supervising teacher. The intern appropriately wonders at the magnitude of the class and the aggregate of individual lives and the vast amount of subject material to be covered. By doing so, the intern becomes aware of the need for objectivity and organization.

Second, the intern is motivated by the needs of the students in the supervising teacher's class and is stimulated to develop plans and write projects that fit those needs. The intern is aware that ideas of previous classes at the college or university now take on new meaning in the framework of the real needs of the assigned classroom.

Third, intensive planning takes place as the intern adds the finishing touches to plans and adjustments are made to provide for the varying needs of the individual students. This intensity of purpose can be labeled as devotion, which is one of the facets of teaching referred to by some as the "art" of teaching.

Fourth, after the interest, the motivation, and the intensive planning, the intern begins teaching. The emotion often accompanying this portion of training is panic. Some interns conceal it rather well but some are obviously nervous and ill at ease. Recognizing the probability of this anxiety is half the battle in overcoming it. Even the best prepared, the most self-confident student teaching intern has many questions prior to taking over the entire class for that first exciting lesson. Most interns mentally catalog a list of alternative possibilities for use in case of a perceived failure of the lesson. During those few minutes just before the first class, some interns become very tense; this is normal. Planning for this specific occurrence helps in alleviating it.

To avoid the development of such anxiety, the intern should make plans to keep busy with the students until the time to begin the lesson. This helps the transition from the previous activity, and the motivation for the students at the beginning of class is more easily established. By helping the students with other activities, the intern forgets self and is concerned more with the students' needs. Once the intern gets into the lesson, awareness develops that teaching that lesson to that class can be totally engrossing.

Fifth, during the initial full-class lesson, the intern finds that the lesson really does fit together after all and that the students really are just regular people. During those few seconds while waiting for students to think and respond, the intern silently thanks the supervising teacher for insisting on thorough planning as well as specific suggestions for implementation of this lesson. As the

lesson continues, the intern begins to breathe normally again and senses a satisfaction at the opportunities encountered during the lesson.

Sixth, as the intern begins to assemble classroom plans and activities and as successes, even small ones, are won with particularly difficult individuals, the students are delighted with the challenge offered them by the intern. This may or may not be overtly shared with the intern and the supervising teacher but both should be aware that it is happening.

After the first class on the first day, the anxiety dissipates and the pleasures of teaching begin. The importance of effective planning is now preeminent; from this moment until the end of the student teaching internship, classroom instruction is the major activity of the intern.

Flexibility in adapting the previously planned activities and materials is crucial. Accepting changes at the last minute is frequently necessary. Sometimes these changes come in the form of suggestions from students on better ways of getting to the same objective. Individuals with tendencies toward being perfectionists sometimes enter the teaching profession; their characteristics have a tendency to make students needlessly uncomfortable. The classroom is not a place to impose perfection, and the student teaching intern should be satisfied with a realistic level of performance by the students in his classroom.

The supervising teacher is there for support of the intern and the intern should feel that support during the classroom lesson. By planning ahead, both can develop a system of signals that the student teacher would like some assistance from the supervising teacher. Intervention under these circumstances is not only acceptable, it is much appreciated. In addition, it causes the flow of classroom activity to proceed uninterrupted, which is a major benefit to the students both academically and emotionally. Such an arrangement also increases the probability of positive classroom control.

Arrangements for various types of intervention by the supervising teacher should be made prior to the very first lesson. There are times that he should intervene for the protection of the students, for clarity in case of incorrect information, and for the self-confidence of the student teaching intern. Such intervention should be established as a part of the teaching arrangement so that the students in the classroom do not identify it as a negative factor toward the intern.

▼ GUIDELINES FOR THE SUPERVISING TEACHER

1. Your intern is probably anxious about that first full-class lesson. You cannot disperse that anxiety, but you may help alleviate it somewhat. Be kind.

2. Share with the intern particular problems with difficult students. You may want to remove certain students from this first class by involving these students in an activity with you during this first lesson.

3. Insist on thorough planning. It pays huge dividends for you to be a difficult taskmaster.

4. Mentally prepare your intern for lesson implementation by verbally walking through it together. The intern may consider this a waste of time, but insist on it.

5. Offer any materials, props, resources, and suggestions that you feel enhance the intern's lesson implementation. Later the intern may seek these as their importance in the lesson delivery is realized.

6. Finally, when you have done all you can, avoid the impression of watching the intern teaching until you feel a comfortable security in the position as teacher has been achieved. Plan an appropriate seating area in the back of the classroom and blend into the background. You must release the intern with your class to allow growth.

▼ GUIDELINES FOR THE INTERN

1. This is it! You have worked for nearly 4 years to get to this point. You have stored much knowledge, made lesson plans, practiced vocal delivery, and made all the preparations necessary for teaching. You are ready to implement the plans put together by you and the supervising teacher.

2. Self-confidence is a major key to success for the beginning teacher. Many interns may laugh at the idea of self-confidence due to a lack of it. However, you can profit from convincing your students that you have self-confidence, and once you have convinced them that you possess it, you will find you have nearly convinced yourself. If you have good plans and feel well-prepared, self-confidence comes more readily.

3. Be as prepared as possible. Be sure your plans are workable and realistic in terms of time.

4. Retain poise, calmness, and dignity.

5. Be realistic about the situation. You are placed here to learn how to teach. You may make a few mistakes. Even the most seasoned pro does that, so do not allow the possibility of mistakes to bother you. Instead, use your time efficiently by developing methods of handling your errors. Think positively.

6. Be yourself. Students can see right through a person. Be genuine all of the time with them.

CASE 19–1

▼

Mrs. Atkins felt that her intern was not sufficiently concerned about planning, especially her first series of lessons. She hesitated to use fear as a motivator but her suggestions were unheeded. Finally, Mrs. Atkins phoned the college coordinator and discussed the situation. The next day the coordinator visited the classroom and discussed the problem with the intern who agreed to plan effectively. No sooner had the coordinator left than the intern reproached Mrs. Atkins for calling the coordinator.

1. What should the supervising teacher have done initially?
2. What options were open to Mrs. Atkins now?
3. How should she continue to seek the advice of the college coordinator?
4. How should she proceed on her own?
5. What would happen if the supervising teacher allowed the student teaching intern to fall on her face before the class due to poor planning? To what extent would this be allowable? ▼

CASE 19-2
▼

Joe was the intern in Mrs. Graves's high school English classes. As Joe began his first full-class teaching, he resisted using notes. Although in format he had a well-developed lesson plan, it was apparently not practical. Joe insisted that he really did not need notes for reference as he taught the class. He convinced Mrs. Graves that he had prepared sufficiently and that he would remember everything.

Well, Joe did not remember everything. When he stood before the first class of the day, after the bell rang and he closed the door, he turned to the class and his mind went blank!

1. Mrs. Graves was aware of the situation. Should she do anything? If so, what?
2. Do you think Joe learned his lesson about using notes?
3. How would the class react to him next time?
4. What long-range measures should Mrs. Graves take?
5. What implications does this situation hold for all beginning student teaching interns? ▼

CASE 19-3
▼

Sixth grade time was valuable and Mr. Wilson hoped his intern would be well organized and use student time wisely. Mr. Wilson had talked with other teachers with whom his intern had served field experiences. The intern had a propensity for adlibing and wasting time. Mr. Wilson tried to tactfully express his concern about this to the intern but it apparently was not effective. The intern wrote well-developed plans and professed a high degree of organization. Yet, when he began teaching the full-class lessons, the intern was easily distracted from the subject and much student time was wasted.

1. What caused the gap between the planning by the intern and his delivery of the lesson material?
2. How could a videotape record of a class assist in this situation?
3. Should the supervising teacher interrupt the lesson at the point of diminishing returns?
4. Because tact had not worked earlier, what should Mr. Wilson try next?
5. Because observation by the college coordinator during the very early stages of taking over the class could easily make the intern more nervous, what benefit would there be from such an observation? ▼

CASE 19-4
▼

Coach Elroy felt that lesson plans were a waste of time and shared this philosophy with his intern, Jeff. However, the department chairperson communicated to Jeff that he expected to see his lesson plans 1 week prior to his first full-class teaching.

1. Without Coach's cooperation, how could Jeff write effective lesson plans?
2. What responsibility did Jeff have to the department chairperson?
3. Should Jeff discuss the coach's feeling about lesson plans with someone? With whom?

4. What other people in the school could Jeff use for assistance in unit and lesson planning?
5. In a case such as this, Jeff has the opportunity to learn more than most student teaching interns because of his involvement with other teachers in addition to his supervisor. What are some of the things he will be learning about personalities of teachers? ▼

CASE 19–5
▼

Lily loved biology and thought she would enjoy student teaching until it was time for her to plan her first full-class presentation. She seemed overwhelmed and initially planned too little material. After conferences with the supervising teacher, her re-planning was grossly overdone. Still filled with anxiety, Lily asked the supervising teacher to leave the classroom for the first presentation. She assured the teacher that she would feel more confident and would be able to teach better. The supervising teacher had some doubts about leaving her class with a beginner for the entire period.

1. As the student teaching intern, why would you make such a request?
2. As the supervising teacher, how would you react to such a request?
3. What legal constraints operated for the supervising teacher?
4. Would the student teaching intern actually make a better presentation to the class without the supervising teacher present? Why or why not?
5. What additional approaches could the supervising teacher take in this situation other than leaving the classroom during the initial lesson? ▼

CASE 19–6
▼

Wilbur had already announced to the math classes in which he was assigned to student teach that he was a retired military officer and that teaching was for him just something to do for a few years before he completely retired. He has already explained to several of the students that they could call him Captain. Students had expressed to the supervising teacher that Wilbur really did seem impressed with himself but that they were unimpressed.

The supervising teacher was concerned that the students would become antagonized by Wilbur and make his student teaching assignment difficult for him and disrupt the positive classroom climate. The actual presentation of the lessons could be the most likely time for bad feelings to develop into inappropriate actions. During announcements and short presentations, Wilbur was overly authoritarian and the students had openly resented his attitude.

1. What action should the supervising teacher take in helping Wilbur assess the situation?
2. How should the students be prepared to deal with the situation?
3. In what ways could the coordinator assist this supervising teacher?
4. What options does the student teaching intern have at this point? What is the best way to help him understand these options?
5. What kind of screening could have occurred in the teacher preparation program at the college or university to assist Wilbur in coping with this kind of antagonistic behavior? ▼

RECOMMENDED READING

Anderson, Linda M. (1989). Classroom instruction. In Maynard C. Reynolds (Ed.), *Knowledge base for the beginning teacher* (pp. 101–115). New York: Pergamon Press. (I&S)
This chapter reviews the knowledge base on classroom instruction to assist in increasing student learning through a cognitive-mediational perspective. The kind of instruction that increases higher order learning is discussed and advocated.

Gall, M. D., Joyce P. Gall, Jacobsen, Dennis R., & Bullock, Terry L. (1990). Listening, participating, and taking notes in class. In *Tools for learning: A guide to teaching study skills* (pp. 86–109). Alexandria, VA: Association for Supervision and Curriculum Development. (I&S)
This chapter deals with showing teachers how to help students improve their in-class learning by improving their listening, participating, and taking notes in class. Twenty specific skills are explained that can be implemented by students immediately.

Grossnickle, Donald R., & Thiel, William B. (1988). *Promoting effective student motivation in school and classroom: A practitioner's perspective.* Reston, VA: National Association of Secondary School Principals. (I&S)
This monograph was written to help teachers and administrators recognize and overcome the obstacles to student motivation. Models, examples, and cases are used to demonstrate methods of increasing student motivation.

Johnson, Eric. (1987). *Teaching school* (rev. ed.). Boston: National Association of Independent Schools. (I&S)
A veteran of 30 years of teaching experience has compiled realistic suggestions for practical applications in the classroom. Johnson has assembled a how-to for the entire instructional process. This is concise and to the point; it is strongly recommended for the student teaching intern and the supervising teacher.

Jones, Beau Fly, Palinscar, Annemarie Sullivan, Ogle, Donna Sederburg, & Carr, Eileen Glynn. (Eds.). (1987). *Strategic teaching and learning: Cognitive instruction in the content areas.* Alexandria, VA: Association for Supervision and Curriculum Development. (I&S)
This book contains a wealth of information from several authors related to developing the framework for strategic teaching and for applying those strategies in the content areas. Areas included are science, social studies, mathematics, and literature.

Ortman, Patricia E. (1988). Keeping it up: Instructional methodology. In *Not for teachers only: Creating a context of joy for learning and growth* (pp. 27–37). Washington, D. C.: Author. (I)
Ortman gives the student teaching intern a good review of several important teaching concepts: individual differences, discovery learning, modeling, mastery learning, transfer of learning, and reinforcement. Her suggestions are appropriate for helping the student maintain confidence through effective teaching.

United States Department of Education. (1986). Research about teaching and learning: Classroom. In *What works: Research about teaching and learning* (pp. 18–43). Washington, D. C.: Author. (I&S)
Research findings are given on a number of classroom topics including managing time, tutoring, study skills, student ability and effort, and on specific disciplines such as science, mathematics, reading, and writing. Comments and references to document the research findings are of much assistance to both the supervising teacher and the student teaching intern.

20 INSTRUCTIONAL EVALUATION

The evaluation process used by an intern during student teaching should be an outgrowth of the unit and lesson plans that are developed in initial planning. In methods classes at the college, the intern has probably been exposed to a number of types of lesson and unit plan schemes, and the supervising teacher may be able to offer some additional types of organization for planning and evaluation that are more appropriate for particular situations. Classroom teachers generally have taken the theory offered in methods classes and adapted it to the reality of the classroom. Therefore, the planning methods offered by the supervising teacher may in the long run be more valuable to the intern.

As objectives are developed by the intern in planning with the supervising teacher, and as activities are chosen to meet those objectives, the intern must decide how to determine if those objectives have been met. Once the decision has been made, the evaluation process itself progresses with little difficulty. The secret is in the appropriate planning; it is critical for the intern to realize that teaching can be compared to a three-legged milking stool with evaluation as one of those three legs, combining with planning and implementation to maintain balance on the stool. Interns sometimes have a tendency to postpone developing their evaluative procedures until the last minute and then rush into an inappropriate activity for the evaluation.

Another natural weakness that supervising teachers should be aware that interns sometimes develop is that of planning rather monotonous evaluations. Because the evaluation with which the intern is most familiar is the paper and pencil test, that type of evaluation may be used more frequently during student teaching if adequate guidance is not given during the planning stages.

Good planning for evaluation is difficult and takes much time on the part of the intern who may be inexperienced in the use of a variety of forms of evaluation. The supervising teacher needs to offer advice on a wide range of evaluation problems, and the intern could profit from observation visits with other teachers in the area of evaluation.

Among problems that the intern must anticipate are those of evaluating for individual personal and cultural differences. Maintaining a classroom standard, evaluating special needs students who have been mainstreamed, dealing with students who have other teachers who use different evaluation techniques, and being able to work with parents in explaining the grades that students eventually take home are critical skills for the intern to develop.

129

Adequate record keeping is a must. There is no substitute for documentation. The intern must be able to explain at any time just what the classroom achievement status is for any one of the students, both to the supervising teacher or the principal and to parents and students. It is imperative to keep records up to date.

Among the variety of records the student teaching intern must keep up to date are attendance records, classroom discipline records, progress records, and records of the current academic standing of students (see Appendix K). In addition to the written records in the grade book, it is wise for the intern to keep a modicum of information about each student in his head. Parents may run into the intern in the grocery story and ask how their child is. If the intern says the child is doing fine and the report card comes home the next week and it is not fine, the parent will have questions about the qualifications of the intern. If the response the intern makes to the same question is: "Oh, I don't remember. He's a nice kid, though," the parent will begin to question whether their child should be taught by this person.

Patterns of record keeping vary from teacher to teacher. It is useful to develop a code so that several entries could be made in a small space. The typical grade books furnished to teachers by most schools are designed for records of 6 or 9 weeks per section. The student names are listed on the left-hand side of the book and the rest of the space is divided into cells, one per school day for the grading period. Codes that may be usable for the student teaching intern include such devices as using "A" for absent; if the student comes in tardy, overwrite a "T" on the "A." If the student brings in an excuse for his previous absence, mark a diagonal through the "A." Thus in a very small space, the intern has a record of attendance.

In that same small cell in the grade book, a record of homework can be made: a zero meaning no homework was turned in, a check meaning homework was turned in, and if the homework is turned in late, put a check through the zero that is already there (see Appendix L).

Special columns in the grade book should be devoted to tests, projects, and special accomplishments. As the student teaching intern gets to know other teachers in the assigned school, it is helpful to ask those teachers to share their record-keeping systems. People who have been in teaching for some time develop coding systems that can say a lot in a small space. The supervising teacher already has a record-keeping system in place, and the student teaching intern should adopt that system. Other records for which the intern shares responsibility with the supervising teacher and the Guidance Office are records related to standardized testing and, for the high school students, tests for various college interests, for example, National Merit tests, ACT, and SAT.

Methods of instructional evaluation vary greatly depending on the grade level and the subject with which the intern is working. In elementary school, one intern probably uses several methods of evaluation with the same class due to the varied subject materials and content the group will have covered.

In addition to being well planned and well recorded, evaluation must be fair, both to the individual as well as to the group. As important as fairness is in evaluation, the intern should give the student the benefit of any doubt and temper all the grades with professional mercy. The grade book is no place to feed a grudge.

When *reporting to parents* is mentioned to most teachers and interns, one often pictures either a report card or a note written to the parent in regard to some inappropriate action, behavioral or academic, on the part of the student. Communication with parents can prove to be a beneficial factor in classroom management as well as for the academic progress of individuals within the group. Interns should plan a positive communication program with the parents, and with the aid of the supervising teacher, take the necessary steps to ensure the establishment and maintenance of such a program (see Appendix M).

State laws and school district regulations mandate the report card. Student anxiety produced by the report card must be dealt with by the intern. One method is to prepare the students throughout the term to do their best and accept themselves through positive self-concepts.

Notes from the intern to the parents (approved by the supervising teacher) are another standard method of communication. These notes should convey messages of a positive nature about the student, for example, good behavior, some good work done. The intern should use praise cautiously but should give the student commendations when appropriate (see Appendix N). In the elementary school, a good rule of thumb is to send at least one personal communication home to a student's parents during each reporting period. Spaced halfway between report cards, a note can lend reassurance to both parents and students. It need be nothing more than the following:

Dear Mr. and Mrs. Jones:

Johnny seems to be enjoying school this year. I talked with him earlier about the conditions of some of his homework papers and since that time he seems to have made a real effort to improve. I appreciate his cooperation and I feel we're going to have a good term.

I will be happy to set up a conference after school at your request.

(signed)
_____
Student Teaching Intern in Mr. Smith's Class

Interns should be aware that any remark written on a student's papers is also a message to parents. Some students use a poorly worded comment written on a homework or test paper written by the intern to the disadvantage of the intern if any animosity exists. Notes on such papers should be well thought through and sincerely and carefully stated and proofread.

Parent conferences are a method of reporting to parents. These are usually scheduled before or after school. Some schools provide PTA meeting times or offer teacher-parent contact. Care must be given to make special arrangements with those parents who cannot get to the school during regular hours. Most principals agree to meet with the intern, the supervising teacher, and the parents at the school after the parents' working hours. Other possible sites for such conferences are the public library or the main office of the school district. Discretion is urged on the selection of any other site as it is generally recognizable that some sites are inappropriate.

Conferences with parents can be rewarding and enlightening to student teaching interns. Usually such conferences are held at the request of either the parents or the intern based on an academic or behavior problem. Some schools routinely schedule parent conferences and the intern, on the advice of the supervising teacher, may choose such a schedule.

Whatever type of reporting to parents is chosen by the intern, it should be kept positive and objective and must be approved by the supervising teacher. Care must be used so that reports are realistic. If reports are glowing, parents will be surprised if the grades are poor.

▼ GUIDELINES FOR THE SUPERVISING TEACHER

1. In early observations, both with you and with other teachers, suggest that the intern observe specific methods of evaluation and make notes in a professional notebook.
2. Help the intern to realize and practice the concept that different methods of evaluation are sometimes good for different students covering the same material.
3. Help the intern to understand that those students who do not test well with paper and pencil tests may be better evaluated with an individual oral test. A major difficulty with this is the security of the evaluative situation and the time for such individual tests. The results, however, are worth the added time and load.
4. As the supervising teacher, do not allow the intern to proceed with teaching until you have seen and approved the methods of evaluation to be used.
5. It helps the intern to have access to your grade book to be aware of current performance of students in the classroom. The intern should maintain a separate grade book and should keep it well documented, up to date, and secure.
6. Stress the necessity for immediate feedback to students with the evaluative measures chosen. Consider, for example, the intern in high school English who assigned a six-page essay to all five of his classes. In his planning he had not considered how much time he would need to grade those essays in addition to the time necessary to continue ongoing planning and preparation. This particular intern became so weighted down with the work of grading the essays that he became physically ill and was forced to stay out of school for a week to recover.
7. Discuss with the intern the importance of good communication between the school and the home. Openness in this area contributes to a healthier mental state for the student. Frequently, school-home communications suffer because of a lack of time on the part of the teacher and a lack of accessibility on the part of the parent. If you can aid the intern in identifying these problems, then less difficulty develops for the intern.
8. A variety of methods of reporting to parents can be suggested by the supervising teacher. In addition to the 6 or 9 week report card, the intern could develop a type of periodic written memo (see the format for a Happy-Gram in Appendix O), a schedule of telephone calls to parents, a planned sequence of group or individual conferences at the school, and possibly even visits by the intern to the homes of the students.

▼ GUIDELINES FOR THE INTERN

1. Plan your evaluation immediately on setting your objective. Never wait until it is evaluation time to plan for it.
2. Your supervising teacher may be able to help you by giving you samples of evaluation procedures used in the past. Do not hesitate to use such materials as examples of what you can develop to fit your own material.
3. As you plan, your thinking naturally flows in terms of evaluation. It is important to make note of these ideas when they occur to you. Experience shows that those ideas that seemed to be important can be replaced very soon by other ideas of apparently equal importance, and the former are forgotten.

4. Be flexible. As you move through the work, a more appropriate assessment mechanism may be found. Do not hesitate to change for the sake of improvement.

5. Be careful about the directions you give to students concerning their evaluations. Students should be told as they begin new material just how they will be evaluated. As you develop evaluative material, think step-by-step through the classroom procedure in which you will be using that material. Anticipate the actions and questions that students might have. Prepare for these in the directions by giving students a sense of security about the evaluation and by developing improved classroom control due to good planning.

6. As you develop paper and pencil tests, remember to consider the ease with which you may be able to grade the papers. You may want to include all your essay questions in one section of the test. With the objective questions, you may want to leave the blanks down either the left-hand or the right-hand margins for the student to fill in the answers (see example in Appendix P). For essay answers, you may request that the students use lined paper and write on alternate lines.

7. Ask the supervising teacher for permission to sit as an observer during her parent conferences. Many useful interpersonal skills can be gathered through such observations. Learn how the supervising teacher has materials and records available, is professionally ready for meeting the parents, allows them sufficient time to question and discuss their child, remains pleasant throughout the meeting, and ends the meeting at the appropriate time on a positive note.

8. You may feel more comfortable in your first few parent conferences if you role play through a typical situation with a friend. Parent conferences are rough on the beginner at first. When you stop to think that a parent conference is sharing time for someone the parent and the teacher (intern) care about, the task becomes less difficult.

9. Remember that success in teaching your class depends on what you know about your students individually. Be careful about accepting second-hand advice and information except from your supervising teacher, who is your greatest source of information. Parents are a unique source of information about your students, both in what they say and in what they avoid saying.

10. As you deal with parents, remember to be a professional educator and keep the best interests of the student uppermost in your mind. Always be courteous and understanding with parents; try to give them the benefit of any doubt, remembering that those students with the least amount of school contact on the part of their parents usually are in the greatest need of such contact.

CASE 20–1

▼

Three preparations per day in English were all in a day's work for Suzie who was interning in Ms. Wright's classroom. In her excitement of getting students motivated and preparing materials, Suzie frequently failed to specify her planned evaluation procedures to Ms. Wright. Knowing the critical nature of the early development of such procedures, Ms. Wright felt that she must take steps to help improve Suzie's planning for evaluation.

1. Should Ms. Wright offer specific methods of evaluation?
2. Should she merely indicate the obvious need of such methods to Suzie and expect her to follow through with her own materials?

3. How could Ms. Wright involve Suzie in obtaining evaluative methods from other teachers in the school?

4. How should the coordinator be involved?

5. How can student teaching interns avoid having this happen to them? ▼

CASE 20–2
▼

Les, the intern in Coach Martinez's physical educational classes, had stated early in his student teaching that all physical education students should receive a grade of "C" no matter what they did. The coach realized someone must change Les's attitude before report cards went out and parents began calling him about their children's grades. When Coach Martinez explained the problem to Les, he was told: "You grade them; I'll teach them."

1. How should he respond to Les?

2. How will the evaluation practices that Les uses in this assignment affect his evaluation methods for the rest of his career?

3. Besides having an incomplete awareness of his responsibility in the area of evaluation, Les seems to have a problem in terms of his respect for Coach Martinez. How should Coach handle this?

4. What issue here is more important than the responses that Coach has to give to the parents of his students?

5. What responsibility does the coordinator have in this situation? ▼

CASE 20–3
▼

Mr. Spencer noted that his student teaching intern gave frequent paper and pencil tests and seemed to be planning his entire evaluation strategy on such devices. Because there were a number of students in the class who could benefit from alternative kinds of evaluation, Mr. Spencer offered several evaluation alternatives, but the intern insisted on continuing to use only paper and pencil tests.

1. How should Mr. Spencer deal with his intern?

2. Should he force the intern to use other evaluation methods? Why?

3. Should he allow him to learn by experience, thus penalizing the students in the classroom?

4. How could Mr. Spencer help his intern to want to use different methods of evaluation?

5. How could his own insecurity be affecting the intern to the point that he was uncomfortable with anything except paper and pencil tests? ▼

CASE 20–4
▼

Elsie, the intern in Mrs. Castro's first grade, felt that true evaluations of student work were inappropriate. She felt that all reports to the home should indicate only good, positive messages. Mrs. Castro could appreciate Elsie's point of view, but she felt it necessary to enlarge Elsie's horizons to include those needs that the children had indicated by her evaluative data.

1. Should she insist that Elsie maintain the established evaluation system? Why?

2. How should she attempt to involve the college coordinator and any relevant theoretical materials available?

3. How could Mrs. Castro involve Elsie in researching this topic with other teachers in the school?

4. What opportunities could be developed for this same research with those teachers who were also parents of school-aged children?

5. What experiences from her own life could Mrs. Castro give Elsie to help her consider this more realistically? ▼

CASE 20–5 ▼

Eleanor felt that everything that a child did should be reflected on the evaluation report. During her student teaching, she attempted to record every response, written and oral, and make anecdotal records on each of the third grade children. Mrs. Packard, the supervising teacher, realized that this was ineffective and could not continue. During the mid-point of the term, Eleanor seemed to be wearing down somewhat, but instead of finding a better solution to the evaluation situation, she was beset with guilt feelings, as if she were incompetent. Mrs. Packard was concerned about the immediate problems Eleanor was experiencing, the effect of those problems on her students, and the long-range effect on Eleanor's professional life.

1. How could the supervising teacher help Eleanor?
2. What resources on the college campus might help in this kind of situation?
3. What role should the college coordinator play in resolving this problem?
4. Is there any hope for people such as Eleanor to become effective teachers?
5. What responsibility does she have to help herself without further guilt feelings? ▼

CASE 20–6 ▼

Seaton loved his student teaching in the advanced biology classroom. He was a live wire in the classroom and the students seemed to be making progress. The supervising teacher was satisfied with Seaton's work and the only complaint was that Seaton worked too hard.

In an effort to move the students along as fast as possible and keep them interested, Seaton assigned 10-page compositions to accompany their major project to five sections of biology classes at the same time. This was done without a prior discussion with the supervising teacher. When she discovered what had been done, it was too late to revise the work schedule for the students. Seaton was unable to visualize the problem until the day the papers and projects were due and he began grading them. He seemed to get nowhere fast. As his grading took most of his time, his planning suffered and so did his classroom performance. Yet he felt driven to return the compositions and projects in a timely fashion.

1. How could the supervising teacher help Seaton, aside from grading the compositions and projects for him?
2. Should the teacher take over the class temporarily while Seaton gets back on his feet? Why?
3. What constructive assistance could the coordinator offer?
4. How could this situation have been avoided?
5. How can student teaching interns plan their time as realistically as possible? ▼

RECOMMENDED READING

Anrig, Gregory R., Daly, Norene, Futrell, Mary Hatwood, Robinson, Sharon, Rubin, Louis, & Weiss, John G. (1987). *What is the appropriate role of testing in the teaching profession?* Washington, D. C.: National Education Association. (I&S)

This book contains the proceedings of a cooperative conference sponsored by the American Association of Colleges for Teacher Education, the Center for Fair and Open Testing, the Educational Testing Service, and the National Education Association. In addition to a wide range of the uses of testing, and the place of testing in the pedagogical training of teachers, the moral as well as the political imperatives of testing are discussed.

Baker, Frank B. (1989). Computer technology in test construction and processing. In Robert L. Linn (Ed.), *Educational measurement* (3rd ed.) (pp. 409–428). New York: Macmillan Publishing Company. (I&S)
Baker includes an extensive review of the technology involved in using microcomputers for item development and test development. Steps in processing the material such as item writing, test construction, scanning, scoring, and reporting are explained. The chapter is excellent information for both the supervising teacher and the intern.

Choppin, B. H. (1988). Objective tests. In John P. Keeves (Ed.), *Educational research, methodology and measurement: An international handbook* (pp. 354–358). New York: Pergamon Press. (I)
Objective tests and test items are defined. Areas of application and item formats in addition to the advantages and disadvantages of objective tests are discussed. This material is important for the beginning teacher to understand.

Evertson, Carolyn M., Emmer, Edmund T., Clements, Barbara S., Sanford, Julie P., & Worsham, Murray. (1984). Evaluating your classroom's organization and management. In *Classroom management for elementary teachers* (pp. 147–162). Englewood Cliffs, NJ: Prentice-Hall, Inc. (I&S)
This chapter covers some major indicators of the effectiveness of classroom organization and management. Methods of improving the management of instructional activities are offered.

Herman, J. L. (1988). Item writing techniques. In John P. Keeves (Ed.), *Educational research, methodology and measurement: An international handbook* (pp. 358–363). New York: Pergamon Press. (I&S)
The range of current item writing techniques for objectives measures is given. Item writing algorithms and linguistic-based approaches to item development are discussed. Rules and examples are included.

Perrone, Vito. (Ed.). (1991). *Expanding student assessment.* Alexandria, VA: Association for Supervision and Curriculum Development. (S)
This book is a collection of outstanding writings by 13 authors who propose that those of us in education seriously review our educational goals and then determine how we can effectively assess those goals. Each individual chapter is a good reading assignment for the supervising teacher to give the student teaching intern.

21

EVALUATION OF THE STUDENT TEACHING INTERN

During student teaching, the intern feels that everyone is watching; paranoia is sometimes a condition of internship. What the intern does not realize is that very few are in a position to evaluate the internship. Students are watching, but they are interested only in what is done to them. Parents of students are watching but they usually cannot evaluate the intern; they only hope the intern helps their child. Teachers down the hall are watching, but they observe only surface activities. The principal is watching, but the intern should be aware that the principal is also observing many teachers and that the relationship with the intern is only one of many responsibilities. The department or grade chairperson may be watching, but these people depend on the supervising teacher for basic information before expressing professional opinions about the intern.

Two other major participants remain in the intern's world: the supervising teacher and the college coordinator. Both of these individuals should be involved with the intern in evaluating progress throughout the term. The intern should expect to sit down with the coordinator and supervising teacher at the beginning of the term to review any standard evaluation forms (see Appendix Q for sample evaluation forms) and to discuss those criteria for successful completion of student teaching.

It is not sufficient for the intern to be told: "Just go in there and do a good job. I know you'll do fine!" This is the point in their careers that interns can feel lost. Even an effervescent, enthusiastic intern is probably hiding a multitude of fears about pending evaluations. Direction at this stage of the professional training is imperative for the intern. Responsibilities should be explicitly pointed out.

One method of approaching the initial evaluation conference is for the coordinator and/or supervising teacher to outline the evaluation materials to be handled during the term by all concerned. Frequently, both the college and the school district require final evaluation forms completed by the supervising teacher. Discussing these point by point aids both the intern and the supervising teacher to bring out related aspects of the intern's responsibility that should be considered. Most colleges expect the supervising teacher to submit a mid-term evaluation. This can serve as good discussion material, both at the beginning of the term and at the time it is being completed to turn in to the student teaching office.

The college coordinator has a different sequence of evaluations to complete. In many programs, the coordinator routinely completes an observation sheet each time visits are made to the intern. Arrangements should be made for the supervising teacher and the intern to be given copies of these periodic evaluations. Usually, general topics such as professional manner, classroom management, lesson preparation, and presentation ability are cited on these observation report forms; of course, space is usually provided for any narrative comments of the coordinator. It is a great advantage to the intern to discuss this report with the coordinator following the observation.

A final evaluation by the coordinator is expected. This report includes a rating of the intern on specific teacher qualities and a comprehensive assessment by the coordinator of the probability of success of the intern as a teacher.

Probably the most important reference for the intern is done by the supervising teacher. This is the main reference that hiring officials want to see before offering employment to a beginning teacher. They know that the supervising teacher knows the intern best of all because she has been the main evaluator during the student teaching experience.

It is most important that the student teaching intern have a positive attitude about evaluation. A few find it very difficult to accept criticism. This is a very immature response. One of the major purposes of student teaching is growth in teaching competencies, and this cannot take place without constructive criticism. Most interns definitely want feedback.

One important part of the evaluation of interns is their ability to handle the evaluation of the students in their classes. The interest shown and ability to work with grading procedures, student progress folders, and other aspects of student evaluation are true indicators of teaching potential.

▼ GUIDELINES FOR THE SUPERVISING TEACHER

1. Maintain an ongoing evaluation of your intern by developing a schedule for such evaluations. Short, periodic evaluations provide a good record as well as material for conferences with the intern.
2. As the coordinator visits your intern, confer with both of them, sharing your records. Maintain notes of such conferences.
3. Develop an evaluation file on your intern. This file should include samples of the intern's work, lesson plans, daily records, anecdotal records, and personal notes. Ask the coordinator for copies of the periodic observation evaluations for your file.
4. Provide the intern with evaluation opportunities and record these in your file.
5. Remember the value of positive reinforcement. Emphasize to your intern the high standards you expect.

6. Maintain evaluation dialogue with your intern constantly throughout the term.

▼ GUIDELINES FOR THE INTERN

1. You are student teaching in order to learn how to teach. Your competence as a teacher is expected to grow as your experience grows.
2. Welcome evaluations from your supervising teacher as you daily strive to develop appropriate teaching competencies in your classroom.
3. Feel confident in yourself and in your teaching ability. Readily develop a style of teaching that is comfortable for you. Seek evaluative comments from your coordinator and supervising teacher and build on them in developing your personal style.
4. Spend as much time as possible discussing with your supervising teacher and coordinator just what they expect of you. Ask them to be specific; you have sufficient "worry material" during student teaching without their intangible generalizations about evaluation.
5. Self-evaluation is important during student teaching. As you begin to openly analyze your objectives during student teaching, you already have begun an important professionalization process. Honest self-appraisal is a real asset to any teacher. Through reflective thinking, you will undoubtedly make a great amount of professional growth.

CASE 21–1

▼

Greta disagreed with the mid-term evaluation that Mr. Smiley, her supervising teacher, had written about her. Greta called the coordinator to see what could be done and explained that she had received a low mark on the preparation of lesson plans, but that Mr. Smiley had said she could use his lesson plans and need not write her own.

1. What role should the coordinator play in this situation?
2. Should Greta grin and bear it and begin writing lesson plans no matter what Mr. Smiley said? Discuss.
3. Would it be wise to involve the principal?
4. Is Mr. Smiley doing the right thing to encourage Greta to use his lesson plans? Discuss.
5. What options are available for Greta to adapt Mr. Smiley's lesson plans? Would such plans be effective?
6. Is there a way that Greta can tactfully appease both the supervising teacher and the coordinator? Explain. ▼

CASE 21–2

▼

Tim's coordinator gave him a low evaluation mark in instruction and classroom management when, in fact, Tim had precisely copied the method of his supervising teacher. Unaware of this, the coordinator gave Tim and the supervising teacher a copy of the evaluation report, which cited the methods used as "unimaginative, dull, and out-dated." The supervising teacher became agitated and vented her frustration on Tim. Poor Tim!

1. How can the coordinator help?
2. What actions should Tim take to sooth the situation?
3. Would it be inappropriate for Tim to request permission to use different teaching methods?

4. Does the coordinator have a right to evaluate the methods of the supervising teacher? Discuss.
5. What responsibility should the supervising teacher assume in defending Tim?
6. What valuable lessons for Tim are demonstrated in this situation? ▼

CASE 21–3
▼

Mindy was a young woman who was excited about being a teacher. Her supervising teacher, Ms. Stone, was nearly the same age and they became good friends as the student teaching term wore on. In fact, they became such good friends that Ms. Stone realized too late that her suggestions were meaningless to Mindy. The mid-term evaluation was soon due and in all professional fairness Ms. Stone was aware that she should give Mindy a below-average rating in some performance areas. Determined to be professional, she attempted a serious conference with Mindy, who at first seemed surprised and then countered with, "But I thought you were my friend!"

1. How could Ms. Stone help Mindy?
2. What chances does Mindy have of succeeding in this classroom?
3. How could the involvement of the grade chairperson or the department chairperson assist Ms. Stone?
4. Does this situation mean that an intern and supervising teacher should not be close friends? Discuss.
5. What psychological preparation could assist Ms. Stone prior to discussing this with Mindy?
6. What guidelines can be useful in avoiding such situations? ▼

CASE 21–4
▼

Cecil was a 6'5", 210-pound intern in physical education. He was getting his teaching degree in the off seasons while playing for a major league football team. During the student teaching, his supervising teacher felt that Cecil was trying to get by on the waves of his popularity. His classes frequently were "rap" sessions about professional football. Cecil was insulted when the supervising teacher suggested they preview the evaluation forms.

1. How could the supervising teacher help instill in Cecil the desire to do as well in teaching as in football?
2. Do you think converting the evaluation forms to score sheets with penalties, completed passes, field goals, and touchdowns would help?
3. Would such a conversion be worth the effort?
4. Do you feel that Cecil has the potential to become a successful teacher of physical education? Discuss.
5. What characteristics of professional athletes might be assets for teachers?
6. What personal qualities should Cecil spend time developing? ▼

CASE 21–5
▼

Harvey was about mid-way into his student teaching when he realized that his evaluation at the end of the term would be concerned with many activities he had not planned or experienced. He felt, however, that what he was involved with in his high school music classroom was appropriate for a teacher of music. He and his supervising teacher also agreed that a number of teacher activities required by music teachers were not included on the evaluation form.

1. What other form of evaluation could be used for the student teaching experience in Harvey's case?

2. How should the coordinator be involved in developing additional evaluation material?
3. How could the supervising teacher determine the acceptability of any additional evaluation materials?
4. What is the major purpose of a mid-semester evaluation?
5. In what other subject areas might there be a need for different evaluative criteria? ▼

CASE 21-6
▼

Denise was at the end of her student teaching in shorthand class. She had enjoyed the high school students she had worked with and had accomplished quite a bit with them. Her supervising teacher was very proud of her and insisted that she get an "A" in student teaching. The college coordinator disagreed and felt that Denise was closer to average and should get no higher than a "B."

Because the two individuals had to agree on the grade for the student teaching assignment, a decision had to be made; grades were due to be turned in immediately.

1. What events would contribute to the development of such different opinions?
2. Whose responsibility is it to work out a solution?
3. Should the grade recommended by the supervising teacher have more weight than the grade given by the coordinator?
4. How could Denise be involved in this decision?
5. How should a coordinator and a supervising teacher avoid the development of such a situation?
6. To avoid this kind of situation, what are colleges and universities doing with grades for student teaching? ▼

RECOMMENDED READING

Association of Teacher Educators. (1988). *Teacher assessment.* Reston, VA: Author. (I&S)
This monograph is a product of the Association of Teacher Educators' Commission on Teacher Assessment. Purposes of assessment, as well as political, measurement, and legal issues, are included in this discussion.

Balch, Pamela M., & Balch, Patrick E. (1987). Evaluating a student teacher. In *The cooperating teacher: A practical approach for the supervision of student teachers* (pp. 123–141). New York: University Press of America. (S)
Methods of evaluating the student teaching intern are discussed, including a horizontal evaluation model (intra-individual), a vertical model (skill based), and a humanistic evaluation model (attitudinal). A comparison of these models is given.

Heywood, John. (1982). *Pitfalls and planning in student teaching.* New York: Nichols Publishing Company. (I&S)
This text contains a full range of information for the student teacher; however, the section on appraisal and self-appraisal is especially recommended. A scheme for self-evaluation for teachers and student teaching interns is given in addition to an Experimental Pupil Evaluation Form for Teachers and a Student Teaching Evaluation Form.

Posner, George J. (1989). What have your learned from your field experience? In *Field experience: Methods of reflective teaching* (2nd ed.) (pp. 141–146). New York: Longman, Inc. (I&S)
Posner offers the student teaching intern the unusual opportunity to self-evaluate by writing a progress report that includes context, goals, and learnings. Also included is a list of questions to guide future professional planning by the intern.

Stanley, Sarah J., & Popham, W. James. (1988). *Teacher evaluation: Six prescriptions for success.* Alexandria, VA: Association for Supervision and Curriculum Development. (I&S)

This book is worthwhile reading for a supervising teacher who is seeking direction in evaluating an intern. Six alternative teacher evaluation approaches are presented, each recommended by different individuals. All six react to the same situation; each approach is followed by a "from-the-field" reaction, typically from a school principal or central office administrator involved in teacher appraisal.

22 CERTIFICATION

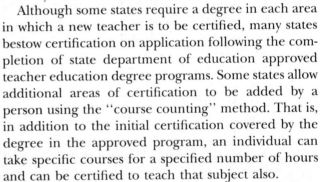

Becoming certified to teach is one of the last major steps that teachers-to-be take in their career preparation; it is a part of the final process of becoming a professional educator.

Consideration of the certification process should occur as the teacher trainee first begins the college program. However, because most students are not aware of or concerned about the certification process until graduation, the term of student teaching is a good time to take a long look at the process. No national certification to teach currently exists; however, research efforts are underway to develop such a certification program. Until those are available, certification requirements will vary from state to state.

Although some states require a degree in each area in which a new teacher is to be certified, many states bestow certification on application following the completion of state department of education approved teacher education degree programs. Some states allow additional areas of certification to be added by a person using the "course counting" method. That is, in addition to the initial certification covered by the degree in the approved program, an individual can take specific courses for a specified number of hours and can be certified to teach that subject also.

Some states require, in addition to a bachelor's degree, specific activities such as competency tests, extended internships, and beginning teacher programs. There are states, such as Alabama, Georgia, Florida, New York, North Carolina, and Oklahoma, that have developed their own tests. These tests vary from state to state and test scores are not reciprocal. For instance, if the candidate wishes to be certified in Florida, passing scores on a test on the generic teaching competencies and on a test on the special subject matter area are both required. Other states, for example, Louisiana, Mississippi, Tennessee, and West Virginia, require the National Teachers' Examination. For the testing schedule and information, write: National Teachers Exam, Educational Testing Service, Box 911-P, Princeton, NJ 08541. Usually the application deadlines for any of these tests are rather early; determine which tests, if any, are needed. The candidate should contact the state department of education of the state in question for specific information.

If a teacher-to-be is otherwise qualified and applies to be certified in a state requiring either a test or extended internship, that state department of

143

education usually grants a temporary certificate under which the graduate may teach, giving a certain amount of time during which the test is to be passed. It is possible, and practical, for the extended internship requirement to be satisfied by actual on-the-job classroom teaching.

If the student teaching interns plan to teach within the state they are trained, the college will probably furnish certification information regularly throughout the training program. In some states, the Department of Education automatically awards the appropriate certificates to graduates of the state-approved teacher education degree programs. In other states, the graduate must present an application, transcript, and processing fees to the Department of Education. Some states are now requiring all certification applicants to submit fingerprints to be processed through state police and Federal Bureau of Investigation files.

Students who graduate in one state and apply for certification in another should be aware that certification requirements vary from state to state. It is also normal procedure for the state department of education in the state in which certification is sought to write to the graduating institution for an institutional recommendation.

A student teaching intern can easily become confused with the variety of certification information, and, for that reason, it is important to know whom to ask for information. The intern should be clear about what questions are to be answered and may wish to actually make a list such as the following:

1. What is the appropriate source of certification information?
2. What are the requirements for certification in the state in which I want to be certified?
   a. Will my bachelor's degree (or master's degree) satisfy all the certification requirements?
   b. Does my state participate in the Interstate Reciprocity Agreement, in which member states agree to accept for certification those who complete state-approved teacher education degree programs in other member states? These states currently include: Alabama, Alaska, California, Canal Zone, Connecticut, Delaware, District of Columbia, Florida, Hawaii, Idaho, Indiana, Kentucky, Maine, Maryland, Massachusetts, Nebraska, New Hampshire, New Jersey, New York, North Carolina, Ohio, Oklahoma, Pennsylvania, Rhode Island, South Dakota, Utah, Vermont, Virginia, Washington, and West Virginia.
   c. Does my institution belong to the National Council for Accreditation of Teacher Education? Graduates of colleges and universities that are NCATE accredited are accepted in most school districts across the nation as certifiable.
   d. Can I be certified in a related area of study by "course counting" and taking additional course work without an additional degree?
   e. Is a competency test required in my state? If so, should I take it before or after graduation?
   f. Is an extended internship required in my state? If so, can I work this off while I teach with a temporary certificate?
3. What about the actual certification process?
   a. To whom do I apply?
   b. When do I apply?
   c. Where do I get my application?
   d. Is there a fee? How do I pay? To whom?
   e. Are there any papers I need to send with my application? Some states require fingerprints submitted with applications; information on this is available where you get the certification application forms.

Each college or university with a teacher training institution has a person designated as the certification adviser, and it is to this person that the student teaching intern should direct specific questions. Your college library reference section may have certification materials from other states; ask the librarian. For more detailed information about certification in any state write the Department of Education in that state (See Table 22–1).

TABLE 22–1 Sources of Certification Information

Write: State Department of Education

STATE	ADDRESS & TELEPHONE
Alabama	Montgomery 36130-3901 (205/242-9700)
Alaska	Alaska Office Building, Juneau 99811 (907/465-2800)
American Samoa	Pago Pago, Tutila 96799 (OS633-5159)
Arizona	Phoenix 85007 (602/542-5156)
Arkansas	Little Rock 72201-1071 (501/682-4204)
California	Sacramento 95814 (916/445-4338)
Colorado	Denver 80203-1705 (303/866-6806)
Connecticut	Hartford 06106 (203/566-5061)
Delaware	Dover 19901 (302/736-4601)
District of Columbia	415 Twelfth Street, N.W., Washington, D.C. 20004 (202/724-4222)
Florida	Tallahassee 32399 (904/487-1785)
Georgia	Atlanta 30334 (404/656-2800)
Guam	Agana 96910 (OS671/477-4978)
Hawaii	Honolulu 96804 (808/548-6405)
Idaho	Boise 83720 (208/334-3300)
Illinois	Springfield 62777 (217/782-2221)
Indiana	Indianapolis 46204-2798 (317/232-6665)
Iowa	Des Moines 50319-0416 (515/281-5294)
Kansas	Topeka 66612 (913/296-3202)
Kentucky	Frankfort 40601 (502/564-4720)
Louisiana	Baton Rouge 70804-9064 (504/342-3602)
Maine	Augusta 04333 (207/289-5800)
Maryland	Baltimore 21201 (301/333-2200)
Massachusetts	Quincy 02169 (617/770-7300)
Michigan	Lansing 48933 (517/373-3354)
Minnesota	St. Paul 55101 (612/296-2358)
Mississippi	Jackson 39205 (601/359-3513)
Missouri	Jefferson City 65102 (314/751-4446)
Montana	Helena 59620 (406/444-3680)
Nebraska	Lincoln 68509 (402/471-2465)
Nevada	Carson City 89710 (702/885-3100)

TABLE 22–1   *continued*

Write: State Department of Education

STATE	ADDRESS & TELEPHONE
New Hampshire	Concord 03301 (603/271-3144)
New Jersey	Trenton 08625-0500 (609/292-4450)
New Mexico	Sante Fe 87501-2786 (505/827-6516)
New York	Albany 12234 (518/474-5844)
North Carolina	Raleigh 27603-1712 (919/733-3813)
North Dakota	Bismarck 58505-0164 (701/224-2261)
Northern Mariana Islands	Saipan, CM 96950 (OS322-0311)
Ohio	Columbus 43266-0308 (614/466-3304)
Oklahoma	Oklahoma City 73105-4599 (405/521-3301)
Oregon	Salem 97310 (503/378-3573)
Pennsylvania	Harrisburg 17126 (717/787-5820)
Puerto Rico	Hato Rey 00919 (809/751-5372)
Rhode Island	Providence 02908 (401/277-2031)
South Carolina	Columbia 29201 (803/734-8492)
South Dakota	Pierre 57501 (605/773-3243)
Tennessee	Nashville 37219 (615/741-2731)
Texas	Austin 78701-1494 (512/463-8985)
Trust Territory of the Pacific Islands	Saipan, Mariana Islands 96950
Utah	Salt Lake City 84111 (801/538-7510)
Vermont	Montpelier 05602-2703 (802/828-3135)
Virginia	Richmond 23216-2060 (804/225-2034)
Virgin Islands	St. Thomas 00802 (809/774-2810)
Washington	Olympia 98504 (206/586-6904)
West Virginia	Charleston 25305 (304/348-2681)
Wisconsin	Madison 53707 (608/266-1771)
Wyoming	Cheyenne 82002 (307/777-7675)

It is essential for student teaching interns to realize that certification is for a limited period and renewal requirements vary from state to state. Keeping a certificate is important. Various infractions of criminal and civil law as well as state school board rules can lead to suspension or revocation. A number of states routinely check for revocation in other states prior to issuing the initial certification.

▼ GUIDELINES FOR THE SUPERVISING TEACHER

1. Firsthand information is often the best, and it is important that you discuss certification with your intern.
2. Feel free to relate how you became certified as well as how you renew and extend your certificate.
3. Share any special problems relative to certification that fellow teachers have experienced.

4. If your state requires the development of certain classroom competencies, share this information with your intern and assist her in the development and improvement of these competencies.

5. Assure your intern that the purpose of certification is to ensure that the students in the classroom have qualified teachers who are knowledgeable, trained, and worthy of their respect.

▼ GUIDELINES FOR THE INTERN

1. As you begin to consider certification, you may decide that just one more roadblock to becoming a teacher has been put in your path. The purpose of certification is to help in your professional development. Try not to be discouraged.

2. Begin asking questions about certification early.

3. Find the appropriate person on campus or in the school district in which you are student teaching and keep yourself up to date on certification requirements you must meet and on any impending changes. Promptness pays off. Do not be shy or assume that someone will tell you when the time is right. Someone probably will; do not wait for that, however.

4. Accept your professional responsibility early and know what is expected of you. If you do not know the answers to the questions given above, find someone who does know.

5. Ask a qualified person so that you can be assured of factual information. You will be more comfortable in your interning classroom if you are confident about your certification process.

CASE 22–1
▼

Nellie was unaware that certification was a part of her professional preparation until her supervising teacher referred to it one day in a conference. The supervising teacher was surprised that the process had not been covered in Nellie's courses at the college. Knowing that Nellie needed the information about obtaining a certificate to teach as soon as possible, the supervising teacher considered suggesting that Nellie visit the school district personnel office.

1. Should the supervising teacher call the college to find the name of the certification adviser, or should she leave this up to Nellie? Why?
2. How could she suggest that this kind of information be included in the methods courses prior to student teaching?
3. What action should she suggest Nellie take?
4. How could the college coordinator assist Nellie in this situation?
5. What kinds of information do you think Nellie will recommend be included in the teacher education program prior to student teaching in the future? ▼

CASE 22–2
▼

Hal was working toward a teaching degree in English and was student teaching in the high school. Someone had told him that if he took 12 additional semester hours in speech and drama he could be certified in speech and drama. He felt this would be a professional asset and improve his marketability when he went job hunting. He could not remember who had given him the information, and he felt a vague need to verify whether he could really add speech and drama to his certificate. In sharing this with his supervising teacher, he was told: "Oh, you don't need anything but English!" He relayed this to his coordinator who felt the need for tactful counseling as she did not want to come between the supervising teacher and the intern.

1. Should the coordinator share with both the intern and the supervising teacher the name of the college's certification adviser? Why?
2. What other steps could be taken to improve the situation?
3. How can Hal obtain the information he needs without offending his supervising teacher?
4. What problems could develop if Hal tries to get his supervising teacher to understand his desire for additional certification areas?
5. What lessons can Hal store for future reference to use when he is a supervising teacher? ▼

CASE 22–3 ▼

Mr. Kaiser was concerned about the professional attitude of his student teaching intern, Arnold. It seems that Arnold had discussed certification requirements with the campus certification adviser and had found that, with the addition of a few courses here and there, he could be certified in mathematics, science, and social studies, as well as in his major, technology education. Arnold was interested in pursuing as many certifications as possible. Mr. Kaiser's concern was that, although Arnold may have the certification, he really would not be prepared to teach all those subjects.

1. How could he voice his objection to Arnold?
2. Why did Mr. Kaiser have the right to object to Arnold's plan?
3. How could Mr. Kaiser explain this professional dilemma to the coordinator without betraying Arnold's confidence?
4. How could it be possible to be certified in so many subjects?
5. How can such wide certification be justified on sound professional grounds? ▼

CASE 22–4 ▼

June, a student teacher in Mrs. Crumpton's first grade, was excited about teaching and getting her own classroom following graduation and certification. Uncle Sam had other plans, however; he transferred June's husband to a military base in Europe. Although no problems arose about the graduation date, June was unable to decide whether she should apply for certification before she left for Europe.

1. Should she wait until she and her husband were transferred back to the United States?
2. Suppose the requirements changed in the interim?
3. Would she want to teach on the base in Europe?
4. Would she need certification from the Department of Defense Dependent Schools or from the state in which she was living at the time of transfer?
5. Mrs. Crumpton felt unable to help answer these questions. To whom should she refer June?
6. What advice would you give June as to taking tests for certification such as state competency tests or the National Teacher's Exam? ▼

CASE 22–5 ▼

Marcella loves teaching. Her student teaching had been a successful experience and she was looking forward to her first job in a high school home economics class. After looking through the openings for home economics teachers across the nation, Marcella decided to take a position in a neighboring state. During her interview with the school administrator, her certification was discussed. For the first time, Marcella realized that her home state certification would not be sufficient in the state in which she wanted to teach. She was perplexed. At this point in her life, she had completed a college degree in teacher education and fulfilled what she thought were all the requirements for her to become a teacher. With disappointment in her heart, she considered her alternatives.

1. How could Marcella become certified in the state in which she wished to teach?
2. Would her new state require a teacher certification test? How could she find out?
3. Would there be a probationary period for her to teach prior to her receiving a regular certificate in that state?
4. Was it worth the effort? So much paper work was involved, should she just wait in line for a job in her home state?
5. How could Marcella's dilemma have been solved earlier in her college program? ▼

CASE 22-6
▼

James was proud of being a teacher and was enjoying student teaching in physics. He felt that teachers should be as well prepared as possible for their noble profession. During his student teaching, he became aware of a teacher on the faculty who had been hired primarily to coach football but also to teach a few classes in math. The coach had laughingly said that he had no certification in mathematics and did not intend to get it, that he had a winning football team and that was what really counted. James was astounded that the administration would allow this.

1. With whom should James discuss this problem?
2. What, if anything, should he try to do about it?
3. How should the coordinator and the supervising teacher respond to James's complaints relative to this situation?
4. In what ways could James help the coach to understand his feeling about certification? How should James feel if the coach continues to rebuff him?
5. How would you react under the circumstances? ▼

RECOMMENDED READING

Association of Teacher Educators. (1986). Qualifications and responsibilities of Affiliated Supervisory Personnel. In Association of Teacher Educators (Ed.), *Guidelines for professional experiences in teacher education: A policy statement* (pp. 17–18). Reston, VA: Association of Teacher Educators. (S)
This material speaks to the qualifications and responsibilities of the individuals who are to be involved as affiliated supervisors. Criteria are to be jointly established by the institutional affiliates to ensure the maintenance of high quality professionals. The entire set of guidelines (pp. 1–21) are standards that are highly regarded in the teacher education profession.

Cronin, Joseph M. (1983). State regulation of teacher preparation. In Lee S. Shulman & Gary Sykes (Eds.), *Handbook of teaching and policy* (pp. 171–191). New York: Longman, Inc. (I&S)
Cronin reviews the reasons for regulating teacher preparation programs including concerns in the areas of accreditation, certification, and licensure

for teachers. He speaks specifically to the issues of current reforms, an overreliance on testing, the overextension of teacher training, the overatomization of teaching competencies, and the costs of screening and selection.

Feistritzer, C. Emily. (1990). *Alternative teacher certification: A state-by-state analysis 1990.* Washington, D. C.: The National Center for Education Information. (I&S)
This article includes comprehensive data on the location of alternative certification programs across the United States. State listings and requirements for certification for those who hold a bachelor's degree and data on certificates issued are also listed.

Floden, Robert E. (1988). Analogy and credentialing. In John Sikula (Ed.), *Action in Teacher Education, The Journal of the Association of Teacher Educators: Tenth-year anniversary issue, commemorative edition* (pp. 13–19). Reston, VA: Association of Teacher Educators. (I&S)
Floden speaks to the purposes of credentialing and

to the similarities and differences between other professions such as law and medicine and that of education. He responds to critics of certification and points out that in fact education has a better system of credentialing than the health or legal professions.

Huling-Austin, Leslie. (1988). Factors to consider in alternative certification programs: What can be learned from Teacher Induction Research? In John Sikula (Ed.), *Action in Teacher Education, The Journal of the Association of Teacher Educators: Tenth-year anniversary issue, commemorative edition* (pp. 169–176). Reston, VA: Association of Teacher Educators. (I&S)
The author discusses the characteristics of some alternative certification programs, their populations, and the potential for induction and reten- tion. *Also discussed is the beginning teacher research at the Research and Development Center for Teacher Education at the University of Texas at Austin.*

Westerman, John E. (1989, Summer). Minimum state teacher certification standards and their relationship to effective teaching: Implications for teacher education. *Action in Teacher Education, 11* (2), 25–32. (S)
This article presents a review of the potential for a relationship between state department of education standards and effective teaching. A knowledge of these effective teacher characteristics and professional education curriculum standards research may guide the supervising teacher in helping the student teaching intern develop into a more effective teacher.

23 LEGAL STATUS

The legal status of the student teaching intern is a perennial question with both interns and supervisors. Although the degree and approved program status of the intern is prescribed by state law and interpreted by state board of education rules, the legal responsibility and liability of the intern pose questions for both supervising teachers and interns.

Many state legislatures deal with the classroom role of the student teaching intern in only a general sense. Because this area of school law is developing through the accumulation of case law, student teaching interns should keep abreast of current cases in their own states.

Most states require the intern to comply with local school board rules and regulations and to observe all duties of the classroom teacher. In the application process for the student teaching internship, the candidate signs a statement agreeing to abide by all the laws affecting the state, district, and school in relation to the classroom assignment. Any abridgement of that agreement places the student teaching intern in jeopardy of losing his internship position, and he will not likely be placed for such an experience in that school district again. School district administrators take very seriously the agreement they enter into with the student teaching intern and they expect the same attitude from the intern in return.

Under the circumstances agreed on by the district and the student teaching interns, the interns are generally afforded the same legal status as their supervising teachers when they are in the school. This agreement is usually a part of the student teaching application that the student, the university representative, and the district representative sign.

Although some professionals consider the student teaching intern to be covered by district liability insurance, every intern is encouraged to purchase personal liability insurance to cover the period of student teaching. This liability insurance is available from various organizations of professional educators as well as from independent insurance agencies. Physical education, technology education, and science classes are examples of particular liability coverage needs for the intern.

A major source of information relative to the legal status of the student teaching intern is the appropriate book of state rules for school boards. Most principals have a copy, and the intern should borrow the book or spend some time in the administrative office reading the sections pertaining to preservice teachers. These state rules for school boards are the official interpretation of the laws passed by the state legislature and are written in language easily comprehended. If the principal does not have such material, she may be able to secure a copy for the intern.

It is imperative that the student teaching intern be aware that the majority of lawsuits in teacher liability cases arise from alleged negligence on the part of the teacher. This deserves special attention from the person preparing to teach.

▼ GUIDELINES FOR THE SUPERVISING TEACHER

1. As the supervising teacher, it is sometimes easy to forget that the novice teacher in your classroom may be unaware of the current legal status of a student teaching intern. It is natural to assume that those working with us are as knowledgeable as we are about such professionally related matters as legal status.
2. It is a great help to the intern if you share your experiences relating to school law.
3. With all the matters demanding time on the intern's schedule, it may be difficult to find time for additional reading. If possible, however, share reading materials with the intern to extend knowledge of the legal status.
4. Refer the intern to specific individuals on your faculty who are knowledgeable and have practical experience in the area of school law.
5. Share with the intern a copy of your contract.
6. If your local professional organizations dispense materials relative to the legal status of the teacher and the rights and responsibilities of the teacher, obtain copies of such materials for your intern. Sometimes the intern may be too busy or feels awkward pursuing this type of material.
7. Make it as easy as possible for the beginning teacher to learn as much as possible related to school law during the student teaching process.

▼ GUIDELINES FOR THE INTERN

1. Acts of negligence probably give teachers and interns more problems than any of the other law-related situations. Negligence can be proved only if there is sufficient evidence the intern has not warned the classroom students of hazards, either real or potential. Documentation of this warning is essential and should be kept in a permanent file by the intern.
2. Use all available sources to find information concerning your legal status not only as an intern but also as a teacher when you will have your own classroom.
3. Discuss this in the teachers' lounge. Other teachers can provide a wealth of information, and probably most of it will be in the form of specific cases. Analyze all that you hear and read.
4. Find other professionals interested in discussing these matters with you. What you learn is more meaningful and will be retained longer by your having discussed and reflected on someone else's ideas.
5. Obtain a copy of the state school board rules from your principal. Make an effort to read them and understand them.
6. Be aware of the responsibilities under which you are working. You are in a position to be involved in activities with far-reaching results.
7. Maintain what would be classified as "reasonable" behavior and you will be relatively safe.

8. Avoid taking chances, both as a student teaching intern and as a teacher. Lawsuits are expensive, even if you win. Aside from the legal implications of a lawsuit, you might experience difficulties with your state teaching certification.

9. Consider purchasing personal liability insurance, available for a minimal fee, for the period of time you are in school as a student teaching intern.

10. Because much of the developing law involving your type of position is based on case law, attempt to avoid being party to any such cases.

CASE 23–1
▼

C alvin was interning in the technology education classroom in the middle school. At the beginning of each unit he carefully outlined safety procedures for the students and watched alertly to ensure that students obeyed safety regulations. The students had learned how to use the equipment and generally were careful to avoid horsing-around.

One day, as a student was cutting a piece of wood on the table saw, he asked another student to hold the heavier side of the wood as it passed through the saw. As the wood ran through the saw, the student holding the heavy side moved with the wood up against the wall. The wood caught and injured his hand.

Immediately the intern saw what was happening and turned off the main power switch. After rescuing the student with the injured hand, Calvin went with him to the office for first aid, leaving the supervising teacher in charge of the class. As he walked down the corridor with the student, Calvin's mind was full of questions. Aside from the safety of the student, the intern was concerned with his own legal status and what would happen to him.

1. What questions do you think would be in Calvin's mind?
2. In what case would the parents have a legitimate cause for a lawsuit?
3. How would an inquiry into this accident affect Calvin's completing his student teaching internship?
4. Why would it be important for him to immediately call his coordinator?
5. With legal issues involving students more and more each day, how would this affect his teaching record?
6. How could he prepare himself to deal with the possible accidents that could happen in a shop class? ▼

CASE 23–2
▼

M yrtle was thoroughly enjoying the first grade class in which she was interning. With no major problems on the horizon, she was trying to prepare herself professionally as well as possible. She wanted to read the state rules under which the schools and teachers operated, but when she asked the principal if she might borrow a copy, he shrugged off her request and told her, "Well, you really don't need to read that. We'll tell you everything you need to know here."

Myrtle was dumbfounded. She had never imagined that an administrator could say such a thing.

1. Should she give up and forget about the rules and their implications for her professional life? Why?
2. Would it be appropriate for her to discuss this with her supervising teacher? With the college coordinator?
3. Where could Myrtle go to find a copy of the state rules?
4. Would it appear that she was trying to make waves if she pursued this matter further?
5. Does she have the right to read the rules? Explain your answer. ▼

CASE 23-3
▼

During a conference with the parents of one of his sixth grade students, Johnny realized that the frustration level of the parents was increasing. Johnny had been the student teaching intern in the sixth grade for 2 months. During that time, this student had experienced more difficulty than previously with homework, class work, and tests. The parents were alleging that the intern was not an appropriate teacher for their child.

Johnny had tried several resources but with no success. He and the supervising teacher realized that the student was beginning to display learning problems that would require more time than they had to give to one student. It was difficult to get the parents to understand this.

As the conference wore on, the situation became more disturbing. Finally, the father stood up and stated that it was the responsibility of the school to teach his son and that if they could not do that, he would sue the school, the supervising teacher, and the intern. He intimated that the problem was probably the use of the student teaching intern in the classroom, anyway. As the parents left the conference, Johnny reflected on his future.

1. Did he want to continue in a profession in which he could be sued for doing the best he could for a child?
2. Would he be considered the reason for the child's failure?
3. Would the school take the full responsibility for this or would he have to stand alone?
4. Would the college be involved in any such lawsuit?
5. What interpersonal techniques could Johnny contribute in an effort to salvage this situation before it deteriorates further? ▼

CASE 23-4
▼

Physical education classes offer many hazards to students. Freddie was aware of the legal hassle that some of the teachers in her field had undergone, and she wanted to plan to avoid any such problems.

She considered having the parents of all her students sign a paper absolving her of any responsibility. Before she checked this out with her administrator, she wanted to consider all the ramifications.

1. How would her supervising teacher consider such a request?
2. Because the intern would be in the school only one term, would the supervising teacher be willing to go along with this?
3. What reaction would parents have?
4. Realistically, what would be the chances of getting such a statement from all the parents?
5. What could be done with the students whose parents refused to sign such a statement?
6. Could she legally absolve herself of the responsibility of these students? Explain. ▼

CASE 23-5
▼

Louise was student teaching in Mrs. Max's 11th grade English class. Although much younger than Mrs. Max, Louise was much more traditional in her expectations of students in their dress and conduct. She had expressed her disapproval about the lack of student concern over sloppy clothes and unkempt hair. One day, her reactions reached the boiling point when she asked a student to tie his shoes or leave class. The student refused, saying that he had a right to wear his shoes any way he wanted. As the student and Louise glared at each other, the other students turned to Mrs. Max.

1. What, if anything, should Mrs. Max do in this situation?
2. What options does Louise have?

3. What rights does the student have?
4. What steps could have been taken earlier to prevent this occurrence?
5. In what way could Louise's attitude toward the student be a reflection of what she thought of the supervising teacher's lax attitude? ▼

CASE 23–6
▼

Mr. Bannon's new student teaching intern, Bob, was a pious young man on his way to the seminary. He was getting his teacher certification to earn his way while he continued his education for the ministry. He felt strongly about having a morning devotion.

Without prior warning, Bob announced one morning to his ninth grade homeroom that they were to begin having Bible reading and prayer each day and that everyone would participate. There were surprised faces among the group as Bob proceeded to open the New Testament and begin reading. A student left his desk and walked out of the room; then two others followed. As Bob's face turned red with rage, the group began looking at each other in bewilderment.

1. What immediate action must be taken? By whom?
2. How should the college coordinator be involved?
3. What responsibility does the school administration have in this situation?
4. What rights do the students have?
5. What could the college preparation have done to have helped to avoid such a situation occurring?
6. Who should respond to the parents' phone calls and visits to the school about this incident? Why? ▼

RECOMMENDED READING

Association for Supervision and Curriculum Development. (1987, August). *Religion in the curriculum.* Alexandria, VA: author. (I&S)
This report from the Association for Supervision and Curriculum Development Panel on Religion in the Curriculum examines practices in the schools of today, the basis for those practices, and a baseline for beginning the examination of religion in the public schools. Attitudes affecting textbook publishing and curriculum development are reviewed. This issue, although not a legal one in itself, sometimes causes legal difficulties for the unprepared professional.

Association of Teacher Educators. (1988). Legal issues. In Edelfelt Johnson (Ed.), *Teacher assessment* (pp. 26–32). Reston, VA: Author. (I&S)
This discussion of legal issues related to teacher assessment includes references to specific court cases. The right of the states to regulate entry into the profession is cited; also included are 10 principles to be applied in considering teacher assessment programs. Student teaching interns are usually approaching their state professional tests and may have particular interest in this information.

Clune, William. (1983). Courts and teaching. In Lee S. Shulman & Gary Sykes (Eds.), *Handbook of teaching and policy* (pp. 449–471). New York: Longman, Inc. (I&S)
This chapter offers the supervising teacher and the student teaching intern an overview of the effects that courts have had on educational reform. The author includes four propositions in his generalizations on the relationship between judicial reform and educational change.

Lunenburg, Fred C., & Ornstein, Allan C. (1991). The state role in education. In *Educational administration: Concepts and practices.* Belmont, CA: Wadsworth Publishing Company. (I&S)
This chapter deals with good background information for the student teaching intern on the various levels of state government including the state courts, the state board of education, and the state

department of education. Guidelines and strategies for reform and renewal and policy development are included.

McCarthy, Martha M. (1989). Legal rights and responsibilities of public school teachers. In Maynard C. Reynolds (Ed.), *Knowledge base for the beginning teacher* (pp. 255–266). New York: Pergamon Press. (I&S)
This chapter covers a review of the law as it pertains to professional educators. The material is comprehensive in terms of topics and general in terms of specific coverage. An extensive bibliography offers additional valuable information. This material is highly recommended for both the supervising teacher and the student teaching intern.

Mitchell, Douglas E., & Kerchner, Charles T. (1983). Labor relations and teacher policy. In Lee S. Shulman & Gary Sykes (Eds.), *Handbook of teaching and policy* (pp. 215–238). New York: Longman, Inc. (S)
Mitchell and Kerchner speak with depth to the policy framework involving labor relations for teachers. This material is recommended for the supervising teacher to share as appropriate with the student teacher. Diagrams illustrate the support of labor work structures by labor relations.

Zirkel, Perry A. (1988). Teacher evaluation: A legal overview. In John Sikula (Ed.), *Action in Teacher Education, The Journal of the Association of Teacher Educators, Tenth-year anniversary issue, commemorative edition* (pp. 21–29). Reston, VA: Association of Teacher Educators. (S)
The student teaching intern may not be ready for an article of this nature. However, it is sound information for the supervising teacher to review and share where appropriate with the intern. Federal law, state law, and case law concerning teacher evaluation are reviewed. A reference point for this information should assist the supervising teacher as well as the intern.

·24· ETHICS OF THE TEACHING PROFESSION

A discussion of ethics in teaching early in the semester can serve to guide the intern and can allow the supervising teacher to know much about the professional ideas of the intern. Frequently, the supervising teacher discovers that a review of professional ethics reaffirms a prior personal commitment to teaching. It is important for the intern to realize that such a commitment exists. Modeling of professional ethics is one of the most important aspects of the supervision of the student teaching assignment.

Any list of ethical prescriptions should be considered in relation to the particular school involved. As possible, university teacher training programs attempt to place students for field experiences in a variety of settings during their preparation. These different exposures help the intern identify the implications for professional ethics across a wide spectrum of student populations: social, economic, and cultural.

Terms such as *equal educational opportunity, ethical standards, worthy member of society*, and *professional service* may have different implications for different people. Because of those differences of opinion, the student teaching intern should investigate widely and think clearly about the need for ethical behavior.

Fairness to the student, the parents, and the school have a high priority. Maintaining confidentiality in respect to grades and other school achievements is extremely important. Trusting students is important to their psychological and emotional development; it is critical to give them an opportunity to accomplish and to achieve at what for them is a doable task, something of which they can be proud.

Ethical behavior for teachers means doing what is good and honorable for the student and avoiding what is bad, painful, or showing lack of honor to the student. It is important for the supervising teacher to help the student teacher to understand the various cultural groups represented in the classroom so that the definition of honor for each group can be recognized.

An ethical teacher is one who practices equity. Such a teacher makes no differences between students on the basis of sex, race, creed, or handicapping condition. The ethical teacher sees the possibilities for growth, health, and happiness of students and how those possibilities can be enhanced in his classroom.

The ethical teacher observes convention. This includes convention of school

157

and community rules. She attempts to operate within established policy, though not blindly.

The ethical teacher is compassionate and makes every effort to help students help themselves. Some feel that the ethical teacher strives to put student learning above subject matter content.

According to the Code of Ethics of the Teaching Profession developed by the National Education Association (Kim & Kellough, 1991), the professional educator has two primary commitments: first, to the student and, second, to the profession. Such commitments are taken for granted in many cases. However, it is important for the supervising teacher and the intern to spend time discussing methods of ensuring ethical behavior during the entire professional life of the intern. Such behavior tends to bond teachers together. The intern should be aware that a lack of such behavior tends to exclude him from such bonding.

A major test that indicates the level of ethics involved is reflected in the answer to the question: "Would I want a teacher to treat me (or my child) in such a manner?" If we can treat each student in each situation in a way that we would appreciate being treated, then the behavior or the treatment passes the test of being ethical.

▼ GUIDELINES FOR THE SUPERVISING TEACHER

1. Expose your intern to those members on your faculty that exemplify the code of ethics of teachers so that important lessons on ethics can be learned without having to be taught.
2. Be an example so that there are daily learning situations in dealing with value-oriented topics for your intern.
3. Use positive approaches rather than criticism when discussing school in particular and education in general.
4. Help your intern see examples of benefits to students when teachers have behaved in ethical ways.
5. Explain to your intern the benefits of good public relations on the part of the teacher.

▼ GUIDELINES FOR THE INTERN

1. Try to strictly obey all the school rules governing your conduct while you are involved in student teaching.
2. View your intern experiences as valuable and use these experiences in developing your teaching career.
3. Avoid discussing actions or problems that occur in the classroom with unauthorized individuals.
4. Maintain a sensitive but objective attitude toward your students.
5. Avoid prejudging a student for any reason—race, sex, ethnic or economic background.
6. Be aware that the attitudes of students develop simultaneously with subject mastery.
7. Respect the rights of the student as required by law (P.L. 94-142).
8. Remember the dynamic impact that you can have on your students and pursue a positive one.

9. Keep in mind the example you set for your students. Be fair and honest.

CASE 24-1
▼

Ingla had always wanted to be a physical education teacher. Working with the cheerleader sponsor as a student teacher added another dimension to her professional preparation. Because it was spring term, Ingla was able to assist with tryouts for the following year by girls who wanted to be cheerleaders. She enjoyed the procedure until something happened that disturbed her.

Although to Ingla it was obvious who the cheerleaders would be for the next year, when they were announced, it appeared that a less talented girl had won out over a very talented minority student. This disturbed Ingla and she attempted to discuss it with her supervising teacher. She was told that it was none of her affair. Still perplexed, Ingla worried about the injustice committed.

1. Under what ethical constraints was Ingla operating?
2. How does such a discovery affect Ingla's opinion of her supervising teacher?
3. What would probably happen if she insisted on discussing it with the supervising teacher?
4. In what ways could the coordinator help Ingla? Should she confide in him?
5. Were any other options open to Ingla? What? ▼

CASE 24-2
▼

Mike was student teaching in Ms. Breen's third grade classroom and he was delighted when he had received his placement assignment. He knew that a parent of one of Ms. Breen's students was the owner of a local automobile dealership. Early in the term, Mike scheduled a parent conference with the automobile salesman-parent. After briefly discussing the child's progress, Mike changed the subject to automobile sales and discounts to teachers. The parent was really put on the spot. He did not want to say or do anything to this student teacher that would hurt his son.

1. What could the parent do?
2. With whom should the parent discuss the situation?
3. What effect would a case conference on Mike's problem have?
4. Should Mike be withdrawn from student teaching? Should he be allowed to continue?
5. If you were the coordinator, what would you say to Mike?
6. How could long-range changes occur in Mike's philosophy? ▼

CASE 24-3
▼

Faye and Barbara were college roommates and had been assigned student teaching placements in different sections of the city. As they compared notes of materials, supplies, and resources available to their students in biology, they became aware of financial discrimination between the schools within the same district. They became enraged about the situation and tried to decide between themselves the best course of action.

1. Who would be interested in listening to these two?
2. Were there other individuals in the school district who were aware of the situation? If so, why had they done nothing?
3. How would questioning the practice hurt their chances of employment in the district?
4. If you were Faye or Barbara, what would you do?
5. How can such differences be eliminated? ▼

CASE 24-4
▼

Nelson was a politically active young man prior to his student teaching assignment in junior high civics. Political activity was high because of an upcoming election. Nelson's candidate needed handbills distributed door to door throughout the town. Nelson promised an "A" to every student who would distribute 300 handbills.

The next morning, the principal called Nelson to his office and asked him to explain his actions.

1. What gave Nelson the right to reward students in such a manner for political activity?
2. How could he punish those students who did not participate?
3. What conversation probably transpired between the principal and Nelson?
4. What do you think happened when the opponent of Nelson's candidate found out about this episode?
5. In your opinion, what do you think was the final outcome? ▼

CASE 24-5
▼

Betsy was assigned to student teach in art at the beach high school. Her work in the classroom was barely acceptable. She spent little time planning and preparing her lessons. However, she had greater problems with her social life. After school on Fridays, the students knew they could find her at the local beach bar, which she usually patronized all weekend. When she began missing school on Mondays, the students explained to the supervising teacher how Betsy had partied at the bar until early Monday morning. The supervising teacher knew something must be done.

1. Betsy seems to have a number of problems. Rank them in order of importance to her professional life as a teacher.
2. What action should the supervising teacher take?
3. Should Betsy's parents be involved?
4. How can the coordinator facilitate better adjustment for Betsy?
5. Is there any hope for Betsy's future as a teacher? ▼

CASE 24-6
▼

Randy was a middle school reading student teacher. No one was aware Randy was homosexual until one of his students observed him typing material on the subject professing his inclination and sexual preference. Because this did not fit community norms, the school board requested Randy's immediate withdrawal from the classroom in which he was student teaching.

1. Was the college obligated to withdraw Randy from his student teaching placement? Why?
2. What options were open to Randy at this point?
3. Had Randy's rights been violated?
4. How do you think Randy's sexual preference would affect his teaching ability?
5. What could the solution be for Randy?
6. What suggestions would you have given Randy prior to student teaching? ▼

REFERENCES

Kim, Eugene C., & Kellough, Richard D. (1991). *A resource guide for secondary school teaching: Planning for competence* (5th ed) (pp. 39–41). New York: Macmillan Publishing Company.

RECOMMENDED READING

Broudy, Harry S. (1990). Restoring honor: A modest proposal. In Marcella Kysilka (Ed.), *Honor in teaching: Reflections* (pp. 67–73). West Lafayette, IN: Kappa Delta Pi Publications. (I&S)

Broudy discusses the professional status of teaching due to variations in practice. He points out that until uniformity is established, the label of professional will not be awarded and that the more creativity is stressed the less the teachers will be recognized as professionals. He used the example of whether lawyers or physicians are creative in the practice of their profession.

Flanders, Ned A. (1990). Honor becomes effective teaching. In Marcella Kysilka (Ed.), *Honor in teaching: Reflections* (pp. 83–90). West Lafayette, IN: Kappa Delta Pi Publications. (I&S)

Flanders questions how teaching could have lost honor during a period when teachers are striving to accomplish more than ever under situations that are worse than before. Restoring honor is related to restoring locus of control of the education environment to the teacher.

Ortman, Patricia C. (1988). Central ethical issues. In *Not for teachers only: Creating a context of joy for learning and growth* (pp. 38–45). Washington, D. C.: Author. (I)

This material is presented to help beginning teachers reaffirm their own principles and beliefs. Dilemma are presented involving the purpose of education, teaching values, punishment, sex education, and the teacher as friend of the student.

Sergiovanni, Thomas J. (1992). Moral authority and the regeneration of supervision. In *Supervision in transition: The 1991 ASCD yearbook* (pp. 203–214). Alexandria, VA: Association for Supervision and Curriculum Development. (I&S)

Sergiovanni suggests that supervision move from the psychological to the professional and moral and that at that time supervision will be from within oneself as a teacher. A valuable chart shows assumptions, strategies, and consequences for the following sources of authority: bureaucratic, psychological, technical rationality, professional, and moral.

Strom, Sharon M. (1989). The ethical dimension of teaching. In Maynard C. Reynolds (Ed.), *Knowledge base for the beginning teacher* (pp. 267–276). New York: Pergamon Press. (I&S)

The author reviews the knowledge base of teaching as a moral/ethical activity and gives an extensive review of material promoting ethical sensitivity and moral reasoning. This reading is highly recommended for supervising teachers and student teaching interns.

25 JOB PLACEMENT

Most education students are contemplating a future in teaching. In fact, the task of finding a teaching position at the completion of their education degree program is uppermost in the minds of the majority of education majors.

The college or university placement office is a potential resource in finding a teaching position. Personnel in such offices provide insight into such topics as supply and demand trends, suggested methods of making applications and resumes, recommended interviewing techniques, information about various school districts, and lists of specific teaching vacancies. Computers that streamline services are available in many placement offices.

There will always be a market for good teachers. The difficulty of finding a job, of course, varies depending on a number of factors. One important factor is the school record of each candidate. These records are summarized in sets of credentials that are housed, at the request of the student, in the placement office. These credentials may include a summary of grades, references from supervisors and professors, and other information requested by hiring officials. It is most important that education majors and teachers in the field keep their credentials up to date. A hiring official seldom employs a teacher without first seeing the credentials file.

The importance of maintaining an up-to-date placement file has been proved time and time again. It is wise to obtain references from your professors and supervising teacher while you are fresh on their minds. It is sometimes difficult to make contact with these people as the years go by.

A second reason for keeping credentials up to date is the possibility of receiving a promotion or changing jobs. If a candidate is being considered for a promotion, the hiring officials will want to see the credentials and will be impressed if they are available and current. If there is a change of jobs with the possibility of a move involved, a teacher should get immediate supervisors to send references to the placement office involved. (See sample letter of application in Appendix R.)

The letter of application is many times the first contact between teacher candidates and hiring officials. These letters are usually one page and include information such as application request, name, address, phone number, date of graduation, present or prospective certification including area qualified to teach, reasons for interest in school district, and availability for interview. These letters should be sent to superintendents of schools or personnel directors, whoever is responsible for the screening of teacher candidates.

Great care should be taken with the letters of application. Sloppy erasures, misspelled words, or poorly constructed sentences usually result in elimination of consideration for employment. The supervising teacher is a good proof-reader and adviser for these letters. After receiving the letter of application, the personnel office usually responds by sending an application form with a request to complete and return it.

Because student teaching normally takes place at the end of college training, it is likely that interns will be invited for interviews during this period. These interns must remember, however, that their first responsibility is to their pupils and classroom and any interviews scheduled during the school day must be with complete knowledge and approval of the school principal, supervising teacher, and college coordinator and should be done infrequently.

After applications have been sent to the personnel office, the next step is to make contacts with various principals because principals usually have the major responsibility for hiring their teachers. A short personal resume presenting the candidate's best features should be forwarded to the principals with whom the candidate wishes to have an interview. A resume contains the following information: name, address, telephone number, professional objectives, educational background, work experience, extracurricular activities, hobbies and interests, military service, related professional experiences (if any), and the names, addresses, and telephone numbers of references (see Appendix S for resume format).

Teacher candidates have found that one of the best methods of obtaining employment is through successful substitute teaching experience. Positive contacts with school personnel, no matter the form they take, should improve your chances.

All of the above-mentioned contacts will be of no avail if a candidate does badly during interviews. This one-to-one conference is crucial. The importance of such things as promptness, proper dress, good questions, effective eye contact, good listening ability, noted enthusiasm, and overall ability to sell oneself cannot be overemphasized. Hiring officials can usually be quite selective and, therefore, it is imperative that candidates present themselves in the best possible way.

Availability and willingness to go where jobs develop is also a big factor in being selected. At any given time, there are teaching vacancies in large metropolitan areas as well as in remote rural areas. Good candidates who are available to move around should have little difficulty in finding a teaching position.

Teacher candidates sell themselves short at times. They feel that they are prepared only to teach. This is not true! In fact, many businesses, industries, and governmental agencies are interested in employing good teacher candidates, regardless of their major areas. The traits that make a good teacher are the same traits that enhance success in other areas. The necessary training programs are provided after employment. Successful teacher candidates can have numerous opportunities for employment in areas other than actual teaching if they desire. Each candidate should consider this possibility, and, if interested, make the necessary contacts. Here again the placement office can assist.

▼ GUIDELINES FOR THE SUPERVISING TEACHER

1. Take an interest in the concerns your intern has about finding a teaching position. If you are working with top-notch teaching prospects, you can make a contribution to the education profession by making employment contacts for them.
2. Encourage your intern to register with the college or university placement office. This results in the availability of credentials that can be sent to potential hiring officials.
3. Report the successes of your intern to your principal. If you feel this intern would become a definite asset to your particular school, make this known to your principal.
4. The references you write for your intern are a most important contribution in the intern's quest for a job. Accentuate the positive but at the same time be honest about the potential of your intern.
5. Encourage your intern to make contacts for employment. Finding a teaching position is very difficult in certain geographic areas and requires an all-out effort.

▼ GUIDELINES FOR THE INTERN

1. Register with your placement office prior to becoming a student teaching intern. You probably have little time for such things after student teaching begins. Not only should you register with the placement office but you should also use its services.
2. Become acquainted with all the principals in the schools where you are doing field work. Express your interest in employment to the principal of the school where you are student teaching if possible. Even though there might not be vacancies in that particular school, the principal meets periodically with other administrators who may know of vacancies.
3. Make applications for employment early. One does not have to complete college work before applying for a job.
4. Be very careful in the preparation of your letters of application, school district applications, and personal resumes. Brevity and careful proofreading are two necessities.
5. Use your supervising teacher as a reference. Hiring officials are most interested in this particular reference.
6. Prepare for your job interviews just as you would plan for a teaching lesson. It is a must that you project yourself at your very best. In preparing for these interviews, consider the following suggestions:

a. Have good questions in mind. This shows interest and concern on your part.

b. Arrive at your interviews on time; in fact, it is best to be early. If you are late for interviews, you would probably be late for school as a teacher.

c. During the interviews, try to put across what you could do for the school district if you are employed. Special talents and interests should be mentioned.

d. Be a good listener; you will get your chance to talk.

e. At the close of the interview, be certain to inquire about the next step. Will you be contacted or should you check back periodically? Some hiring officials consider it a lack of interest if you do not keep in contact.

f. Write the interviewer a letter expressing thanks for the interview (see Appendix T for sample letter). Reaffirm your interest in the job.

g. Do not settle for one interview; keep making contacts.

MEMORANDUM

TO: Graduating Education Majors
FROM: A Former Placement Director
SUBJECT: The Job Search

Congratulations future graduates! You are well on your way to becoming a school teacher. It is now time to begin thinking about getting that first job.

Times have changed since I was helping education students obtain employment. In those days, during the 1960s, there were serious shortages in many areas of teaching. Today this is not true; there are few shortage areas, and it is much more difficult to obtain a teaching job. There will always be a need for good teachers, however.

Your first step in the job search should be to submit completed employment applications to school systems that interest you. If you are free to go where the jobs are, your task will be much easier. Educational directories are usually available in your placement services library. After you have submitted your completed applications, request that a copy of your credentials file be forwarded to the school districts involved.

Try to see as many principals as possible because they are the ones who usually make the final hiring decision. If there is a personnel director available in the school system, however, it would be wise to begin in that office. Some personnel directors frown on candidates interviewing principals until they are fully registered with their offices.

When you make contacts with hiring officials, be sure to leave a resume that may help you to be remembered. Also, be sure to send a note thanking them for the interview.

If you have a chance to substitute teach in a school, do so by all means. Principals often hire candidates who have previously served as successful substitutes. Substituting is also a very good experience for potential teachers.

Avoid sitting around and waiting for a job to come your way! Be tactfully aggressive and make as many contacts as possible. If you are restricted to a location with few vacancies, consider applying for positions in other fields. You have the same traits that hiring officials in numerous fields are seeking.

Keep in constant touch with your placement officer. The main purpose of the personnel in this office is to help you find a job. Good luck!

CASE 25-1 ▼

S tudent teaching was drawing to a close for Richard, an intern assigned to a middle school. He had begun his last two weeks of full-time teaching and was progressing very well. One of Richard's fraternity brothers received an offer to teach in a nearby community. Suddenly, Richard appeared to lose interest in his student teaching and began leaving school early in order to contact principals concerning employment.

Richard's supervisor was quite upset. The last two weeks were crucial for the rounding out of Richard's student teaching experiences. The time at the end of the day after the students left was needed for necessary revision of plans and conferences.

1. What steps should the supervising teacher take to revitalize Richard's enthusiasm previously shown to his teaching assignment?
2. If a change in attitude does not take place, should Richard be allowed to pass his student teaching? Explain.
3. Should the coordinator be called?
4. How will this affect the desire on the part of the supervising teacher to assist in helping Richard find a teaching position?
5. Could Richard be jealous of his fraternity brother's job offer and begin to panic that he has not received one? ▼

CASE 25-2 ▼

A nne is a second semester intern assigned to a high school English classroom. She was very concerned about finding a teaching position for the following school year. Anne had been successful in her student teaching and her supervisor was quite concerned about her finding a job. She suggested that Anne register with the college placement office and was surprised at Anne's response: "I prefer to get my own job! Help from the placement office isn't needed."

1. How can the supervisor convince Anne that placement is a lifetime service?
2. Why do you think Anne had this attitude about getting a job without any assistance from the placement office?
3. What are the advantages to having your records available at a central repository?
4. What does the attitude Anne shows here tell you about her?
5. What impression might Anne's response have on the supervising teacher? ▼

CASE 25-3 ▼

B en had completed his student teaching assignment in a fifth grade classroom. He was interested in setting up his placement credentials and was in the process of obtaining references. Ben refused to get a reference from his supervising teacher. He was successful in his student teaching, but was afraid that his supervisor would give him a poor reference. Ben and his supervisor did not have good communication, and he really did not know where he stood. He felt that his selection of references was to be his decision.

1. What should be his coordinator's advice concerning this matter?
2. What chance would Ben have to get a teaching position without a positive reference from his supervising teacher?
3. Would a negative reference from his supervising teacher keep him from getting a job?
4. Should Ben discuss this with the placement office?
5. Should Ben consult with his supervising teacher about whether or not he would receive a positive reference? ▼

CASE 25-4 ▼

Betty completed a successful student teaching experience in a third grade classroom. She worked very well with her third-graders but always felt ill at ease around adults. At the final conference with her supervising teacher and coordinator, the topic of employment came up. The supervising teacher brought up the point that Betty might not be successful with personal interviews because of her bashfulness. Betty agreed and asked if there was anything she could do in order to have a successful interview.

1. What suggestions could the coordinator and supervising teacher give Betty?
2. Would mock interviews be helpful? If so, how could they be arranged?
3. Could a person as bashful with adults as Betty be happy and successful as an elementary teacher?
4. How could Betty have received constructive help with this problem during her teacher training?
5. What are Betty's chances of overcoming her shyness with adults after several years of teaching? ▼

CASE 25-5 ▼

Janice was very concerned about the possibility of getting a job in the high school where she was doing her student teaching. She was assigned in business education and was doing a very good job according to her supervising teacher.

A vacancy for an accounting teacher developed at another high school in the district, and Janice thought this was her chance. She scheduled an interview with the principal to discuss this vacancy. The interview went well until the principal asked what questions she had about the job and her mind went blank; she could not think of one question to ask. She was afraid that the principal considered this an indication of a lack of interest on her part.

1. Do you think the principal would eliminate Janice as a candidate because she had no questions?
2. Give examples of appropriate questions she might have asked.
3. What follow-up procedures could Janice take to show her interest in the vacancy?
4. Should Janice request help from her supervising teacher?
5. What sources of assistance could Janice have used prior to the interview? ▼

CASE 25-6 ▼

Dan was in his next-to-the-last week of student teaching in an eighth grade mathematics assignment. He was quite elated when he was offered a job to teach in a nearby community, 20 miles away. It was his hope that he would be permitted to complete his student teaching in the school where he would be teaching. He made this suggestion to his supervising teacher who did not think it was a good idea at all. Dan decided to call his college coordinator.

1. If Dan's request is granted, what effect would it have on his present class?
2. Why would the supervising teacher veto Dan's request?
3. Would there be any problems in transferring to another school district for the final days of his student teaching?
4. How should the coordinator react to Dan's situation?
5. What could be the legal implications if Dan served as both an intern and as a contracted teacher? ▼

RECOMMENDED READING

Connotillo, Barbara Cahn. (Ed.). (1984). *Teaching abroad.* New York: Institute of International Education. (I)
This is a good source of information on schools abroad. Schools are listed by country. It also includes addresses of embassies and education-related employers who hire for worldwide vacancies.

Edelfelt, Roy A. (1988). *Careers in education.* Lincolnwood, IL: VGM Career Horizons. (I)
The author reviews job descriptions and educational requirements for specific careers in education. Patterns of preparation, benefits, and details relevant to the specific career are included.

Fine, Janet. (1985). *Opportunities in teaching careers.* Lincolnwood, IL: VGM Career Horizons. (I)
The author reviews the career opportunities in teaching and related fields. She includes suggestions on how to plan and get started toward a career in teaching.

Kniker, Charles R., & Naylor, Natalie A. (1981). Career preparation and employment opportunities. In *Teaching today and tomorrow* (pp. 61–83). Columbus: Merrill Publishing Company. (I&S)
Important concerns of student teaching interns include the nonclassroom job opportunities. This chapter discusses these options: business and industry, government agencies, nonpublic teaching, overseas opportunities, adult education, agencies, and service groups. This material includes the steps for applying for a position and has a set of questions to assist the candidates decide if being educators is the right thing for them.

Krannick, Ronald. (1991). *The Educators' Guide to Alternative Jobs and Careers.* Manassas Park, VA: Impact Publications. (I)
Krannick explores career opportunities for educators outside of the field. This should be a rich resource for interns who are restricted to locations offering few vacancies in teaching.

Machado, Jeanne M., & Meyer, Helen C. (1984). The search: Choices and alternatives. In *Early childhood practicum guide: A sourcebook for beginning teachers of young children* (pp. 281–294). Albany, NY: Delmar Publishers, Inc. (I)
Material in this chapter assists the student teaching intern to think through questions about future employment including short- and long-range career goals, career ladders, and ways to find job openings.

Machado, Jeanne M., & Meyer, Helen C. (1984). Resumes, applications, and interviews. In *Early childhood practicum guide: A sourcebook for beginning teachers of young children* (pp. 295–312). Albany, NY: Delmar Publishers, Inc. (I)
This chapter helps the student teaching intern to immediately begin the job search. A resume outline is included with directions and advice on preparing it. The content of cover letters is illustrated with samples; suggestions on how to prepare for a successful interview are included.

Moody, Douglas. (Ed.). (1990). *Patterson's American educator.* Mount Prospect, IL: Educational Directories, Inc. (I)
Part I presents addresses of secondary schools, territories of the United States, diocesan superintendents of Roman Catholic schools, and superintendents of Seventh-Day Adventist schools. Part II lists postsecondary schools and educational associations and societies. This is helpful information for interns not restricted to a particular location.

Moody, Douglas. (Ed.). (1992). *Patterson's elementary education.* Mount Prospect, Il: Educational Directories, Inc. (I)
This book lists addresses of elementary school, diocesan superintendents of Roman Catholic Schools, and superintendents of Seventh-Day Adventists schools. This is a helpful resource for interns looking for school addresses in various locations.

O'Hair, Mary. (1989, Spring). Teacher employment interview: A neglected reality. *Action in Teacher Education, 11* (1), 53–57. (I&S)
The author discusses the importance of training the new educator in employment techniques. Factors given that affect the outcomes of such interviews include: communication, stereotypes, demographics, atmosphere, enthusiasm, and psychological factors.

APPENDIXES

APPENDIX A

Student Teaching Journal

_____
Date

What happened in class today:

How I felt about what happened:

Implications of what happened:

Next steps (what I need to do):

APPENDIX B

Format for Daily Notes
(Steno Pad)

Student Teaching Intern   Supervising Teacher

APPENDIX C

Two-Way Conference Log

Date _____   Time _____

Participants: _____

_____

Points made in discussion:

Recommendations/suggestions:

Other:

APPENDIX D

Three-Way Conference Log

_____ _____
Date   Time

Participants: _____

_____

_____

Points made in discussion:

Recommendations/suggestions:

Other:

APPENDIX E

Lesson Plan Format A

1. Objectives:

2. Teacher activities and materials:

3. Student activities:

4. Evaluation of student work:

5. Evaluation of lesson:

APPENDIX F

Lesson Plan Format B

Subject _____   Period _____

Date _____

1. Name of unit and purpose of the lesson:

2. Teacher procedures to use:

3. Elements of lesson and time required for each:

4. Materials/equipment needed:

5. Methods of evaluating student progress:

6. Method of evaluating lesson effectiveness by teacher:

7. Notes for future planning:

Lesson Plan Format C

1. Comprehensive objectives:

2. Behavioral objectives:

3. Sequence of lesson (with approximate time):

4. Materials needed:
   A. By teacher:

   B. By students:

5. Evaluation of student learning:

6. What changes could improve this lesson next time?

APPENDIX H

Lesson Plan Format D

1. Primary objectives of the lesson:

   Expanded objectives of the lesson:

2. What materials/activities will be used:
   A. By teacher:

   B. By student:

3. List of procedures in lesson with approximate times:

4. Evaluation of student work:

5. Evaluation of lesson implementation:

6. What changes would you make next time in this lesson?

7. What could be added to this lesson if you see that you are about to run out of material?

8. What could be omitted in this lesson if you see that you are beginning to run out of time?

APPENDIX I

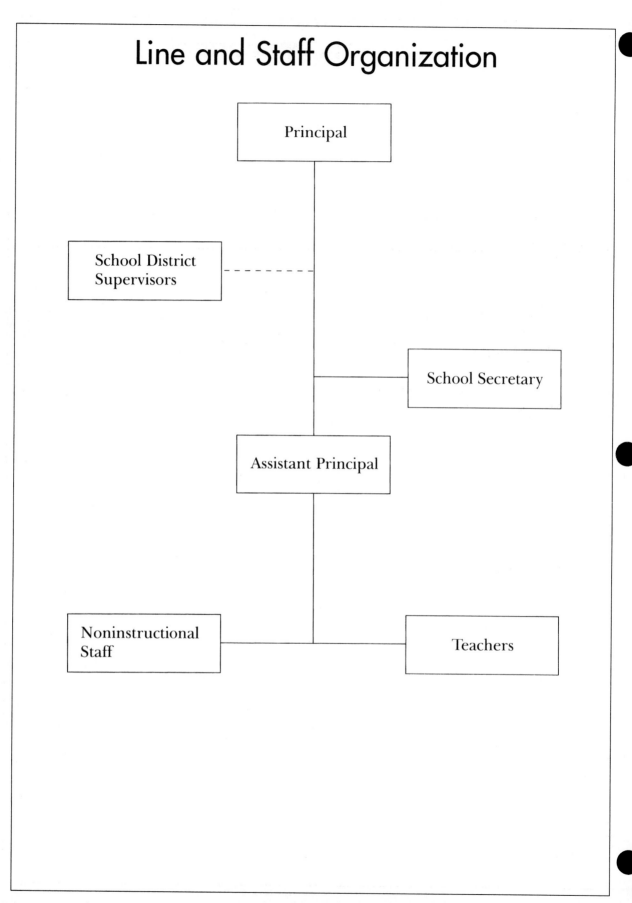

Line and Staff Organization

Principal

School District Supervisors

School Secretary

Assistant Principal

Noninstructional Staff

Teachers

APPENDIX J

Memorandum Format

DATE: _____

MEMO

TO: _____

FROM: _____

SUBJECT: _____

APPENDIX K

Classroom Management Record Form
(10-Day Period)

Code: + motivated, working; — not motivated; \ not working;
O minor misbehavior; X major misbehavior.

Student Names	Days										Notes
	1	2	3	4	5	6	7	8	9	10	

APPENDIX L

Student Record-Keeping Form

Code: ○ absent; Ⓔ excused absence; Ⓣ tardy; + homework turned in; – no homework; * see notes; test scores to be written in numerically.

Student Names	Days										Notes
	1	2	3	4	5	6	7	8	9	10	

APPENDIX M

Parent Phone Log

1. _____ _____ _____

   Date   Phone #   Person called

   Purpose of call:

   Summary of discussion:

2. _____ _____ _____

   Date   Phone #   Person called

   Purpose of call:

   Summary of discussion:

APPENDIX N

Interim Report to Parents

_____
Name of Student

_____
Name of Teacher

_____
Subject

_____
Date

Dear Parent or Guardian:

_____ Work is satisfactory in most areas.

_____ Needs particular help in such areas as _____

_____

_____

_____.

_____ Seems to be enjoying school.

_____ Your child may wish to discuss with you problems related to _____

_____

_____

_____.

Happy Gram

Date:

To:

From:

The GOOD news is:

APPENDIX P

Objective Test Format

Name of Course
Test # ____
Date

Directions:

Write the answer to each question in the blank to the left of the question. Read the questions carefully.

_____ 1. (Write short answer or fill in the blank question here.)

_____ 2.

_____ 3.

_____ 4.

_____ 5.

_____ 6.

_____ 7.

_____ 8.

_____ 9.

_____ 10.

_____ 11.

_____ 12.

_____ 13.

_____ 14.

NOTE: Answers are to be written in the blanks to the left of the questions, enabling the grader to check the answers much more quickly. In the case of multiple choice questions, the answer blank can be shorter because only the selected letter will be written in the blank.

APPENDIX Q

Student Teaching Evaluation

Key: 1 = Outstanding
2 = Good
3 = Acceptable
4 = Needs help
5 = Not observed

I. Personal qualities
   A. Dedication to teaching ____
   B. Personal grooming ____
   C. Enthusiasm ____
   D. Flexibility ____
   E. Creativity ____
   F. Acceptance of students as worthy individuals ____
   G. Other: _____

II. Instructional qualities
   A. Knowledge of principles of teaching and learning ____
   B. Planning and preparation ____
   C. Instructional skill ____
   D. Lesson variety ____
   E. Appropriate questioning techniques ____
   F. Reflective learning techniques ____
   G. Higher level thinking skills ____
   H. Evaluation techniques ____
   I. Knowledge of subject matter ____
   J. Group management and organization ____
   K. Other: _____

III. Professional qualities
   A. Understanding of student growth and development ____
   B. Communication skills
      1. Written ____
      2. Verbal ____
      3. Listening ____
   C. Understanding of student socialization patterns ____
   D. Ability to utilize criticism and suggestions ____
   E. Organizational ability and timeliness ____
   F. Other: _____

APPENDIX R

Letter of Application

March 15, 199__

Dr. John Smith
Director of Personnel
Harrisburg Unified School District
3086 Main Street
Harrisburg, Florida 33209

Dear Dr. Smith:

Our university placement office has posted a notice of anticipated vacancy for an English teacher in your school district for next school year. Please consider me an applicant for this position.

I will graduate in May from Middletown University with a bachelor's degree in Education with a major in English and a minor in Spanish. While attending the university, I was active in the Future Educators' Club, serving as secretary during this school year. I also participated in an intramural volleyball league and was a student ambassador for the university for three years. My enclosed resume lists other pertinent data.

I will be happy to come for an interview and can be reached at the above address or by phone: (317) 555-5555.

Sincerely,

Molly Young
2220 University Drive
Middletown, IN 47304

APPENDIX S

Resume Format

NAME
Address
Phone

Brief statement of qualifications:

Educational history:

Work experience:

Nonwork related experience:

Honors and awards:

Activities, interests, and hobbies:

References:

190

APPENDIX T

Follow-Up Thank You Letter

May 4, 199__

Dr. James R. Smith
Director of Personnel
Escambia District School System
412 North Avenue
Byrneville, North Carolina 28400

Dear Dr. Smith:

I appreciate the opportunity you gave me yesterday to visit with you and to discuss the teaching vacancy in English in your school district. I enjoyed the discussion about the new 10th grade English curriculum that is being implemented this next year.

The professional opportunity that this position offers is exciting; I hope that I will be seriously considered.

Thank you.

Sincerely,

Molly Young
4220 Pine Street
Byrneville, North Carolina 28400

INDEX

ABOUT THE AUTHORS

Dr. Patricia J. Wentz has worked with students in internships and student teaching since 1972. She has served as Director of Pre-Student Teaching Field Experiences, Assistant Director of Student Teaching, Assistant Director of Clinical Studies, Director of Clinical Studies, Director of Teacher Certification and Field Experiences, Director of Teacher Education Student Services, Associate Dean, Interim Dean, and Dean of the College of Education at the University of West Florida. As chair of the Department of Educational Leadership, she currently directs administrative internships with students pursuing their specialist degrees.

Dr. Wentz received a B.S. in English and an M.A. in Counseling at East Carolina University; she received her Ph.D. from Texas A&M University in Educational Psychology and Curriculum & Instruction. Dr. Wentz has served extensively in staff development activities related to student teaching. Her public school teaching experience includes being a junior high school librarian, teaching English and U.S. history at the junior high and high school levels and serving as a high school guidance counselor. Prior to her public school experience, Dr. Wentz worked at the D. H. Hill Library at University of North Carolina at Raleigh and as a newspaper reporter for North Carolina's *News & Observer*.

James R. Yarling teaches at the University of West Florida where he coordinates teaching interns and works in the area of language arts (Department of Elementary and Secondary Education).

After receiving his undergraduate degree in Elementary Education, he worked as an elementary and middle school teacher in Winchester, Indiana, and as an elementary and middle school principal and Assistant Superintendent in West Lafayette, Indiana.

Between 1958 and 1968, Dr. Yarling was Assistant Director of Placement at Ball State University. He completed his doctorate there in 1968 and then accepted a position at the University of West Florida.

Dr. Yarling has coordinated student teachers for the past 24 years, even during his four-year period as Associate Dean, College of Education. He also teaches undergraduate and graduate methods classes and has served as a troubleshooter in the Student Teaching Office. Four outstanding teaching awards have been presented to Dr. Yarling, including the prestigious excellence-in-undergraduate teaching award granted by the Florida Legislature (1989).

ISBN 0-02-425491-6

9 780024 254917